Abstracts

from

Newspapers

of

Edenton, Fayetteville, *and* Hillsborough North Carolina

- 1785-1800 -

Compiled by:
Raymond Parker Fouts

Southern Historical Press, Inc.
Greenville, South Carolina

This volume was reproduced
from a personal copy located in
the Publishers private library

Please direct all correspondence and book orders to:
SOUTHERN HISTORICAL PRESS, Inc.
PO Box 1267
Greenville, SC   29602-1267

PREFACE

These abstracts were made from microfilm of the original newspapers, obtained from the North Carolina State Archives at Raleigh, North Carolina. Information concerning dates and sources is included at the beginning of each year. All issues located are noted, though nothing may have been abstracted from them.

Advertisements are recorded only from the first issue in which they appear in legible form.

Please note that these abstracts are arranged by place of origin and by date within that designation. This arrangement places the earliest date in the last section, as it occurs in the newspapers from Hillsborough.

Each item has been assigned a number, within parentheses. The name index and location index refer to these numbers, unless otherwise noted.

TABLE OF CONTENTS

EDENTON

1787	The North Carolina Gazette; or The Edenton Intelligencer	1
1788	The Edenton Intelligencer	1-3
1799	The Herald of Freedom	3-8
1800	The Encyclopedian Instructor, and Farmer's Gazette	8-10
	The Post-Angel or Universal Entertainment	10-14
	The Edenton Gazette	15-16

FAYETTEVILLE

1789	Fayetteville Gazette	16-19
1790-1791	The North Carolina Chronicle; or Fayetteville Gazette	19-51
1792-1793	Fayetteville Gazette	51-80
1795	The North-Carolina Centinel & Fayetteville Gazette	80-85

HILLSBOROUGH

1785-1786	The North Carolina Gazette	85-87

INDEX	89-105
LOCATION INDEX	107-111

ABSTRACTS FROM NEWSPAPERS OF EDENTON, FAYETTEVILLE,

& HILLSBOROUGH, NORTH CAROLINA

1785-1800

EDENTON

1787 - All issues missing except for the following from Sondley Reference Library-December 19.

THE NORTH-CAROLINA GAZETTE; or THE EDENTON INTELLIGENCER.
No. IX. Wednesday, December 19, 1787 (Vol. I.

(1) This enquiry is made for the purpose of collecting the proper materials for a Gazetteer of the United States.. Those gentlemen who may be so obliging as to favour the above design, by communications, are requested to forward them to Mess. R. AITKIN or W. SPOTSWOOD, Philadelphia, Mess. SPOTSWOOD and CLARK, Book-sellers, Baltimore, Rev. Mr. KEITH, Alexandria, Dr. Hugh WILLIAMSON, Edenton, North Carolina, Dr. D. RAMSAY, Mess. WRIGHT and Co., Charleston, The ___ A. BALDWIN and Joseph CLAY, Esqs. Georgia, Samuel SMITH, D. D. Princeton, Mr. LOUDON Printer, New-York and the Rev. Samuel AUSTIN, or Jedediah MORSE, New-Haven, with their names..and residence, that the author may have the pleasure of knowing to whom he is indebted for their friendly assistance. Jedediah MORSE.

(2) Taken up, By the Subscriber, in Perquimens County, at the Mouth of SUTTONss Creek, A Large Grey Stray Horse... James SUMNER. Nov. 12th, 1787.

1788 - All issues missing except for the following from American Antiquarian Society-April 9; from Louisiana State Museum-June 4.

THE EDENTON INTELIGENCER
No. 25.) Wednesday, April 9, 1788. Vol. I.

(3) To be Sold By the Executors of Thomas WHITE, deceased, All the Estate of the said deceased, consisting of 591 Acres of Land..Slaves..Horses, Beef Cattle..Sheep, Hogs, Household Furniture, &c.. Part of the Land is of the best quality in the County of Chowan, and 500 Acres of it is situated on Albemarle Sound, known by the name of Bluff Point... March 17, 1788.

(4) Notice. The Subscriber proposes to form a New Town, by the name of Campbellsburgh; situate on the West side of Chowan River, between Thomas COCHRAN's and said CAMPBELL's on the place formerly called the Old Tar Landing, in Bertie County, North-Carolina.. Those Gentlemen desirous of becoming adventurers in the above, may apply to the following Gentlemen: Josiah COLLINS, Esq. in Edenton, Mr. Benjamin BRYER, in

1

(4) (Cont.) Windsor. Doctor Patrick GARVEY, in Winton. Captain David MEREDITH and the Subscriber, near the Premises... James CAMPBELL. Bertie County, Feb. 23, 1788.

(5) Claims, For the Payment of Taxes, May be had at One Fourth of their Nominal Value.. Apply to W. SKINNER. Perquimans County, March 10th, 1788.

(6) For the Edenton Intelligencer. Mr. MURPHY. In your Paper of the 9th of January last, I read an Ordinance of the General Assembly, in favor of Thomas VAIL.. Allow me to call your attention to the proceedings of the House on this business-they _in_-velop three matters of the greatest moment to every Citizen of the State. 1st. The unconstitutional usurpation of the Legislature on the Judiciary. 2nd The impeachment of the sacred character of a Judge, and 3dly. An attack upon the momentous Palladium of our Liberties, the Trial by Jury..listen to the Resolution. "Whereas it has been represented to the General Assembly, and confirmed by several depositions, and these of Record, and by the testimony of the Sheriff, who was present at the Trial, that Thomas VAIL, of the County of Chowan, has been indicted in the Superior Court of Law and Equity, for the District of Edenton, for Forging and Publishing knowing to be Forged, in November, 1786, an Obligatory Note, and that on the Trial of the said indictment, The Jury found him not Guilty; yet by accident the said Verdict was recorded as guilty of passing it, knowing it to be Forged, and whereas it appears that the said VAIL, has heretofore supported a fair and unblemished character." ... A Juryman

(7) Boston, March 8. At New-Durham, in New-Hampshire, on Monday the 4th instant, at a tavern..were Col. TASH, Capt. Peter DROWN, a son of Colonel TASH, and one Elisha THOMAS-THOMAS having got into a dispute..when Captain DROWN interfered, and attempted to reason with THOMAS..THOMAS drew a knife, and plunged it into Captain DROWN's breast, of which wound, in a few hours he died. The Friday following his remains were honorably interred.. THOMAS..made his escape; but on Wednesday the 6th was taken and committed to jail in Dover, (N. H.) THOMAS left at home his wife and six children-On Saturday last, his wife, taking her youngest child to one of the neighbours, set out for Dover to see her husband. In the night the other five being in bed, the eldest (a boy) waked..with the house..in flames..he in vain attempted to save his four brothers and sisters..himself only escaping to tell the news!

(8) The copartnership of BLACK and AMIS will be dissolved the 15th instant... Alex. BLACK, Thomas AMIS. April 4, 1778.

(9) The Sub. Has For Sale, at his Store, in Murfree'sboro', on Meherrin river..Hard-Ware and Pewter..for Cash, Tar or Tobacco. J. VOLLINTINE. Murfree'sboro', Feb. 10.

(10) To Be Sold, At Public Vendue, On the 10th Day of April next At MOORE Yard, on GARDNER's Creek in Martin County: A New Vessel of Four Hundred Barrels burthen... Maurice MOORE, March 13th, 1788.

(11) Edenton, Printed by Maurice MURPHY.

__33.__) Wednesday, June 4, 1788. Vol. I.

(12) Taken or Stolen, out of the House of Captain John SMALL, A Quadrant, Makers name Andrew NEWELL?, Boston, engraved on a heart as usual on a piece of Ivory, and the subscriber's name also... Rufus SUMNER, Edenton, May 14.

(13) The Subscriber begs leave to inform..that he has opened a Tavern at Ga es Co rt-House and has supp ed himse f with good Liquour... Thomas FINNEY.

(14) The copartnership of W_ O_ and VOLL_TIN_ be n mu ual y and am_ a ly disolved the 1st of April..apply to Joseph VOLLINTINE of M_rfre_borough... E. WATSON, J. VOLLINTINE

(15) Ran away from the Subscriber living in Martin County the 3d of May, a Negro Man named SAN_, or SAMBAY, between 30 or 40 years old, about 5 feet 8 or 10 inches high; he is between a black and yellow complexion, thin visage and well made..his nose is rather sharper than common for a negro, and uses his left hand more than the right..reward of 20 Pounds..in any other State, 30 Pounds. S. WILLIAMS.

(16) George LADNER, Painter, Gilder, and Glazier, (lately from New-York) Takes this method of informing..that House, Sign, and ship painting is done in general...

1799 - The following are the only issues located: From Harvard University-March 27; May 1.

THE HERALD OF FREEDOM
Edenton: Printed By James WILLS
Vol. XIV. Wednesday Evening, March 27, 1799. Number 680.

Advertisements of no more length than breadth inserted in this paper for 5s. the first time, and 2s. 6d. for every continuance. None need be sent from any distance without the Money.

(17) List of Laws, Passed at the third Session, of the 5th Congress of the United States, Begun and held at the city of Philadelphia, in the state of Pennsylvania, on Monday the 3d of December, 1798, and ending the 3d March '99. ... 5. An act for the relief of Jonathan HASKILL.. 7. An act for the relief of GAZZAM, TAYLOR and JONES, and of Samuel WATT of the city of Philadelphia.. 16. An act for the relief of Thomas LEWIS.. 19. An act allowing James MATHERS compensation for services done for the United States, and expenses incurred in rendering said services, as sergeant at arms to the Senate.. 45. An act for the relief of Comfort SANDS and others.

(18) Baltimore, March 9. Official. (Letter to Secretary of the Navy.) United States frigate Constellation, Bassaterre roads, St. Christopher's, 16th of February, 1799. My dear Sir, I enclose you a newspaper that gives a very accurate account of my capture of the Insurgente, French frigate... Thomas TRUXTON.. Jeremiah YELLOTT, Esq.

(19) Extract of a letter from Andrew STERRETT, a young gentleman of this city, third Lieutenant of the frigate Constellation, to his brother. "United States frig-ate Constellation, St. Kitts, February 14, 1799. Dear Charles,.. She proved to be the French national frigate Insurgente, of 40 guns and 40_ men.. One fellow I was obliged to run through the body with my sword, and so put an end to a coward. You must not think this strange, for we would put a man to death for even looking pale on board this ship.. I send you a list of the killed and wounded on board our ship. A. STERRETT." James M'DONERIGH, midshipman, wounded. John ANDREWS, ordinary seaman, do. Thomas WILSON, do. since dead. Neal HARVEY, killed for cowardice.

(20) Philadelphia, March 2. The schooner Vandyke, Benj. GUILD, which sailed from Baltimore about the beginning of January last, after being boarded by two New Provi-dence privateers and dismissed, was boarded by a third, the John and Edward, of New Providence, commanded by John B. MILLER, off the west end of Cuba..people of theVan-dyke were treated with great barbarity, and the English Captain drew his knife on the American commander..-the vessel was plundered..and..to proceed for New-Providence

(20) (Cont.) The schooner belongs to Sylvanus DUAR and Sons, of Duxbury, Massachusetts, but was freighted by merchants of Baltimore. The above particulars are signed by the following persons, and dated February 28, 1799. Benjamin GUILD, James CHANDLER, Thomas CARROL, Benj. BATTERSHALL, John ROXBURG, Snow Maryland of Baltimore.

(21) March 15. Appointment-by Authority. William MACPHERSON, Esq. to be a Brigadier General in the army of the United States.

(22) Norfolk, March 23. Yesterday arrived the armed schooner Ann D. H. HINCHMAN?, master, from Martinico, last from Dominico, in 13 days. The day previous to..leaving Martinico, arrived there the schooner Sally, S. RIPLEY, master, from Boston bound to Martinico...

(23) Edenton, Wednesday Evening, March 27. The paragraph inserted in our last, announcing the death of Mr. John Ward FENNO, we are happy to contradict; the report appears to be unfounded.

(24) By the President of the United States of America. A Proclamation. Whereas combinations to defeat the execution of the laws for the valuation of lands and dwelling houses within the United States, have existed in the counties of Northampton, Montgomery and Bucks, in the state of Pennsylvania, and have proceeded in a manner subversive of the just authority of the government..certain persons, in the county of Northampton..have been hardy enough to perpetrate certain acts, which I am advised amount to treason..the said persons exceeding 100 in number, and armed and arrayed in a warlike manner..on the 7th..March, proceeded to the house of Abraham LEVERING, in the town of Bethlehem, and there compelled William NICHOLS, Marshall of the United States, in and for the district of Pennsylvania, to desist from the execution of certain legal process..call forth military force, in order to suppress such combinations ... Done at the city of Philadelphia, the 12th day of March..1799, and of the Independence of the said U. States of America, the 23d. John ADAMS. By the President, Timothy PICKERING, Secretary of State.

(25) State of North-Carolina. Pasquotank county, March 4, 1799. Notice is hereby given, to all the creditors of Armwell LOCKWOOD, deceased..is dead, and that the subscriber qualified as administrator to his estate in last December term... Holland LOCKWOOD, Adm.

(26) State of North-Carolina. Chowan County, March 21, 1799. Notice is hereby given, to all the creditors of Doctor John CUNNINGHAM, dec...is dead, and that the subscribers qualified as executor and executrix to his estate at March term... Elisha NORFLEET, Ex'r. Peggy CUNNINGHAM, Ex'rx.

(27) For Sale, By MOODY and AVERY, French Brandy, 4th proof, West-Indian Rum, New England ditto, Sugar and Molasses, Salt, Burton Ale, Red Lead and Yellow Ochre, ground in oil...

(28) Notice. I once more request all those indebted to the estate of Thomas YOUNG-HUSBAND, dec. to disharge their debts, and those who have claims against the same, to call for settlement on Mr. J. DEAN or Mr. MACURD, near Currituck court house..legally authorised..by my power of attorney... P. YOUNGHUSBAND, Executor of Thos. YOUNGHUSBAND, dec.

(29) Ran away from the Subscriber, AARON, a stout, likely, black fellow, about 5 feet 10 inches high, and 26 years old.... He formerly worked in the Lebanon Swamp, and has a wife in Nixonton. If he is not lurking thereabouts, he has probably got a

4

(29) (Cont.) free pass, and found employment as a shingle weaver, on the Virginia side of the Dismal; a Mr. WILLIAMS, Mr. CAPRON and Mr. DOUGHTY, are particularly requested to have him apprehended, if he should apply to them for work. I will give 25 Dollars to any person who will deliver him to me. Thomas FITT. Lazy-Hill, Feb. 20, 1799.

(30) Jones County, February 15th, 1799. Those it may concern will please to take notice, that the lands advertised for sale as below, for the taxes due thereon, for ..1797, and as yet is said to belong to the estate of David ALLISON. The sale of said lands..is postponed until the second Monday in May, 1799, the 13th day of said month, when the same, or so much thereof will be sold..as will pay said taxes. Edmund HATCH.

Sheriff's Sale. Jones County, North-Carolina, November 27th, 1798. 1280 Acres on the head of gum swamp, beginning at a pine near John ISLAR's line. 8320 acres on the north side of white oak river and west side of HUNTER's creek, beginning..at the mouth of pometer branch and said HUNTER's creek-James WICKS's corner. 460 acres joining the Onslow county line, beginning at..John SAUL's corner on the road. 5120 acres on the north side of Trent river, beginning at a pine-Samuel DELIHUNTER's beginning of his 100 acre patent. 13705 acres on the north side of Trent river and head of BACHELOR's creek, beginning at Hezekiah MERRITT's beginning pine of his 100 acre patent. 35200 acres on the south side of Trent river, beginning at a tree called..the Royal Oak, beginning of two patents in the name of Daniel SHINE. 1408 acres on the south side of Trent river, including the headwaters of Rattlesnake branch..the beginning of Jacob JOHNSTONs 200 acre survey, on the head of Tocohoe branch. 1280 acres on the north side of white oak river including part of the pocoson..Joseph HATCH's and Richard JONES corner. 640 acres beginning at..Jonathan KEYS's corner of his 250 acre survey. The foregoing Lands appear on record, as the property of David ALLISON, late of Philadelphia. 1280 acres on the north side of white oak river and west side of great branch..James TAYLOR's corner of a 300 acre survey. 640 acres on the north side of Trent river, on the head of miry branch.. beginning..south from MERRITT's and his own beginning.. 1280 acres on the north side of Trent river, near the head of the beaverdam, beginning at..Hezekiah MERRITT's third corner of 100 acre survey, dated the 22d day of October, 1782. 1408 acres on the north side of Tocohoe creek.. 1920 acres on the south side of Trent river, and northwest side of Catfish lake, between the head of mill creek and island creek, beginning at two bays in Mr. George POLLOCK's line of survey of 640 acres. 1408 acres on the south side of Trent river, including the waters of reedy branch and little cypress creek, joining the Onslow county line, beginning at a pine in said county line, in John SHINE's line. 2100 acres on the north side of Tocohoe creek, on the head of JOSHUA's branch, beginning at..Jacob JOHNSTON's corner. 3120 acres on the north side of white oak river and southwest side of Catfish lake, and on the head of the black swamp, beginning at..George·POLLOCK's and James LEECH's corner. 1280 acres on the north side of Tocohoe creek, including the head of great branch, beginning at ..the second corner of Rachel GERMAN's 150 acre survey. The foregoing Lands appear to be granted to David ALLISON; but it is reported to be the property of Mr. A. DUBOIS of the city of Philadelphia.

1920 acres on the north side of Trent river, including the Juniper pocosin, beginning at..the last corner of Willie GURGANUS's 100 acre survey. 640 acres on the north side of Trent river, including black swamp pocosin, beginning at..James WESTBROOK's corner near William MORGAIN's house. 1300 acres on the south side of Tocohoe creek, beginning at..Hall JARMAN's corner. 1280 acres on the south side of Trent river, beginning at..David ALLISON's second corner of his Royal Oak survey. 640 acres on the north side of Trent river, including HERRITAGEs pocosin, beginning at..

(30) (Cont.) his and Thos. THORNTON's corner. 2560 acres.. 640 acres in Dover pocosin, beginning..on the east side of KENT's old field, the beginning of his grant in
Craven county for 19200 acres. 15360 acres, including the BACHELOR's creek and Dover
pocosin,..surveyed by James JOYE. The foregoing Lands were granted to David ALLISON;
but are reported to be the property of Solomon MARKS and Henry BECK. Edmund HATCH,
Sheriff.

(31) Onslow County, February 15, 1799. Those it may concern will please to take notice, that the Lands advertised for sale as below, for the taxes due..for..1797, and
as yet is said to belong to the estate of David ALLISON, the sale..is postponed until
the second Friday in May, 1799, the 10th day..when the same, or so much thereof, will
be sold..as will pay the said taxes. Lemuel DOTY. .. Onslow County, North Carolina,
November 28th, 1798. 59025 Acres of land in the Jones county line in the white oak
pocosin, and on the head waters of white oak and new rivers, beginning at an oak in
the Jones county line, known by the name of the Royal Oak. 7 113 acres of land on
the head of holly shelter and shaking creek, joining Newhanover county line, beginning
at a cypress near SEYES' in the county line, the corner of James CARRAWAY's and Daniel
WHEATON's land. 6336 acres of land including the Devil's pocosin, beginning at a
forked laurel, on the path leading from Aaron DAVIS's to William KING's. 4220 acres
including the back swamp pocosin, beginning at a fence in SHIPPER's line on long ridge
7040 acres of land.. 704 acres of land including the flat pond, beginning at the four
mile post in the nine mile road near NIXON's line. 2112 acres of land beginning at
Aaron DAVIS's corner..in Duplin county line. 2816 acres... Lemuel DOTY, Sheriff.

(32) For Sale, The Shop, lately occupied by Dr. John CUNNINGHAM, dec., the shop Furniture, and all the Drugs and Medicines, which are well assorted, and a compleat
Electrifying Machine, and sundry Medical Books. Also for sale, the Houses and 4 Lots
of said deceased... Elisha NORFLEET, Ex'r. Peggy CUNNINGHAM, Ex'rx. Edenton, March
4, 1799.

(33) Whereas, my wife Celia, has absconded from my bed and board without any just
cause of complaint whatever. I do hereby forwarn any person..from crediting, harbour-
ing, or in any manner dealing with her, as I am determined to prosecute those who do,
as she has a house and home to which she may resort when she thinks proper. Nicholas
JORDAN. March 1st, 1799.

(34) For Sale, The House and Lotts, the property of the Subscriber, whereon he now
lives... Thomas SEAMAN. Edenton, Feb. 12, 1799.

(35) Dismal Swamp Canal. At a Meeting of the Directors of the Dismal Swamp Canal
Company. February 13th, 1799. Ordered, that the holders of new Shares, pay unto
James BOYCE, Esq. Treasurer, on or before the 2d day of April next, the sum of 50
Dollars, for each Share. This is the first payment required on the new subscription.
Tho's. NEWTON, A. SLAUGHTER, James G. MARTIN, Directors. Attest, Robert BROUGH, Clk.

(36) State of North-Carolina. Camden County, March 4, 1799. Notice is hereby given,
to all the creditors of Caleb FORBES, deceased..is dead, and that the subscribers
qualified as executors to his estate last term... John BROCKET, William HUGHES, Ex'rs.

(37) State of North-Carolina. Pasquotank county, March 12, 1799. Notice is hereby
given, to all the creditors of Job CARVER, deceased..is dead, and that the subscriber
qualified as executor, to his estate, in March term... William T. MUSE, Ex'r.

(38) 10 Dollars Reward. Run away from the Subscriber, ..a French negro man, named
HECTOR. He is about 30 years old..about 5 feet 9 or 10 inches high... F. BRIOLS.
Chowan County, March 8, 1799.

(39) For Sale, The House and Two Lots..where the Subscriber now lives, in the town of Edenton..also..several unimproved lots, in the said town. Michael PAYNE. Edenton, Feb. 18, 1799.

(40) Notice. All those that are indebted to us..are requested as speedily as possible to make payment... Thomas BISSELL and Son. Who has for Sale, A quantity of high proof Antigua Rum..And..Sugar.

(41) Notice. Will be Sold, on the 25th of April next, at the dwelling-house of Mrs. Sarah ARMISTEAD, on Cashie river, Fourteen Guns, the property of William ARMISTEAD, jun. dec. and Robert ARMISTEAD...Executors. March 15th, 1799.

(42) State of North-Carolina, Chowan county, March 14, 1799. Notice is hereby given, to all the creditors of Jeremiah GALLOP, late merchant of the town of Edenton, deceased, that the subscriber qualified as administratrix to his estate at the last county court of Chowan... Ann GALLOP, Adm'rix. On Thursday, the 11th of April, will be Sold, the whole Stock in Trade of Jeremiah GALLOP, dec. consisting of..Dry Goods,..Groceries..Household and Kitchen Furniture, &c. &c....

Vol. XIV. Wednesday Evening, May 1, 1799. Number 684.

(43) Philadelphia, April 18. His Honour, Judge PETERS, and Wm. NICOLS, Esq. the Marshal, this day arrived from Northampton; the troops, we are informed, will return in about 10 days. Mr. Thomas GRENVILLE, who had been sent on a secret embassy to Berlin, had been shipwrecked and lost. Yesterday Conrod MARKS came to this city, and surrendered himself to the Deputy Marshal of the district of Pennsylvania..Judge PETERS some time since issued a warrant for apprehending him, on a charge of treason .. This man has been among the most active of the insurgents of Buck's county, of which he was an inhabitant.

(44) Edenton, Wednesday Evening, May 1. The ship Roanoke, Capt. Ebenezer PAINE, from Cadiz, laden with..Brandy, Wine and Fruit, lately struck on the bar at Occacock, and went to pieces...

(45) Married, on Sunday evening last, by the Rev. Charles PETTIGREW, John BEASLEY, of mean parentage, but clear blood, by profession a quack Doctor, to Nancy SLADE, of clear blood, and oldest daughter of Mr. William SLADE, all of this town.

(46) Died, on Monday afternoon, after a short illness, Mrs. Jamima ALLEN, aged 75 years, of this town.

(47) For Sale, By John WHITE, At the Corner Store, formerly occupied by Mr. Thomas B. LITTLEJOHN. Wines..Brandy..Rum, White Wine Vinegar..Porter...

(48) Notice. Being under an absolute necessity (in regard to my health) to shift my residence from this state; I offer for sale, all my property, both personal and real, in the town of Edenton, consisting as follows: Lots No. 23 and 45, on which stands a Dwel-House, 38 by 18 feet, with piazzas in front and back.. Also, one water Lot opposite No. 5..two other houses.. Also, a Ware-House, 200 feet long, with a cellar and loft the same length..; the Wharf on this Lot extends from Water street towards the channel 255 feet long, and 66 wide, then extends 145 feet long, and 20 wide, with a head 55 feet long and 20 wide, which forms a dock on the East side, that makes a complete harbour for small vessels. Also, two water Lots, opposite to Lots No. 6 and 7, on which Lots extends a Wharf from Water street line, towards the channel, 175 feet long and 132 wide.. Also, the Land Lots No. 6 and 7 opposite to

(48) (Cont.) these two water lots.. Also, one Lot, No. 131. I have likewise for sale 12 Negroes.. The income of this property has completely maintained my family for several years back, and also has enabled me to add more or less to it every year. Samuel BUTLER. Edenton, April 23, 1799.

(49) Marshal's Sale. By order of the Honourable the _____ miralty for the North Carolina ___ be Sold, on the 4th of May ensu ___ beth TOWE, in Pasquotank county, ___ sing Sun, of Richmond, with he ___ niture and apparel. Also, a few ar_ ___ing of her Cargo. John S. WEST ?. April 10, 1799.

(50) Letters remaining in the Post-Offi_, April the 1st, 1799. Benjamin ATKINSON, 2. Capt. A___, James BAKER, Gates, 2. Tho_____, Levy BATEMAN, John CASEY, John _____, ____ CAMPBELL, Capt. Richard CLARK, Ar_____, Christopher DUCKETT, John EVER-TON, _____, Hugh FAGAN, 2. Alexander FERGU___, ___ FOSTER, Messrs. John and Thomas MILL, _____, Mrs. Tamer HAUGHTON, Henry HAR___, ___mon HOPKINS, John HAR-VEY, Tho_____, George WYATT, Timothy HUNTER, G____ VEY, Wm. JORDAN, John JACOCKS, _____, John KELLY, Wm. LABOYTEAUA?, Ric_____, ____ter P. LAWRENCE, Daniel LATHAM, F____, Mrs. Ann LESTIE, E. LYON, Isaac M___, ___and MUSE, John MAINER, John NOTH___, ___NORCOM, John NICHOLS, Wm. PAYNE, ___PER, Rev. Chas. PETTIGREW, J. P___, ___PERSON, Chas. ROBERS, John RAWNS___, ___SMITH, Joshua SKINNER, Ambrose S___, ___SAWYER, 2, W. SCOTT, L. STOBY, Ste_____, ___John STEWART, Thomas STACY, Wm.___, ___ey STOBY, John TAGERT, Solomon W___, ___WEBB, Elizabeth WHIDBEE, Micha_____, ___shua WIRE, WIGGANS and BOND, _____, Chas. BLOUNT, Benners VAIL, John____, ___ard WEBSTER, James WARD. Hend. STAN___

1800 - All issues missing except for the following from American Antiquarian Society-May 21.

THE ENCYCLOPEDIAN INSTRUCTOR, and FARMER'S GAZETTE.
Edenton: Printed by James WILLS, & Edited by Robert ARCHIBALD.
(3 Dollars per Annum.
(Num. 2. Vol. I.) Thursday Evening, May 21, 1800.

(51) New-York, April 30. City of New-York, ss. Eliajah STURTEVANT, mate of the ship Charlotte, commanded by Capt. GREENFIELD, and belonging to Messrs. BROTHERS, COSTER, and Co. being duly sworn, saith, that the said ship departed from Sandy Hook on the 21st inst. on a voyage to Amsterdam, in company with the ship Warren, Captain CAMP-BELL. That..the morning of the 23d, at 6 o'clock,..the British frigate Cleopatra.. hove in sight, and fired a gun. At 10 A.M. the Captains of the Charlotte and Warren were ordered on board the Cleopatra..were taken possession of by a crew and prize master..and bore away for Halifax..at 2 o'clock P.M. this day the deponent with the other mates and crews were permitted to come on shore... Eliajah STURTEVANT. Sworn before me this 29th day of April, A. D. 1800. T. WORTMAN, Notary Republic.

(52) Philadelphia, May 8. Circuit Court of the United States. The following persons concerned in the insurrection in Northampton and Bucks counties, who submitted to the mercy of the court, received the judgment annexed to their respective names, viz. George HUBER, to be imprisoned..6 months, pay a fine of 150 dollars, and give security himself in 800, and two sureties in 400 each, for his good behaviour for one year.
    STOCKS, 6 months imprisonment, fined 200 dols. bail 400, sureties 200 each. John KLINE, jun., 6 months imprisonment, fined 100 dols. bail 400, sureties 200 each. Daniel KLINE, 6 months imprisonment, fined 150 dols. bail 500, sureties 250 each. Jacob KLINE, same sentence. Adam RIESCH, 6 months imprisonment, fined 150 dols. bail 400, sureties 200 each. William GETTMAN, 6 months imprisonment, fined 100 dols. bail 400, sureties 200 each. George GETTMAN, same sentence. Abram SAMSELL, 3 months imprison-

(52) (Cont.) ment, fined 50 dols. bail 100, sureties 50 each. Peter HAMSBERGER, same sentence. Abram SHAMS, 4 months imprisonment, fined 100 dols. bail 200, sureties 100 each. George MUMBOWER, 6 months imprisonment, fined 150 dols. bail 300, sureties 150 each. Henry MUMBOWER, four months imprisonment, fined 100 dols. bail 200, sureties 100 each. Peter HUGER, same sentence. Peter GABLE, 2 months imprisonment, fined 40 dols. bail 200, sureties 100 each. Daniel and Jacob GABLE, same sentence. Henry SMITH, 8 months imprisonment fined 200 dols. bail 600, sureties 300 each. Valentine KUDER, 2 years imprisonment, fine 200 dols. bail 1000, sureties 500 each. Jacob EYREMAN, 1 years imprisonment, fined 50 dols. bail 1000, sureties 500 each. Michael SMYER, 9 months imprisonment, fined 400 dols. bail 1000, sureties 500 each. Phillip RUTH?, 6 months imprisonment, fined 200 dols. bail 400, sureties 200 each. Conrad MARKS, 2 years imprisonment, fined 800 dols. bail 2000, sureties 1000 each. John EVERHART, 6 months imprisonment, fined 100 dols. bail 500, sureties 250 each. And that they respectively stand committed until sentence be complied with. The jury on the trial of Anthony STAHLER, gave in their verdict NOT GUILTY.

The trial of Frederick HAINY and John GETTMAN for treason, was concluded on the 30th ult..verdict, GUILTY. The Grand Jury..return..an indictment against Anthony STAHLER (who was tried for treason, and acquitted) for conspiracy. Captain JARRET.. from Northampton..on a charge of conspiracy..sentence directs that he be imprisoned for..2 years, pay a fine of 1000 dollars and give bail for his good behaviour for two years. The offenders found guilty of treason..Judge CHASE..pronounced sentence of death on..John FRIES, Frederick HAINY, and John GETTMAN. To be executed on the 23d May instant, at Cross Roads, in Quaker Town.

(53) Halifax, May 12. On Wednesday last the Superior Court of law and equity for the district of Halifax closed its sessions-when sentence of death was passed by the Hon. Judge HAYWOOD, on Elijah T. DUNNAVANT and ____ SMITH, for horse-stealing, and Sherrod PHILLIPS, for negro-stealing. -They are to be executed on Saturday next.

(54) Halifax, May 19. On Saturday last, pursuant to their sentence, Elijah T. DUNNAVANT and ____ SMITH, were executed on the commons of this town.-The Governor was pleased to grant a pardon to Sherrod PHILLIPS.

(55) Newbern, May 10. William BLACKLEDGE, Esq. is appointed Clerk of the District Court, for North-Carolina District, vice Francis HAWKS, Esq. resigned.

(56) Newbern, May 10. The schooner John, Capt. Jacob COOK, arrived here from Jamaica...

(57) Edenton, Wednesday Evening, May 21. A New-York paper says, that BOWLES, the celebrated Indian Chief of Muskogee, was a prisoner to the Spaniards at Pensacola.

(58) Notice. This is to forwarn any person..from purchasing..of a Note of Hand of 500 Dollars, given by me to James FISK, of Edenton, which Note has been duly paid... John VAIL. Newbern, May 8, 1800.

(59) Take Notice. Proposals will be received by either of the Subscribers, until the 7th of June next, for building an Academy, in the town of Edenton... J. COLLINS, Sen., S. TREDWELL, J. BLOUNT, Building Commissioners. Edenton, May 22, 1800.

(60) 50 Dollars Reward. Runaway from the Subscriber, on the 1st day of November last, a Negro Man named ISAAC, about 22 years of age, 6 feet high, yellow complexion, thin visage..is remarkable talkative, and has a remarkable small foot..a shoe maker by trade. He formerly belonged to Abner NASH, Esq. of the state of North-Carolina,

9

(60) (Cont?) deceased, and is well known in..Newbern.. Perhaps he has altered his name to that of Jacob SPELMAN, and may pass as a freeman..reward of Sixty Dollars.. to deliver him to the Subscriber, in Jones county, North Carolina, near the town of Newbern. Durant HATCH. May 5th, 1800.

(61) Advertisement. On the 30th day of May next, will be Sold, at the Court-House in Edenton, a part of that valuable Tract of Land, lying on Albemarle Sound, and near the town of Edenton, formerly belonging to Col. James BLOUNT, dec... Edenton, 14th April, 1800.

(62) Advertisement. To be Sold,..at public vendue, by consent of the mortagee, on Friday, the 23d day of May next..part of that..Tract of Land, situated in the county of Gates, belonging to Mr. Josiah GRANBERY, whereon he now lives, to satisfy a judgment obtained in the Federal Circuit Court, for the North-Carolina district, by Messrs. John FIELD and Son, of the city of Philadelphia... 23d April, 1800.

(63) Henry WILLS, Wishing to remove his residence from the town of Edenton, will sell..a Dwelling House, in King street, near the Court-House, 57 or 58 feet front, now occupied by Capt. Thomas COX..it stands on four lots of ground, extending back to Queen street.. Also, his House and Lot, on Market Street, commonly called Cheapside... Edenton, February 13th, 1800.

(64) Post Days for the arrival and departure of the Northern and Southern Mails, from the 1st of May, to the 1st Nov. 1800... Hend. STANDIN, P. M.

(65) For Sale, The House and Lot, Opposite Absalom LUTEN's, on the Main Street.. For terms apply to the Printer, or the Subscriber, near Hertford. Jas. T. WARD, February 10, 1800.

(66) State of North-Carolina. Chowan county, May 1, 1800. Notice is hereby, to all the creditors of Robert MOODY, late of Edenton, merchant, deceased, that the Subscriber qualified as administrator on the estate of the said deceased at March county Court last... Lem. STANDIN, Adm.

(67) Boarding-Cheap. The Subscriber respectfully informs those gentlemen..who may wish to send their Sons to the Academy now established in this town, that he will board young Gentlemen, for Forty Pounds, currency, per year. He still continues to carry on the Boot and Shoemaking business, in the house lately occupied by Wm. SLADE, Esq. in Market street... Henry KENNEDY. Edenton, May 1, 1800.

(68) All persons indebted to James WILLS, for Newspapers, Advertisements, &c. are hereby notified, that unless they pay up their respective balances on, or before the 25th inst..must not be surprised to find that necessity has drove him to put their several accounts in the hands of an officer, for collection, indiscriminately.

1800 - Post Angel - All issues missing except for the following from the University of North Carolina Library-September 10; November 12.

THE POST-ANGEL, or UNIVERSAL ENTERTAINMENT.
Edenton: Printed By Joseph BEASLEY, For Robert ARCHIBALD.
(2 1-2 Dollars per Annum.)
(Vol. I. Num. 2.) Wednesday Morning, September 10, 1800.

Conditions. (For subscription) One dollar and a half paid in advance, every six months so long as subscribers may please to continue... Robert ARCHIBALD. Edenton, August 9th, 1800.

(69) Eulogium, On the Character of General WASHINGTON. By Major William JACKSON.
To John ADAMS, President of the United States. Sir, ...

(70) New-York, August 25. Robbery! Last evening between 10 and 11 o'clock at the
three mile stone, on the Kingsbridge road, Mr. Joseph HITFELL (or HITSELL) was
stopped by two foot pads armed with clubs, who seized him by the collar and attempted
to search his pockets...

(71) Philadelphia, August 39. Important Detection. Information having been received by Robert WHARTON, Esq. from Mr. de la MONTAGUE of New-York, that..persons
were in Philadelphia who had altered sundry Bank Bills, from small to larger amounts;
.. In a few days by the activity of Mr. HAINS, head constable, with other civil
officers, three persons were arrested and lodged in..jail..viz. Roswell BINGHAM,
alias Robert BEERNAN, Levy STEPHENS, and Ephraim FITCH.. Ebenezer SAUNDERS who was
convicted of robbing the mail, and imprisoned in the goal of Annapolis, lately put a
period to his existence by laudanum.

(72) Edenton, Wednesday Morning, Sept. 10. (Died) on the 27th August, 1800, 6
miles above Edenton, Mr. Richard HOSKINS, in the 63d year of his age, he being the
first and only one taken out of his family, left behind him his widow and 13 children, nearly all grown, he is much lamented by all who knew him in particular by
the poor, the fatherless and the widow.

(73) Departed this life on Friday morning the 29th of July last, at his House in
Edenton, Dr. Frederick RAMCKE.. His death must be regretted as a loss to the public,
in being bereaved of the services of a man of unblemished morals, untainted integri-
ty, and singular probity and goodness.

(74) The subscriber intends leaving this state, early in the spring-has for sale on
Friday October the 3d, the plantation whereon he now lives, 402 acres; whereon is a
dwelling house with six rooms and five fire places.. Several never failing springs,
and near the house an orchard, having about 200 apple trees, peach and other fruit
trees..oxen, cows and calves, and horses.. There may be erected a very good grist-
mill on the above land one mile from the river cashie, and a very good road down to
the river... Henry HARRAMOND. September 8th, 1800.

(75) Twenty-Five Dollars Reward. Run away from the subscriber, on the 10th of May
last, a negro man, named BRISTO about 20 years of age, 5 feet 8 or 10 inches high,
of a dark complexion, and is well made.. I will give the above reward to any person,
that will deliver him to the subscriber, or to Mr. H. FLURY in Edenton... Daniel
YOUNG. Windsor, Sept. 6th, 1800.

(76) Advertisement. Notice, on last evening the 3d day of September, run away from
the subscribers, two negro men, namely SAM a black-fellow, about 30 years of age..
about 5 feet 10 inches high, and very stout made. QUAK a light yellow complected
fellow, about 30 years of age, his hair rather yellowish.. He has a broad round
full face and a flat nose for a mulattoe, he is about 5 feet 10 inches high, and also
stout made.. And we do hereby offer a reward of Twenty-Five Dollars for either of
them, delivered to us at Washington, in Beaufort county... George HILL, Michael
HILL. (N.C.) Beaufort county, Sept. 4, 1800.

(77) For the following anecdote, we are obliged to the Carolinian Observer: Anecdote of POCAHUNTA, a Savage princess, and captain SMITH, an Englishman. POCAHUNTA
was daughter to POWHATAN, the leader of an Indian tribe.. A descendant of the Princess POCAHUNTA is now living in this state, the daughter of Mr. John WALL, a comedian

(77) (Cont.) who married into the royal Indian family.. The present young Princess performed on the stage in Edenton about two years ago, under the name of Miss Pocahunta WALL!

(78) All persons indebted to Henry WILLS, are respectfully requested to..pay up their accounts on or before the 1st day of October next, as he proposes about that time to leave the State.. The House and Lots known as the property of H. WILLS, below the Court-House, will be sold... Edenton, August 21st, 1800.

(79) Take Notice. On Friday, the 12th of September next, I shall attend at Joseph ROGERS's near BALLARD's Bridge, and on Saturday the 13th at Mr. O'MALLEY's tavern in Edenton, for the purpose of taking entries of, and receiving duties for, riding chairs and carriages of every description... Edm. NORCOM, Collector of the Revenue for Chowan county. August 12th, 1800.

(80) For Sale, 500 Acres of good Juniper Swamp, situated on the fork of Great Alligator, about half a mile from Convent-Lagding.. For terms apply to James HATHAWAY in Edenton, or Woolsey HATHAWAY, in Tyrrell county. Edenton, August 23d, 1800.

(Vol. I. Num. 9.) Wednesday Morning, November 12, 1800.

(81) Philadelphia, October 29th. Isaac TICHENOR, Esq. is elected Governor and Paul BRIGHAM, Esq. Lieutenant Governor of the State of Vermont...

(82) From a Charleston paper of Oct. 1. Tremendous Storm. On Saturday night, from 11 to 12 o'clock, as tremendous and destructive a storm, was experienced in this city and harbour, as has happened for nearly 20 years.. At 12 o'clock at night, the tide was above two feet high on the wharves..vessels were..stove to pieces and sunk in the docks, and nearly all the wharves from GIBBES' on South bay, to Gen. GADSDEN's suffered.. Mr. POPE's, Mr. GEYER's, Mr. BEALE's, Mr. CHAMPNEY's, and Mr. NICHOLAS's wharves, were injured to a considerable amount.. The two story house of Mr. CRATZBURGH, in Butcher town, was levelled..and a large part of it carried by the wind nearly 100 yards..the melancholy fate of Mrs. CRATZBURGH, who was crushed to death in the ruins.. The house of the late deceased Mr. THORNEY was unroofed totally, and the chimney blawn down..a large portion of the slating of Mr. RAVENAL's new house, the upper end of Broad street, torn off.

(83) Edenton, Wednesday Evening, Nov. 12. The subscriber takes the liberty to inform..that she has taken the store lately occupied by Mr. Henry WILLS, and has just received from New-York..Wet and Dry Goods..she will sell on very low terms for cash. Dorothy SKINNER. Edenton, Nov. 12, 1800.

(84) Notice. To all the creditors of Kinchen TAYLOR, late of Tyrrel county deceased ..is dead, and that the subscriber qualified as administrator to his estate in July term last... James HOSKINS, Adm. November 5th, 1800.

(85) Advertisement. On the 29th day of October last, came to the house of the subscriber, a negroman who says his name is BRANDY, and that he is a free-man that he was born in Guinea and carried to France, and..brought to this country by CASU a Frenchman, about 12 or 18 months past, who landed at Beaufort. He is about 30 years of age, of a black complexion, about 5 feet 8 or 10 inches high, has the marks in the face of a guinea negro..speaks French.. If any person has any lawful claim..give me private notice, and upon information of his being a slave I will..confine the said negro..as he is at this time at my house and says that he will stay there. Nathan ARCHBELL. Beaufort county, Nov. 1st, 1800.

(86) One Cent Reward. Run away from the subscriber..an apprentice Lad, by the name of Jacob DEAL... Thomas HANKINS. Edenton, Nov. 3d, 1800.

(87) Dolphin DREW, Takes the liberty to inform..that he has taken the Store in Edenton lately occupied by Mr. Allen RAMSEY, he has opened a general assortment of Dry Goods, suitable to the fall season, just received from Philadelphia and New-York... Edenton, Nov. 1st, 1800.

(88) Advertisement. Will be sold, at public vendue on the premises, on Thursday the 27th day of November next..that valuable Tract of Land lying in Gates county, known by the name of Sunsberry, belonging to Mr. Josiah GRANBERRY, and containing about 230 acres, whereon is a Good Dwelling-House, Kitchen, Smoke-House, Barns, Stables..also a Store and Counting-House, and two good Ware Houses.. At the same time..will be sold all the other property belonging to the said GRANBERRY, consisting of Negroes, Horses, Cattle, Sheep, Hogs, Household and Kitchen Furniture, Plantation Utensils, and variety of other articles..to satisfy sundry Mortgages and Executions against the said Josiah GRANBERRY... Edenton, October 20, 1800.

(89) For Sale, One undivided sixth part, of all..tracts..of Land, called the Lake Company's Land, belonging to Josiah COLLINS, the Elder, Nathaniel ALLEN, Samuel DICKINSON and Francis PEYRINNAUT, lying in the county of Tyrrel, on the river Scuppernong, & Lake PHELPS, containing by estimation 100,000 acres. Also one undivided half part, of a tract of the same Land, on the east-side of the Canal leading from Lake PHELPS to Scuppernong river, which purchased by Samuel DICKINSON, Esq..containing by estimation, 8,000 acres, more or less. Also one undivided sixth part of 32 negro men slaves, 31 negro-women, and upwards of 20 negro boys and girls..an excellent set of Water Grist and saw Mills, and perhaps the most compleat set of Machinary for cleaning Rice, of any in the United States..which undivided parts of said Lands,..were conveyed by Samuel DICKINSON, Esq. to Francis PEYRINNAUT, by deed of Bargain and sale..the 15th day of October, 1798. The terms of sale will be made known on application to Nathaniel ALLEN, Stephen CABARRUS and William SLADE, attornies of the said Francis PEYRANNAUT, at Edenton, or either of them. October 24, 1800.

(90) Notice. Having made a conveyance to Mr. Francis PEYRINNAUNT, of one half of all my landed property, negroes, &c. in the county of Tyrrell, on the 15th day of October, 1798, to secure the payment of 6,630 dollars and 58 cents and the interest thereon, redeemable in two years-I now give..notice, that I am determined to hold the property in possession, and consider the transaction as it really was intended to be a Mortgage on the estate, and still redeemable on the payment of the principal and interest. I therefore caution all persons from becoming purchasers, upon any other title than what a Mortgage will convey. S. DICKINSON. Edenton, Oct. 15th, 1800.

(91) Those concerned are requested to take Notice, that I have this day put into the possession of Mr. Alexander MILLEN, all the Notes and Accounts due me,..to settle the same,..and in general to transact all my business in this state... H. WILLS. Edenton, October 21st, 1800.

(92) Letters remaining in the Post-Office at Edenton, 16th October, 1800. David BLACK, Mormaduke BAKER, Joseph BIXBY, 3, Ddm. BROWN, James BULL, John BROWN, James BURTON, Thomas BRITT, Monsr. BRIOLS, Christopher CLARK, Benj. COAKLEY, Nathaniel DOWNS, Margaret DUBOIS, John FRANKFORD, James FISK, John GOELET, Lewis GUIAN, David GOODMAN, James GREGORY, Thos. GAGE, Rhichard GARRETT, Wm. HINTON, Isaac HUNTER, John CAMPBELL, Jame HULEHAN, Wm. JORDAN, C. W. JANSON, Thomas JENNINGS, Jos. INGRAHAM, 2,

(92) (Cont.) William KNIGHT, Isaac LOCKWOOD, Elizabeth LEUIS, Robert STACY, Warren LUU?, Wm. MARBLE, Andrew KENSEY, Jacob DEMORD, John MERRICK, Matthew HEASTY, David OTIS, Jacob PARKER, Rev. Chas. PETTIGREW, Francis PUGH, John PETERS, Jhubald PINKHAM, Chas. ROBERTS, 2, Sheriff of Chowan, Wm. RUSSELL, Ann REYNOLDS, George REED, John SWIFT, Archibald LEUIS, Samuel SELBY, Benj. SAUNDERS, Jacob SHURBERN, Thomas STEPHEN-SON, James SMITH, George SKIPWORTH, John SLEIGH, Benjamin WILLIAMS, George WOFF, James WILSON, Wm. WILLIAMS, John D. WHITE, Thos. VAIL, James WOOD, Thomas WILLIAMS, Benjamin WOODARD, John WALLICE, Timothy WALTON, John YOUNG. Hend. STANDIN, P. M.

(93) Notice. The members of the Dismal Swamp Canal Company, are hereby informed that their anuual general meeting happens on the fourth Monday of this month... Thomas NEWTON. October 9, 1800.

(94) State of North-Carolina. Chowan county, Oct. 22d, 1800. Notice is hereby given, to all whom it may concern, That Richard HOSKINS, late of Chowan county is dead, and that the subscribers qualified as executors of his last will and testament at Septem-ber term of Chowan county court 1800... Samuel HOSKINS, Baker HOSKINS, Executors.

(95) State of North-Carolina. Pasquotank county court, September Term, 1800. Whereas William ALBERTSON & Co. hath sued out an original attachment, against the estate of William SIDE, late of the town of Nixonton, in the state aforesaid, Mariner, returnable before this court, at this term; it is ordered that public notice be given ..said William SIDE, by advertisement in Mr. ARCHIBALD's paper for three months.. That unless he appear at the next term..on the first Monday in December next; & re-plevy his estate and plead to the said action, final judgment therein will be entered up against him. By order, William T. MUSE, Clerk.

(96) State of North-Carolina. Pasquotank county court, September term, 1809. Where-as John Gray BLOUNT assignee of Robert MORRIS, hath sued out an original attachment against the estate of John WAITE, late of the town of Nixonton..merchant, returnable before this court at this term. It is ordered that public notice be given to the said John WAITE by advertisement in Mr. ARCHIBALD's paper..that unless he appear at the next term..on the first Monday in December next, replevy his estate, and plead to the said action, final judgment therein will be entered up against him. By order, Wm. T. MUSE.

(97) State of North-Carolina. Pesquotank county, Oct. 22d, 1800. Notice is hereby given, to all whom it may concern, that John PRICE, late of Pasquotank, is dead, and that the subscribers qualified as executors, of his last will and testament at Sep-tember term of Pasquotank county court, 1800... Jonathan PRICE, William BRUER, Executors.

(98) Notice. The subscriber has lately received a large and handsome assortment of Woolens, suitable for the present season.. Also, Window-Glass, 8 by 10; and Shot.. will dispose of by whole sale... Wm. LITTLEJOHN. Edenton, October 1st, 1800.

(99) I Have for Sale, Liverpool Salt, Ditto Earthen and Stone Ware..London bottled Porter..Brandy..Sherry and Malaga Wines. John LITTLE. Edenton, 27th Sept. 1800.

(100) For Sale, One Thousand Bushels of Turks-Island Salt; about twelve hundred bushels of Liverpool ditto; also..Brown Sugar... James HATHAWAY. Edenton, Sept. 22, 1800.

1800 - Edenton Gazette - All issues missing except for the following from the Univer-sity of North Carolina Library-November 19; December 11.

THE EDENTON GAZETTE.
(2 1-2 Dollars per Annum.)
Edenton: Published by Joseph BEASLEY.
(Vol. I. Num. 10.) Wednesday, November 19, 1800.

(101) From the British Mercury.. These words will immediately present to the reader's mind the name of General WASHINGTON. On the 15th of December (1799) the United States of America lost this great and virtuous citizen, who died in the 68th year of his age, at his house in Virginia, in consequence of a sudden disorder, which carried him off in 24 hours.

(102) Norfolk Borough. At a Husting's Court, held the 28th day of Oct. 1800. The Recorder having laid before the Court, two letters from Samuel COATES, Esq. Chairman of the Committee of Correspondence (with Baltimore, Norfolk and Providence) of Philadelphia, offering relief to the poor in this Borough; which letters, with the answers thereto, are in these words: Philadelphia, 19th Sept. 1800, To Seth FOSTER, Mayor of Norfolk, The citizens of Philadelphia..have appointed Committees to collect a sum of money to relieve the suffering citizens of Norfolk, Baltimore and Providence (as result of the recent fever)... Samuel COATES. Norfolk, Oct. 10, 1800. Mr. Sam COATES, Sir,.. Resolved, That a committee in behalf of the Corporation be appointed to inform..that we are truly thankful for..the kindness of their offer; but are not, at present, under the necessity, that should induce us to make use of it... Thos. NEWTON, Robt. TAYLOR, Tho. BLANCHARD, The Committee.

Philadelphia, 15th Oct. 1800. To Seth FOSTER, Mayor of Norfolk. Our last to thee was the 19th of September..we have received no answer..this committee think it proper to send a remittance without waiting any longer..I..enclose..a draft of George SIMPSON, for 2000 dollars on the Cashier of the Office of Discount and Deposit in Norfolk... Sam. COATES. Ordered, That..the committee..are requested to return the 2000 dollars..accompanying the same with the thanks of this Court for their friendly disposition in our behalf, in time of distress. Teste, Wm. SHARP, C.N.B.C.

(103) Norfolk, Nov. 12. Captain James BARRON is appointed to the command of the United States ship Warren.

(104) The subscriber has just received from New-York, a general assortment of Wet and Dry Goods... John POPPLESTON. Edenton, Nov. 1st, 1800.

(105) State of North-Carolina. Camden county, Nov. 5th, 1800. To all whom it may concern, are informed, that Joseph JONES, Esq., Sen'r. of the aforesaid County, has departed this life, and that the undersigned have qualified as administrators, to the estate of the said deceased, at the present term of this County Court... Charles GRICE, M. FENNEL, Adm'rs.

(Vol. I. Num. 13.) Thursday, December 11, 1800.

(106) General Assembly of North Carolina, House of Commons, Monday, Nov. 17..Tuesday, Nov. 18... Mr. SEAWELL presented the memorial of John TUTLE, of Lenoir county, complaining that the late election, so far as respects Mr. William EASTERLING, was conducted in an illegal manner, and praying an enquiry thereon.. Mr. Henry COTTON, from Northampton, appeared and took his seat Mr. Adam GASKINS, from Hyde county, and Mr. D. GLISSON, from Duplin, appeared and took their seats. A Joint Committee was appointed to enquire if any alterations are necessary in the act passed to perfect the titles of the officers and soldiers of the continental line..and of..entries in the office of John ARMSTRONG.. Mr. BRYAN, from the joint balloting for three en-

(106) (Cont.) grossing clerks, reported that Thomas ROGERS, Wm. HILL and Kenan LOVE, were elected. A bill was received from the senate and read, to authorize Christian JENNETT, the guardian of infants of that name of the county of Currituck, to sell and convey to the United States four acres of land at the head land of Cape Hatteras. Also a bill to alter the name of Tobias SUMNER, to that of Joseph John SUMNER. The following message was received from his Excellency the Governor: To the Honourable the General Assembly of the State of North-Carolina... B. WILLIAMS. Raleigh, Nov. 19, 1800.

(107) Massachusetts Legislature. House of Representatives, Wednesday, Nov. 12. A convention of both Houses was formed and precisely at 12 o'clock his Excellency the Governor..delivered the following Speech... Caleb STRONG. Boston, Nov. 12, 1800.

(108) Philadelphia, Oct. 1. A gentleman..informs that he left Providence (R.I.) on Monday last..and the following are..the names of the electors of the President and Vice-President for that state. George CHAMPLIN, Edward MANTON, Oliver DAVIS, Wm. GREEN.

(109) Philadelphia, Oct. 1. The brig Sukey, Capt. Nathaniel BROWN, bound from this port to La Gyura, was captured on the 13th of October by a six gun schooner..and sent into Curracoa.

FAYETTEVILLE

1789 - Fayetteville Gazette - All issues missing except for the following from Department of Archives and History-August 24. From the University of North Carolina Library -September 14, 21; October 12.

AYETTEVILLE GAZE   .
 I.) Monday, August 24, 1789. (No. I.

(110) The following Address of the Governor and Council of this state..presented to General WASHINGTON, President of the United States-to which he has been pleased to return the Answer thereto subjoined. To his Excellency George WASHINGTON, Esq. President... Samuel JOHNSTON. By order and on behalf of the council, James IREDELL, President. By order, William J. DAWSON, Clerk Council. May 10, 1789.

(111) The ubscriber Has For Sale, some likely young _groes, boys and girls, which he will dispose of on very low terms, for produce. John INGRAM. Fayetteville, August 20, 1789.

(112) The Subscriber has just received a good supply of West India Goods..Old Jamaica Spirits, New-England Rum, Sugar, Coffee, Molasses... Samuel MURLEY. Fayetteville, August 20, 1789.

(113) Strayed or Stolen, from Fayetteville..a Dapple Grey Gelding..bred in Rowan county, by Mr. Joseph BRYAN... Samuel MURLE_. Fayetteville, August 18, 1789.

(114) Fayetteville State-House Lottery. Scheme of a Lottery for raising 600 pounds for the purpose of finishing the Brick State-House, in Fayetteville.. 2000 Tickets, at 30s. each-L3000... John INGRAM, Guilford DUDLEY, John SIBLEY, Duncan MACAUSLAN, Robert ADAM, Managers.

Published by SIBLEY & HOWARD.

Vol. I.) Monday, September 14, 1789. (No. 4.

(115) Political. Remarks on the amendments to the federal constitution proposed by the conventions of Massachusetts, New-Hampshire, New-York, Virginia, South-Carolina, and North-Carolina, with the minorities of Pennsylvania and Maryland. By the Rev. Nicholas COLLIN, D. D. & M. A. P. S., of Philadelphia...

(116) American Intelligence. New-York, August 22. The President..has been pleased to nominate, and..appoint the following persons to the offices in the revenue.. For the state of New-York. New-York.-John LAMB, Collector. Benjamin WALKER, naval-officer. John LASHER, surveyor. Sagg-Harbour-John GELSTON, collector. City of Hudson-John TENBROOCK, surveyor. City of Albany-Jeremiah LANSING, surveyor. For the state of Connecticut. New-London-Jedediah HUNTINGTON, collector. Nathaniel RICHARDS, surveyor. Stonington-Jonathan PALMER, surveyor. Middleton-Asher MILLER, surveyor. New-Haven-Hezekiah ROGERS, surveyor. Fairfield-Samuel SMEDLEY, collector. For the state of New-Jersey. Perth-Amboy-John HALSTED, collector. Burlington-John ROSS, collector. For the state of Massachusetts. New-bury-Port.-Stephen CROSS, collector. Jonathan TITCOMB, naval-officer. Michael HODGE, surveyor. Gloucester-Eps SARGENT, collector. Samuel WHITMORE, surveyor. Salem and Beverly-Joseph HILLER, collector. W. PICKMAN, naval-officer. Barth. PUTNAM, surveyor. Beverly -Josiah BATCHELOR, surveyor. Ipswich-Jeremiah STANEFORD, surveyor. Marblehead-Richard HARRIS, collector. Boston and Charlestown. Benj. LINCOLN, collector. James LOVELL, naval-officer. Thomas MELVIL, surveyor. Plymouth-William WATSON, collector. Barnstable-Joseph OTIS, collector. Nantucket and Sherburne. Stephen HUSSEY (or HUFFEY), coll'r. Edgartown- John PEASE, collector. New-Bedford-Edward POPE, collector. York-Richard TREVETT, collector. Biddeford and Pepperell boro'. Jer. HILL, collector. Portland-N. F. FOSDICK, collector. James LUNT, surveyor. Bath-William WEBB, collector. Wiscasset-Francis COOK, collector. Penobscot-John LEE, collector. French man's Bay. Melatiah JORDON, collector. Mechias-Stephen SMITH, collector. Passamaquody-Lewis F. DES LA DENNIER, collector. For the state of New-Hampshire. Portsmouth-Joseph WHIPPLE, collector. Eleazer RUSSEL, naval-officer. Thomas MARTIN, surveyor. For the state of Pennsylvania. Philadelphia-Sharp DELANY, collector. Frederick PILE, naval-officer. Samuel MEREDITH, surveyor. For the state of Delaware. Wilmington. George BUSH, collector. For the state of Maryland. Baltimore-Otho H. WILLIAMS, collector. Robert PURVIANCE, naval-officer. Robert BALLARD, surveyor. Chester-John SCOTT, collector. Oxford-Jeremiah BANNING, collector. Vienna-John MUIER, collector. Snow-Hill-John GUNBY, collector. Annapolis-John DAVIDSON, collector. Nottingham-George BISCO?, collector. Town-Creek-Robert YOUNG, surveyor. Nanjemoy-John Coates JONES, collector. St. Mark's-Robert CHESLEY, surveyor. George-Town-James M'Cubbin LINGHAM, coll'r. For the state of Virginia. Hampton-Jacob WRAY, collector. Norfolk and Portsmouth-William LINDSAY, collector. Philemon GATEWOOD, naval-officer. Daniel BEDINGER, surveyor. Suffolk-Archibald RICHARDSON, surveyor. Bermuda Hundred-William HETH, collector. Christian ROAN, surveyor. Petersburgh-John GIBSON, surveyor. York-Town-Abraham ARCHER, collector. West-Point-John Spotswood MOORE, surveyor. Tappahannock-Hudson MUSE, collector. Urbanna-Stage DAVIS, surveyor. Port-Royal-George CATTLETT, surveyor. Fredericksburgh-William LEWIS, surveyor. Yeocomico, including Kinsale-Vincent REDMAN, collector. Dumfries including Newport-Richard SCOTT, coll'r. Alexandria-Charles LEE, collector. Samuel HANSON, surveyor. Cherry-Stone-George SAVAGE, collector. South-Key-Thomas BOWNE, collector. Louisville-Peyton SHORT, collector. For the state of South-Carolina. George-Town-John COCKDELL, collector. Charleston-George Abbot HALL, collector. Isaac MOTT, naval-officer. Edward WAYMAN, surveyor. For the state of Georgia. Savannah-John HABERSHAM, collector. John BERRIAN, surveyor. Gunbury, Cornelius COLLINS, collector.

(117) Fayetteville. The following gentlemen are chosen to represent the counties.. in the ensuing assembly and convention. Montgomery County-Senate-Mr. KINDALE. Commons.-Capt. JOHNSTON and Mr. James TINDALE. Convention.-Capt. JOHNSTON, Messieurs James TINDALE, David NESBIT, James TURNER, and John CRUMP. Wilkes County-Senate.-Col. LENOIR. Commons.-Col. HERNDON and Mr. John BROWN. Convention.-Col. LENOIR, Col. HERNDON, Mr. JONES, Mr. William HALL, and Mr. John BROWN. Randolph County. Senate.-Mr. William ARNOLD. Commons.-Mr. Aaron HILL and Mr. Zeb. WOOD. Convention.-Messieurs Aaron HILL, Zeb. WOOD, Reuben WOOD, and Thomas DUGAN. Choan county. Senator.-Charles JOHNSON, Esq. Commons.-Stephen CABARRUS and Lemuel CREECY, Esquires.-John HAMILTON, Esq. for the town of Edenton. Convention.-Stephen CABARRUS, Charles JOHNSON, Lemuel CREECY, Edmund BLOUNT, and William RIGHTEN, Esquires.-John MARE, Esq. for the town of Edenton. Tyrrell county. Senate.-Jeremiah FRAZIER, Esq. Commons.-Simeon SPRUILL and Samuel CHESSON, Esquires. Convention.-Jeremiah FRAZIER, Simeon SPRUILL, Samuel CHESSON, Hugh WILLIAMSON, and Thomas STEWART, Esquires. Perquimans county-Senate.-John SKINNER, Esq. Commons.-Benjamin PERRY and Ashberry SUTTON, Esquires. Convention.-His Excellency Samuel JOHNSTON, John SKINNER, Benjamin PERRY, Ashberry SUTTON, and Joseph HARVEY, Esquires. Pasquotank county. Senate.-Joseph KEATON, Esq. Commons.-Edward EVERAGIN and Thomas READING, Esquires. Convention.-John SWAN, Enoch RELFE, Devotion DAVIS, Thomas BANKS, and Edward EVERAGIN, Esqrs. Hertford county. Senate.-Robert MONTGOMERY. Commons.-Thomas WYNNS and ____ HILL, Esqrs. Convention.-Robert MONTGOMERY, Thomas WYNNS, ____ HILL, Hardy MURFREE, and ____ , Esquires. Bertie county. Senate.-John JOHNSTON, Esq. Commons.-Francis PUGH and ____ HORN, Esquires. Convention.-John JOHNSTON, Francis PUGH, ____ HORN, William J. DAWSON, and David STONE, Esquires.

(118) Cool Spring Tavern. The Subscriber begs leave to inform the public, that he has opened a Public House, in Fayetteville, near the Cool Spring... Dolphin DAVIS. September 14, 1789.

(119) Extract from the proceedings of Congress. House of Representatives of the United States. Tuesday, July 18... Extract from the Journal, John BECKLEY, Clerk.

(120) Peter PERRY, Has For Sale, at his store the corner of Green and Old streets, near COCHRAN's mill, Rum, Molasses, Gin, Wines, Iron, Steel, Salt, Tea, Coffee, Chocolate, Dry Goods of all sorts. Fayetteville, August 20, 1789.

Vol. I.) Monday, September 21, 1789. (No. 5.

(121) At a meeting of the Subscribers of the Fayetteville Races, at the Cool Spring Tavern, on Thursday the 1 th instant..the races,.shall commence on the Second Wednesday in November next..subscribers are requested to pay their respective subscriptions to William B. GROVE, Esq... Robert ROWAN, Guilford DUDLEY, Managers. Fayetteville, Sept. 17, 1789.

(122) The subscriber wants to hire Two Journeymen Blacksmiths... John LOWREY. Fayetteville, Sept. 20, 1789.

(123) Congress of the United States. Began and held at the city of New-York, on Wednesday the fourth of March, 1789. An Act imposing duties on Tonnage... Frederick A. MUHLENBERG, Speaker of the House of Representatives. John ADAMS, Vice-President of the United States and President of the Senate. Approved-July 20, 1789. George WASHINGTON, President of the United States.

(124) Salem Paper Manufactory. Ladies save your Rags! The Subscriber begs leave to inform..that he is erecting a Paper-Mill in this town..without rags, paper cannot be

(124) (Cont.) made... Gotlieb SHOBER. Salem, Sept. 8, 1789.

Vol. I.) Monday, October 12, 1789. (No. 8.

(125) Fayetteville. We are informed, that Congress have fixed the seat of government for the United States, at WRIGHT's ferry, on the Susquehanna river. The President..has been pleased to nominate..and appoint the Hon. Alexander HAMILTON, of New-
York, Secretary of the Treasury. The Hon. Nicholas EVELEIGH, of South-Carolina,
Comptroller of the Treasury. The Hon. Henry KNOX, Secretary at War. Oliver WOLCOTT,
jun. Esq. Auditor of the Treasury. Joseph NOURSE, Esq. Register of the Treasury.
We also learn, that his Excellency has appointed Major William JACKSON, of Philadelphia, one of his private secretaries.

(126) Ran Away from the subscriber on Saturday last, a mulatto man, by the name of
Bob WOODS, about 60 years of age..country born-5 feet 8 or 9 inches high-rather
thick made. Also, A negro fellow, by the name of LOWDON, about 50 years old-African
born-speaks bad English of low stature-he has a wife in Fayetteville. Any person
who will..deliver them to William Barry GROVE, Esq. or Mr. Peter TARBE, in Fayetteville, or myself at Bladen, shall receive..a generous reward. LALLERSTEDT. October
5, 1789.

1790 - North Carolina Chronicle - All issues missing except for the following from
American Antiquarian Society-February 1; May 10, 24, 31; June 7; July 19. From
Library of Congress-March 29. From North Carolina State Library-September 13 through
December 27. From the University of North Carolina Library-September 6.

THE NORTH-CAROLINA CHRONICLE; or, FAYETTEVILLE GAZETTE.
Vol. I.) Monday, February 1, 1790. (Numb. 23

(127) NOTE: On the bottom margin of the first page of this issue, is the following
handwritten note: "Mr. THOMAS is requested to forward his newspaper, per post, and
oblige his humble servants-SIBLEY & HOWARD." On the right margin of this page:
"This was Dr. John SIBLEY from Sutton, Mass. who now lives at Natchetoches. Mr.
Senator JOHNSON from Louisiana married one of his daughters."

(128) Miscellany. The following observations on the great importance and utility
of Newspapers, are extracted from the first number of the Western Star-a paper published by Mr. Loring ANDREWS, at Stockbridge, Massachusetts...

(129) New-York, December 16. In the gale of wind on Thursday the 26th ult. the
sloop ___, Capt. John ARNOLD, from l'Orient, bound to Providence, and the schooner
Neptune, Captain WILES, from Wilmington, bound to Boston, were stranded near the
south ferry, Narraganset...

(130) Philadelphia, December 18. A correspondent..takes this opportunity to remark
that the tide waters in general on the eastern coast of North America seem at present
to be gradually gaining on the land..most perceivable in high northern latitudes..a
certificate, dated May 19, 1788, from a certain Joseph RICE..offered in the presence
of several credible witnesses to swear to the truth of his assertions: That he the
said Joseph RICE..resides on the banks of Annapolis river, in Nova-Scotia, about 35
miles from the mouth thereof-that along this river are large bodies of ground which
shew the stumps and roots of trees an incredible space below common highwater mark-
that he had often heard an elderly person declare..that the tides extended now 50
miles higher up Annapolis river than formerly.

(131) Pittsburg, November 28. It is with regret we announce to the public, the death of the honourable Samuel H. PARSONS, one of the Judges of the western territory. He had accompanied Captain HEART as far as the Salt Licks, on his way to Glahago, and was on his return, down Beaver Creek, in a canoe, with one man, when coming over the falls, the canoe was dashed to pieces,..both drowned.

(132) Norfolk, January 2. By the ship Union, James TUCKER, master, from Ostend, we have the following...

(133) Fayetteville. Married-At Wilmington, on Sunday last, Mr. Richard WATSON to Miss TOMPKINS. Mr. Peter MAXWELL, to Mrs. Rebecca GUERARD. Mr. Hugh WADDELL, to Miss HERON.

(134) Taken out of Mr. H. I. LUTTERLOH's waggon, on the road between Wilmington and Fayetteville..13 striped silk waistcoat patterns, 2 red cloth ditto, 3 pieces spotted sattinet.. Should any of the above..be offered for sale, it is requested they may be stopped, and information given to Mr. Severin ERICHSON, at Wilmington, or Mr. William MENG, at Fayetteville. Fayetteville, 1st February, 1790.

(135) From a late Philadelphia paper. An Address to the Public, From the Pennsylvania Society for promoting the abolition of slavery.. We..will gratefully receive any donations or subscriptions..made to our treasurer, James STARR, or to James PEMBERTON, chairman of our committee of correspondence. Signed by order of the society, B. FRANKLIN, President. Philadelphia 9th November, 1789.

(136) The Cumberland guard will attend, as usual, at WHITE's mill, in Hawkins county, on the first of October, 1790, to escort families to the Cumberland country, Daniel SMITH, Brigadier-general.

(137) Just Published by the Printers hereof, And for sale..The North-Carolina Almanac, For..1790; By William THOMAS, Fayetteville, Jan. 1, 1790.

(138) Broke Goal on the 5th instant Philip ALSTON, late of Moore county, committed as accessary to the murder of George GLASCOCK... Thomas WRIGHT, Sheriff. Wilmington, January 8, 1790.

(139) POWELL & FAUX, Carpenters, Joiners, Cabinet-Makers, Turners, Carvers, Gilders, and Undertakers, Beg leave to inform..that having been regularly reared in the above branches in Europe, and their many years experience in America..can give satisfaction to all who..employ them.. Undoubted recommendations from Petersburg, Virginia, can be produced, where they have lived almost seven years... Richard POWELL. Fayetteville, January 16, 1789.

(140) To Be Sold, or if not sold, To Be Rented for one or more years, The House in which I now live... James BURNSIDE. Fayetteville, January 9, 1790.

(141) Lost, on the 18th day of December last, a pocket book, containing a Tobacco Note, given by POTTS and CAMPBELL, inspectors, to William SPEARMAN.. Whoever will deliver the above note..in Chatham, shall be handsomely rewarded. William SPEARMAN. Jan. 4, 1790.

(142) Lost, A Pocket Book, containing Three Tobacco Notes, signed by POTTS and CAMPBELL.. Also L7 10s. in money, and a note of hand signed by John REARDEN.. Any person delivering said pocket-book, with its contents, to Major John PORTERFIELD, or the subscriber, shall be entitled to the money, and no questions asked... Amos CHEEK. Fayetteville, January 26, 1790.

(143) For Sale, at the Printing-Office.. An Oration, Delivered before St. John's Lodge, No. 2, of Newbern, the 27th December, in the year of Masonry, 5789. By Mr. Solomon HALLING. Likewise, A Funeral Oration On the Death of General CASWELL. By F. X. MARTIN.

(144) Boston, February 1. Rochester January 7. The night before last..the wife of Lt. Tisdale WINDSLOW..was awakened about 11 o'clock..by fire..mother and eldest daughter..got out..a son about 12 years of age, and a daughter about eight, forced themselves through the flames, leaving two behind them, one of about 5? years..and one of 18 months, who perished..eldest who had followed her mother into the kitchen ..went into a buttery, where she perished.. The son..(lived) until the next morning about 8 o'clock, when death put an end to his suffering. The only surviving child so exceedingly ill of her burns, her life is much despaired of.

(145) Fayetteville. We hear, that the honourable James IREDELL, esq. manifests his acceptance of the appointment as one of the judges of the supreme federal court, by..setting off soon for Columbia, in South-Carolina, to attend said court..to be opened there, on the 12th day of May next.

(146) Died-In this town, on Friday last, Mr. Duncan OCHELTREE, of a lingering drop-sical complaint. He was a respectable merchant a number of years in this town, and for some time past an inspector at one of the tobacco warehouses. His funeral was to have been attended yesterday by the Phoenix Lodge of free masons..he having been master of the Union (a former lodge in this town), but was prevented by the excessive heavy rain...

(147) Notice..That from the first day of May next, no person shall haul any goods, wares,..in Lower Fayetteville, without first entering their carts, waggons, or drays, at the clerk's office... Published by order, R. MUMFORD, Clerk. Fayetteville, March 23, 1790.

(148) Ten Pounds Reward. Stolen from the subscriber, on Wednesday the 24th of last month, a Scale Beam, with Chains... Peter PERRY. Fayetteville, March 29, 1790.

(149) Notice. The Subscriber takes this method of requesting all persons indebted to him on book, to settle the same with Mr. Duncan M'REA, my attorney.. Likewise, any person desirous of renting my House, advertised some time since in this Gazette, may apply to the said Mr. M'REA for terms. James MOORE. Fayetteville, March 15, 1790.

(150) To Be Leased, For the term of five years, from the first day of January next ensuing, A Plantation on the North-West River about six miles from Wilmington, late the residence of Robert SCHAW, esquire, deceased... For terms, apply to the subscriber in Wilmington. Thomas WRIGHT. December 20, 1789.

Vol. I.) Monday, May 10, 1790. Numb. 3

(151) Congress of the United States. House of Representatives, February 24. A Memorial of Thomas BARCLAY was read and committed. A memorial of N. GORE was read and referred to the secretary at war. A memorial of David S. FRANKS was read and laid on the table...

(152) Boston, April 5. Yesterday sailed from this port for Canton, in China, the ship Massachusetts, Job PRINCE, esquire, commander. This vessel was built in German-town, about 12 miles from this town, by the honourable Samuel SHAW, esquire, Consul

(152) (Cont.) of the United States in China...

(153) Alexandria, April 15. A few days ago a duel was fought at Fredericksburg, between a Mr. GLASSELL and a Mr. RITCHIE, both of that place, in which the latter received a wound in his throat, of which he expired in a few minutes...

(154) Fayetteville. The committee of Congress to whom was referred the petition of Richard WELLS and John HART, brought in the following report. Resolved, That the possessors of the continental bills of credit, emitted by the authority of Congress, before the 18th day of March, 1780..shall receive certificates..at the rate of one dollar specie value for 100 dollars of the said bills...

(155) The honourable George MASON, esquire, is elected one of the senators of the United States, from the state of Virginia, in the room of the honourable William GRAYSON, esquire, deceased.

(156) The house of assembly of New-York has passed a resolution, appointing his excellency George CLINTON, Richard VARICK, and John WATS, esquires, commissioners with authority to build a government house, on the ground where the fort stands, and to draw 20,000 dollars out of the treasury of that state for that purpose. The said building to be appropriated for the accomodation of the President of the United States, while Congress remain in that city.

(157) Ran Away, an outlandish negro fellow, named TOBY-has been in this county two or three years, speaks broken English, has his country mark on both sides of his face, about 5 feet 9 or 10 inches high,..about 40 years of age, says he has been in the country about four years, and was landed in South-Carolina... Henry DEBERRY, Sheriff. Montgomery county, April 26, 1790.

(158) Notice. The copartnership of Donald MC NICOLL, & Co. of Fayetteville, as also that of Henry URQUHART, & Co. of Wilmington, being dissolved by the death of Mr. Donald MC NICOLL, one of the partners, the subscriber, one of the surviving partners, requests all persons..render in their accounts for settlement.. He has in his absence,..authorised Mr. Robert MAC FARLANE at his store in Fayetteville, to settle all accounts..and..Mr. Alexander URQUHART to settle all matters..in Wilmington. The remaining stock of goods..being purchased by the subscriber, will be sold by him..at his stores in Fayetteville and Wilmington... Henry URQUHART. Fayetteville, April 27, 1790.

(159) All persons having any demands against the estate of the late Mr. Donald MC NICOLL, deceased..render accounts and..make payments to Henry URQUHART, Adm'r. Fayetteville, April 27, 1790.

(160) To Be Sold, at Public Vendue, In Wilmington, on the 9th day of June next, A Valuable Water Lot in the said town, lately part of the estate of William WILKINSON, esquire, deceased..about 75 feet on Front-Street... John WILKINSON. Wilmington, May 1, 1790.

(161) Ran Away, an outlandish negro fellow, named JEM, about 26 or 27 years of age-has been in this county about two years-5 feet 9 or 10 inches high, speaks broken English-says he belonged to one SANDERS, of South-Carolina, between Charleston and Savannah river... Henry DEBERRY, Sheriff. Montgomery county, April 26, 1790.

(162) Congress of the United States. At the second session, begun and held at..New-York, on Monday, the 4th of January, 1790. An Act providing for the enumeration of

(162) (Cont.) the inhabitants of the United States... F. A. MUHLENBERG, Speaker of the house of representatives. John ADAMS, Vice-President of the United States, and President of the Senate. Approved-February 8, 1790. George WASHINGTON, President of the United States.

(163) Stolen or strayed from the subscriber,..a Bay Horse...reward of 40 shillings ... David ANDERSON. Fayetteville, April 19.

(164) The Subscriber, intending to move from S___bury, will dispose of his house and lot w___ he lives, and his plantation, adjoining the t__, containing better than 200 acres of good L_d... Michael TROY. Salisbury, April 6.

(165) Notice. The subscriber, preparing to leave this st___ requests all..who may have demands..to present their accounts, on or before the 20th of May next... Thomas NEWMAN. Fayetteville, April 19, 1790.

(166) Strayed or stolen from the subscriber, a..Roa_ Horse.. Whoever ___ deliver said horse to the subscriber, in Wilmington, or J. SIBLEY, Fayetteville, shall be generously rewarded. T. HILL. Wilmington, March 20, 1790.

(167) Lost, in Wilmington, about four weeks ago a Silver Watch, made by William ROBERTSON, Greenock, No. 301. Any person deliv__ing said watch to Mr. John BROWN, Wilmington, __ the subscriber, in this town, shall receive four pounds reward. A. FERGUSON. Fayetteville, April 3, 1790.

Vol. I.) Monday, May 24, 1790. Numb 37.

(168) Philadelphia, April 21. Last Wednesday in the afternoon, the remains of the illustrious and venerable Benjamin FRANKLIN, L. L. D. were interred with every mark of tender and respectful sorrow...

(169) Fayetteville. We hear the President..has been pleased to appoint the honourable Samuel ASH, esquire, judge of the district court of this state, and that the first federal court is to be held at Newbern.

(170) On Wednesday the 14th ult. before the supreme circuit court of the United States..at..New-York, William BROWN and James HOPKINS were tried for a conspiracy to destroy the brig Morning Star, and murder the captain and John Lewis LONEY, a passenger.. After a trial..they were found guilty, and sentenced to stand one hour in the pillory, be imprisoned for six months, and publicly whipped...

(171) Ran Away From the subscriber, living in Cumberland county, at the lower Little-River Bridge, on the new road, an old negro fellow, named ROGER..took up with a free woman for his wife, who I have now living at my house. James CAMPBELL. May 13, 1790.

(172) Copy of a letter written by Major-General GREENE, after the action at Guilford court-house, to the society of Friends at New-Garden..I shall be exceedingly obliged to you, to contribute all in your power to relieve the unfortunate wounded at Guilford, and Dr. WALLACE is directed to point out the things most wanted... Given at headquarters, North-Carolina, March 26, 1781, and the fifth year of American independence. (Answer) To Major-General Nathaniel GREENE. Friend GREENE...

Vol. I.) Monday, May 31, 1790. Numb. 38.

(173) Providence, (R. I.) April 3. Last week Mr. Abner MERRIFIELD, of Medway, in the state of Massachusetts, having purchased in this town a chest of tea, and other articles, was proceeding homeward with the goods in a waggon, when his property was seized by a revenue officer, and sent to Boston. By act of Congress..goods and..the waggon and team are forfeited. Blessed effect of our being out of the Union!

(174) Philadelphia, April 21. On Saturday night last departed this life in the 85th year of his age, Dr. Benjamin FRANKLIN, of this city. His remains will be enterred this afternoon at four o'clock in Christ Church burial ground.

(175) Philadelphia, April 21. The indefatigable exertions of John READ, esq. (says a Boston paper of the 20th ult.) in promoting the growth of..Hemp, merit much from his country...

(176) Fayetteville. The honorable John STEELE, esquire, one of the representatives from this state in Congress, arrived at New-York on the 17th ult. and took his seat in Congress the morning following.

(177) The hon. Rufus PUTNAM is appointed Judge of the Western Territory, vice the hon. Samuel H. PARSONS, deceased.

(178) The honourable the Executive of Virginia have appointed John WALKER, esquire, of Albermarle, a senator of the United States, in the room of George MASON, esquire, who refused to serve.

(179) Original Letter from Doctor FRANKLIN, on the death of his brother, Mr. John FRANKLIN, to Miss HUBBARD...

(180) Copper Stills. The subscriber informs the public that he has established a Copper and Tin Ware Manufactory, in this town; where may be had Stills of all sizes... John NAYLOR. Fayetteville, May 31.

(181) Notice. Those who have any demands against the estate of the late Austin CICATY, deceased,..tender their claims, attested, to Francis FONTAINE, who was appointed administrator to the same, by the worshipful court of Cumberland, at their last session... Francis FONTAINE, (Administrator.) Wilmington, May 22.

(182) The following Address was presented to the President of the United States, on Thursday last, by a deputation of the society of Free Quakers from Philadelphia. To George WASHINGTON.. Signed in and by order of our meeting for business, held at Philadelphia on the fourth day of the third month, 1790, by Ty. MATLOCK, Clerk.

Vol. I.) Monday, June 7, 1790. Numb 39.

(183) Fayetteville. Paragraph from a London newspaper, entitled, "The Star.", dated Feb. 19. "On Sunday night, as James JAUNCEY, esquire, of Charlotte-street, Portland Place, was entering the door of Providence chapel, Little Fitchfield-street, Mary-le-bone, he dropped down, and expired immediately. The above gentleman was an American loyalist, and was well known for his constant practice of relieving the poor at chapel doors,. and in the streets."

Vol. I.) Monday, July 19, 1790. Numb. 45.

(184) Proceedings of Congress. House of Representatives, Wednesday, April 28. .. The petition of John BOND, of New-York, merchant, relative to the tonnage law, was read.

(185) Baltimore, June 4. The district Court of the United States for the district of Maryland was opened on Tuesday last the 1st inst. at the Court-house in this town, by William PACA, esquire.

(186) Fayetteville. Died-This morning, at two o'clock, much lamented..Miss Elizabeth HAND. Her funeral is to be attended at five o'clock this evening.. At Salisbury, on the 8th ultimo, Matthew TROY, esquire, a gentleman of uncommon benevolence and humanity to the distressed.

(187) Congress of the United States. At the second session, at..New-York, on Monday the 4th of January, 1790... F. A. MUHLENBERG, Speaker of the house of representatives. John ADAMS, Vice-President of the United States, and President of the Senate. Approved-May 26, 1790. George WASHINGTON, President of the United States. True copy, Thomas JEFFERSON, Secretary of State.

(188) Lands for Sale. Four hundred and 56 acres in Chatham county, about eight miles from the fork of Deep and Hawe rivers, on the east side. 640 acres in Orange county, on..Back Creek, in the Hawfields. 185 acres, including two of the mountains near Hillsborough. 433½ acres, adjoining the lands of George REEVES, about six miles southwest of Hillsborough. 640 acres about eight miles east from Hillsborough, near Mr. CAIN's... Walter ALVES. Hillsborough, June 4, 1790.

(189) INGRAM & HOOPER Have lately received a large supply of Cotton and Wool Cards, which they will dispose of..at their store in Fayetteville... June 14.

(190) The..partnership of THACKSTON, FENNO & Co. expired on the 17th day of..June. All those indebted..are desired to settle with James THACKSTON, in Fayetteville, or John BURGWIN, in Wilmington... John BURGWIN, James THACKSTON. June 28.

(191) All persons having any demands against the estate of Alexander HOSTLER, deceased, are hereby noticed to render them in to the subscribers... William GREEN, Adm'r. Mary HOSTLER, Adm'x. Wilmington, June 20, 1790.

(192) Lands for Sale. 400 acres on the west side of Cape-Fear River, about five miles from Fayetteville, where Elias STONE lives. 150 acres.. 104 acres on the east side of the river, near Mrs. TOMMY's, formerly D. PORTER's. 640 acres.. 640 acres.. 640 acres on the back of LOCK's Creek.. 500 ditto.. 640.. 640.. 200 acres on the drains of Cross-Creek, near John M PHERSON's. 150 acres about eight miles above Mr. ADKINS ferry, on the road to UTLY's, on GOODRICH's Creek. 400.. 150.. Also the house and lot where Mr. RITCHIE lives, opposite Mr. ADAM's store.. Also- the famous Grist and Flaxseed Mill, At present possessed by Mr. John ECCLES... James HOGG. Fayetteville, June 28, 1790.

(193) All persons having any demands against the estate of the late John TURNER, esquire, of Bladen county, deceased... Amey TURNER, Thomas BROWN, Josiah LEWIS, Exe'rs. Bladen, June 26, 1790.

(194) The Subscriber respectfully inorms the public, that he has removed from New-York to Fayetteville, where he intends to carry on the business of Hair-Dressing and Shaving... James ARANTZ. Fayetteville, July 2.

Vol. I.) Monday, September 6, 1790. Numb. 3

(195) From a late Charleston paper.-Sketches of the life and character of the late William DRAYTON, Esq. L. L. D. Judge of the Federal Court for the district of South-

(195) (Cont.) Carolina, and grand master of ancient masons in the said state. The late William DRAYTON, esquire, was a native of South Carolina; and was born in the year 1732 3 0. S... About the year 1747, he was placed under the care of Thomas COR-BETT (now high sheriff of Middlesex, England) who was one of the most ___minent lawyers of that day in the pro____...

(196) Rhode-Island, July 3. Mr. Jacob ISAACS, of Newport, has made such an improvement in the art of distilling salt water into fresh..he can, in a few minutes extract eight pints of fresh water out of ten pints of the saltiest ocean water...

(197) Providence, July 8. On Tuesday evening last, Mr. Joseph BOYS, an in___ ship carpenter fell from the stage of a large India ship building here, and was so much bruised that he died next morning.

(198) Philadelphia, May 11. Among other curiosities presented to Mr. PEALE's Philadelphia Museum..A dressed Skin of the leg and thigh on an Indian, killed in the march of general SULLIVAN into the western country, during the late war. Presented by Zebulon POTTS, esq. member of the supreme executive council of Pennsylvania.

(199) Fayetteville. The honourable John STOKES, esq. is appointed district judge of this state, in the room of W. R. DAVIE, esq. who declined serving.

(200) North Carolina. Treasury Office, August 16, 1790. ... John HAYWOOD, Pub. Tresr.

(201) I Purpose moving to Fayetteville, and intend opening a house of entertainment and boarding, on the first of September, in the house now occupied by Lewis BARGE.. my best endeavours will not be wanting to give satisfaction, having been happy in that respect while living in the public way at Warrenton... John WILLIS. August 8.

(202) Notice. All those that have any demands against the estate of Nathan STEDMAN, senior, deceased... Nathan STEDMAN, Winship STEDMAN, Admr's. Fayetteville, August 30, 1790.

(203) For Sale. The Subscriber's plantation in Bladen county, called Summerton, on the West side of the Waccamaw Lake, containing about 500 acres,..two-story dwelling-house, kitchen.. Cash, negroes, or merchantable produce, delivered at Wilmington, will be received in payment. George GIBBS. Fayetteville, August 16, 1790.

(204) Wanted. As an apprentice to the Sadler's business, a Lad about 14 years of age... Thomas C. MURPHY.

(205) To the Public. Printing-office, ugust 9, 1790. The proprietor of this publication..does..inform..that 52 papers from the beginning, completes the first volume, ..on the 6th day of September next...

(206) Will be sold, on the first Monday of November next at the court-house in Elizabeth Town. A house and lot in said town, being No. 113.. Also 500 acres of land..on Black-River, and a tract of land on Black-River known by the name of SHAW's old Field; the whole in Bladen county, and being the estate of the late James WHITE, esquire, deceased... William H. BEATY, Administrator, Bladen, August 10, 1790.

(207) All persons indebted to the late Doctor John LEWIS of this place, for medecines, attendance..are requested to make payment speedily..to satisfy several large demands against his estate. Traugott BAGGE, (Attorney for Dr. LEWIS's Executor. Salem, August 4, 1790.

(208) The subscriber being under the..necessity of settling his affairs, he gives this notice..debts..be discharged or..suits will be commenced... J. BURGWIN?. Wilmington, August 16, 1790.

(209) Notice. The public is hereby cautioned from receiving..a note of hand, given by Col. James PORTERFIELD to the subscriber, for 25 bushels of Salt dated 8th March, 1790, which note I have lost; and have this day received payment..from said PORTERFIELD... David SMITH. Fayetteville, 4 August 1790.

(No. I, of Vol. II.) - Monday, September 13, 1790 - (Total No. 53)

(NOTE: The pages in this volume are numbered.)

(210) p. 6 Philadelphia, August 9. William PERRY, of the state of Delaware, one of the judges of the territory of the United States, south of the river Ohio. John STOKES, judge of the North-Carolina district, Vice William DAVIE, declines.-Samuel Russel GERRY, collector of the port of Marblehead, vice Richard HARRIS, deceased.-Zachariah RHODES, surveyor of the port of Patuxet, vice John Anthony ABORN, declined. -Thomas ARNOLD, surveyor of the port of East Greenwich, vice Job COMSTOCK, declined. -Joshua JOHNSTON, of Maryland, consul of the United States of America, for the port of London.-Daniel Eldridge UPDIKE, surveyor for the port of North Kington, Rhode-Island.-John STREET?, of Fayal, vice-consul of the United States, for the island of Fayal.-Ebenezer BRUSH, of New-York, consul of the United States, for the port of Surinam.

(211) From the State Gazette of South-Carolina. Died, Early on Monday morning, Thomas SMITH, sen. esquire, aged 71 years; the eldest branch of a numerous and respectable family, that has been handed down for at least a century. ..on Tuesday evening his remains were interred in the family vault in St. Phillip's churchyard, attended by the South Carolina Society (of which he was a member) and a large number of friends.

(212) The following gentlemen are elected to represent their respective counties in general assembly, the ensuing year. Chowan. Senate-Charles JOHNSTON, esquire. Commons-Stephen CABARRUS and Lemuel CREECY, esquires. John HAMILTON, esq. for Edenton. Perquimans. Senate-Joshua SKINNER, esquire. Commons-Ashb___ SUTTON and ___ PERRY, esquires. Bertie. Senate-Francis PUGH, esquire. Commons-David TURNER and David STONE, esquires. Tyrrel. Senate-Thomas STEWARD, esquire. Commons-S. SPRUILL and Samuel CHESSON, esquires. Camden. Senate-Peter DAUGE, esquire. Commons-Charles GRANDY and Enoch SAWYER, esquire. Pasquotank. Senate-Joseph KEATON, esquire. Commons-___ EVERAIGN and ___ READING, esquires. Hertford. Senate-Thomas WYNNS, esquire. Commons- R. MONTGOMERY and Henry HILL, esquires. Anson. Senate-Lewis LANIER esquire. Commons-Captain PICKETT and William WOODS, esquire. Robinson. Senate-H. BROWN, esquire. Commons-Mr. ___ RIGGEN and Mr. ___ BARNES. Carteret. Senate-Malachi BELL, esquire. Commons-William BORDEN and John FUHARD, esquires.

(213) p. 7 Subscriptions Are taken in at this office for a work now printing by Francis Xavier MARTIN, at Newbern, entitled "The Office and Authority of a Justice of the Peace, and also of Sheriffs, Coroners, Constables &c"..collected from different authorities; but chiefly from a work of this kind, published in 1774, by James DAVIS, esquire...

(214) The Public is hereby informed, that..we the subscribers are appointed inspectors of beef, pork, flour and butter, for the town of Fayetteville... John WILSON, D. CRAWFORD, Inspectors. Fayetteville, Sept. 10, 1790.

(215) Strayed or stolen from the subscriber..a yellow Bay Horse... John SIBLEY. Sept. 10, 1790.

(216) Lost. On Friday, the third instant, I delivered a letter to Mr. Jonathan TOMKINS, of Wilmington, directed to Mr. John BLAKELEY, in which was enclosed 17 pounds; also one other letter, directed to Mr. William MILNE, at Mr. M'NAUGHTON's, Wilmington, containing 12 pounds paper currency..I am advised by letter from Mr. TOMKINS, that he supposes he lost said letters on the road from his place to Wilmington, between Mr. MILLET's and Mr. GAUTIER's... William SANDERSON. Elizabeth-Town, Bladen county, Sept. 6, 1790.

(217) Strayed or Stolen, From the subscribers..a chesnut sorrel Horse... BACHOP & PATTERSON. Fayetteville, Sept. 10, 1790.

(218) p. 8 Notice. Whereas..the marshals of the several districts of the United States shall cause the number of inhabitants..to be taken... John SKINNER (Marshal for the district of North-Carolina. Perquimans, August 21st, 1790.

(219) Five Pounds Reward. Ran Away from the subscriber, living in Surry county, North-Carolina, near ALLEN's iron works, on the 29th July last, a negro fellow by the name of CHARLES; about 30 years of age, 5 feet 8 or 9 inches high... William T. LEWIS. August 23, 1790.

(220) L. DEKEYSER, Begs leave to inform..that he has taken Col. PORTERFIELD's large commodious new house, nearly opposite Mr. M'AUSLAN's store, where he intends keeping a Boarding and House of Entertainment... Fayetteville, Sept. 6.

(221) Fayetteville-Printed By George ROULSTONE for John SIBLEY & Co. at Franklin's Head, in Green-Street.. Subscriptions for this paper are taken in at Three Hard Dollars per annum,...

(No. 2, of Vol. II) Monday, September 20, 1790. (Total No. 54.)

(222) p. 13 Treasury Department, July 20th, 1790. In obedience to the order of the house of representatives, of the twentieth of January last, The Secretary of the Treasury, Respectfully reports... All which is humbly submitted, Alex. HAMILTON, Secretary of the Treasury.

(223) p. 14 Norfolk, September 4. Extracts from LINDSAY's Hotel Diary, August 30, 1790. This day arrived the sloop Hope, captain J. RICHARDSON, from Antigua, consigned to Mr. Nathaniel HILL, in 14 days. This day arrived in Hampton Road, from St. Andero, in Old Spain, the ship Vanslookun, captain J. PORTER, in nine weeks.

(224) The subscriber begs leave to intimate to those who stand indebted to James GAMMELL, & Co. formerly of Wilmington and Fayetteville, merchants, that the bonds, notes..belonging to that concern are lodged in his hands for collection.. A. MACNAUGHTON. Wilmington, Sept. 16, 1790.

(225) p. 15 Information Wanted. If Francis TRUAN, a native of France, who came to America, and served in the army commanded by the count d'ESTAING in Georgia..will apply to Monsieur d'GAMBLE, at New-Orleans, he will be informed of a considerable sum of money..for his pension, and bravery in the service of his most christian majesty. The last accounts I had of him was, that he lived in Richmond, Virginia, and carried on business as a merchant. Phill. LAUGZE. Georgia, June 2, 1790. The printers of the United States will be paid by Francis BOSOROUN for inserting the above advertise-

(225) (Cont.) ment, by sending their accounts to him, Charleston, No. 19, Queen-street, near the old battery, next door to the governor's.

(No. 3, of Vol. II.) Monday, September 27, 1790. (Total No. 55.)

(226) p. 22 To Be Sold, By Public Auction, On Monday, the first day of November next..358 acres..on Old Town Creek, near Wilmington, joining Old Town plantation, and lands of captain Thomas WITHERS and Mr. John M'KENZIE... William H. CROUCH. Fayetteville, September 27, 1790.

(No. 4, of Vol. II.) Monday, October 4, 1790. (Total No. 56.)

(227) p. 27 Treaty with the Creek Nation. George WASHINGTON, President of the United States of America. To all whom these Presents shall come-Greeting. Whereas a treaty of peace and friendship, between the United States of America, and the Creek nation of Indians, was made and concluded on the seventh day of the present month of August, by Henry KNOX, secretary for the department of war,.. In witness of all and every thing herein determined between the United States of America, and the whole Creek nations, the parties have hereunto set their hands and seals, in the city of New-York..this seventh day of August, one thousand, seven hundred and ninety. In behalf of the United States, Henry KNOX, secretary of war, and sole commissioner for treating with the Creek nation of Indians. (L. S.) In behalf of themselves and the whole Creek nation of Indians. Signed and sealed by Alexander MC GILLIVRAY, and the Kings, Chiefs, and Warriors of the Cusetah, Little Tallisee, Big Tallisee, Tuckabat-chy, Natches, Cowetas-OF THE BROKEN ARROW, COOSADES, Alabama Chief, OKAYSOYS. Done in presence of Richard MORRIS, Chief Justice of the State of New-York, Richard VAR-ICK, Mayor of the city of New-York, Marinus? WILLET. Thomas Lee SHIPPEN, of Phila-delphia. John RUTLEDGE, junior. Joseph Allen SMITH. Henry IZARD. Joseph his X mark CORNELL, Interpreter... G. WASHINGTON. By the President, Thomas JEFFERSON, By command of the President of the United States, Henry KNOX, Secretary of the depart-ment of War.

(228) p. 29 Boston, September 4. In the city of New-Haven, in 60 families, there have been raised the present season, no less than 442,000 silk worms. In the family of Mr. Abraham THOMPSON, 60,000..were raised;..several young ladies..turned their attention thereto, one of whom, Miss Betsey SHERMAN, actually raised this season 12,000-and..from 1300 cacoons, or silk balls, reeled eight ounces of the best of silk.

(229) Stockbridge, August 24. Progress of Manufactures. Mr. Moses BARNUM, of this town, has, since the month of August, 1789, fulled no less than 5,310 yards of cloth -and of thin cloth, dressed 3,200-in all, 8,510 yards.

(230) New-York, August 31. The sloop experiment, captain BOYD, from Albany, has brought to this port 40 hogsheads of maple sugar, made at Cooper's town, on Otsego Lake: Mr. William COOPER is the proprietor of this valuable specimen...

(231) John JOHNSTON & Co. Have Imported..from London and New-York, a neat and gen-eral assortment of Dry Goods, suitable to the approaching season... Wilmington, Sept. 27, 1790. (p. 31)

(No. 5, of Vol. II.) Monday, October 11, 1790. (Total No. 57.)

(232) p. 37 Boston, Sept. 7. Benjamin BOURNE, esquire, of Providence, by a large majority of votes, is chosen representative to Congress for Rhode-Island district.

(233) p. 37 George-Town, September 11. We are informed that the following singular and melancholy circumstance happened near Port-Tobacco, Charles county, in the after-noon of Saturday last: Mr. Ignatius SMITH and Mr. Zachariah MUDD, two promising young men, were riders at two separate races, a few miles distance of each other, they fell from their horses, nearly at the same minute, and expired instantaneously.

(234) Newbern, September 23. Died-On Friday last, the Reverend Dr. Patrick CLEARY, a Roman Catholic Priest, and a Canon of the Cathedral Church of the island of Madeira. His remains were decently interred in the afternoon of the next day.. On Tuesday, Mr. William HOBDAY. The Coroner's inquest sat on his body, and found, "that his death was occasioned by a wound he received in the lower part of his belly." One Francis JOHNSTON has been committed to the district gaol, on suspicion of having given the said wound.

(235) From the Charleston City Gazette. As there are various accounts respecting Mr. MC GILLIVRAY, the famous chief of the Creek Indians, the following sketch may be depended on, it being related by one of his old school-fellows: About the year 1759, Alexander MC GILLIVRAY, then a youth of 10 years of age, was sent by his father from the Creek nation to this city, and committed to the care of Mr. Farquhar MC GILLIVRAY, a relation of his father's, by whom he was placed under the tuition of Mr. George SHEED.. He was taught the Latin language by Mr. William HENDERSON, one of the mas-ters of the free school.. At the age of 17, Mr. M'GILLIVRAY was sent to Savannah, and placed in the counting house of general ELBERT; he was afterwards some time in the house of Messrs. INGLES and Co....

(236) p. 38 Stolen from the subscriber, last Thursday night, the 23d instant, a Mare..a reward of six pounds is offered to any one who will..deliver her to Mr. Wil-liam MENG, at Fayetteville, or to Richard WEST. Dry Creek, Chatham co. September 30, 1790.

(237) On or about the 18th of September, was stolen from the subscriber, a Bright Sorrel Mare... James CROW. Tyrrel's creek, Chatham co. Sept. 30, 1790.

(238) Notice. That all persons who are indebted to the estate of Major Thomas EVANS, deceased, late of Surry county... John ARMSTRONG, William POINDEXTER, Executors. October 4, 1790.

(No. 6, of Vol. II.) Monday, October 18, 1790. (Total No. 58.)

(239) p. 45 Fayetteville. On Tuesday last died in this town, the honourable John STOKES, esquire judge of the district court of the United States, for the state of North-Carolina, of a fever, with which he was attacked on his way from Newbern, to this place, where he had been to hold the first federal court. ..so conspicuous have been his merits..it is difficult to decide whether as a Soldier, a Judge, a Legisla-tor, or a Lawyer, he was most worthy of admiration. .. At BLEWFORT's defeat, in South-Carolina, he lost his right hand.. His remains were attended to the grave, on Wednesday evening by the Phoenix Lodge of ancient Free Masons, and interred with the usual solemnities.

(240) Robbery! The following account was handed us by Mr. John WELSH, jun., who was robbed in Moore county, on Tuesday last, which we insert as a caution to the public. On Tuesday last I set out from this town for Salisbury, to acquaint the family of Col. STOKES with his dangerous illness..the fellow who robbed me..I have been informed ..to be one Ezekiel COLTER, a most notorious villain.. COLTER is near six feet high, slender made, of a dark sallow complexion, appears to be between 25 and 30 years of

(240) (Cont.) age, and has a large scar on his left cheek, had on a yellow coloured straight bodiced coat, with a white one over it, and homespun linen overalls, the colour of the flax.

(241) p. 46 Horse Keeping. The subscriber informs..that he has..convenient stables and pastures for the purpose of keeping horses the ensuing season. He has 100 acres of meadow and corn-field under one fence, which is only half a mile from Fayetteville ... William COOK. Fayetteville, Oct. 14.

(No. 7, of Vol. II.) Monday, October 25, 1790. (Total No. 59.)

(242) Died-This morning, Mrs. Elizabeth SIBLEY, the wife of Doctor John SIBLEY, and daughter of the Reverend Samuel HOPKINS, of New-Port, Rhode Island.-She has left a husband, with two little sons, to lament her death. The inhabitants of Fayetteville are requested to attend her funeral, to morrow, at 11 o'clock,..from the house of Doctor SIBLEY, to the place of interment... (p. 51)

(243) p. 51 The subscriber begs leave to inform..that he has removed his shop next door below Mr. WILLIS's tavern, and opposite Mr. RITCHIE's store, where he carries on the business of Hair-Dressing and Shaving... S. STAIERT.

(244) p. 52 Philadelphia, August 31. An account of the produce of different kinds of grain, planted in September, 1789, and March, 1790, by Jacob HILTZHEIMER, esq. Speitz.. The above-mentioned produce was presented to the Philadelphia Society for promoting agriculture, at their meeting on the 17th instant.

(245) Fayetteville. State of North-Carolina, ss. By his Excellency Alexander MAR-TIN, Esq. Governour, Captain-General and Commander in Chief, in and over said State. A Proclamation. Whereas,..an act of congress passed at their last session, intitled "An act to accept a cession of the claims of the state of North-Carolina, to a certain district of Western territory."* I Have thought proper to issue this my proc-lamation..announcing the same to the citizens of this state, to those inhabiting that territory..that due observance be had thereto, and their conduct governed ac-cordingly. Given under my hand, and the great seal of the state, at Danbury, the first day of September, A. D. 1790... Alexander MARTIN. By his excellency's com-mand, Thomas ROGERS, P. Sec. *See No. 18 of this paper.

(246) State of North-Carolina, ss. By his Excellency Alexander MARTIN, Esq. Gover-nour,.. A Proclamation. Whereas, the honourable the secretary at war, hath trans-mitted to me an authenticated abstract..of specie due the non-commissioned officers and privates of the North-Carolina line, as their pay for the months of January, February, March and April, in the year 1783: I Have thought proper to issue this my proclamation, notifying the same to the persons aforesaid..that they may apply.. to the treasurer of the United States, for the sums of money annexed to their.. names.-As also specie due the officers of the North-Carolina line, for arrears of subsistance for the years 1782 and 1783, taken from attested accounts lodged in the office. Given under my hand..at Danbury, the tenth of October..1790. By his excel-lency's command, Thomas ROGERS, P. Sec.

Abstract of specie due..for the months of January, February, March and April, 1783, taken from Mr. Ebenezer JACKSON's settlement.

NAMES	Dol.	90ths	NAMES	Dol.	90ths
David CHESTER,	40		Thomas BROWN,	26	60
Francis LARHO,	40		Samson SYKES,	26	60

NAMES	Dol.	90ths	NAMES	Dol.	90ths
Samuel BAXTER,	40		Daniel MC FARTER,	26	60
Bennet MORGAN,	40		Nehemiah PRAVEY,	26	60
Benjamin MOTTE,	40		John CARTER,	26	60
Matthew NEWBY,	40		John WELLS,	26	60
Archibald BUTTS,	29	30	Peter HADSOCK,	26	60
David AMBROSE,	29	30	William THOMAS,	26	60
Joseph BROWN,	29	30	Fountain JORDAN	26	60
William LONG,	29	30	Robert MC KENNY,	26	60
Caleb JORDAN,	26	60	Abraham FOWLER,	26	60
Crawford JOHNSON,	26	60	James IVES,	26	60
John BAILEY,	26	60	Eli MC VAY,	26	60
Francis WESTERDALE,	26	60	William RYALL	26	60
Caesar SANTEE,	26	60	John PLATT,	26	60
Levy WIGGINS,	26	60	William BROWN,	26	60
Benjamin JOINER,	26	60	William BURNETT,	26	60
Joel TAYBOINE,	26	60	Frederick BLOUNT,	26	60
John LEE,	26	60	John SIMSON,	26	60
Benjamin WHITE,	26	60	Robert SEYERS,	26	60
John LEACH,	26	60	Lotte WATSON,	26	60
Vincent SALMON,	26	60	Caleb THOMAS,	26	60
Solomon MIDDLETON,	26	60	p. 53 Richard ROBERTS	26	60
Adam HART,	26	60	Richard HARDWICK,	26	60
Isaac LEWIS,	26	60	Gibbs LAMB,	26	60
Morris MORGAN,	26	60	Samuel SIMSON,	26	60
John WARD,	26	60	Benjamin RIVERS,	26	60
William FAITHFULL,	26	60	Isaac CLARK,	26	60
Roger MC CRAW,	26	60	Joshua HARVEY,	26	60
John GRAHAM,	26	60	Brittain GEORGE,	26	60
James FAULKS,	26	60	William WELCH,	26	60
John HURLEY,	26	60	Levy COLTER,	26	60
John ELLIS,	26	60	Joseph GURLEY,	26	60
John STRINGER,	26	60	Giles BOWERS,	26	60
John SHEPERD,	26	60	Henry MILLER,	40	
John SULLIVANT,	20	40	Ezekiel WHALEY,	29	30
Edward WILLIAMS,	20		David SWEAT,	26	60
Drury BENHAM,	40		Philip DEAN,	26	60
Charles BRIGHT,	40		William COLE,	29	30
Gideon ACKEN,	29	30	Dempsey BRYANT,	29	30
Burrell LUCY,	29	30	John CAMPEN,	26	60
James SISK,	29	30	William PAYFORD,	29	30
William DOUGLASS,	29	30	Dempsey UNDERDOO,	26	60
Leyman BARKO,	29	30	James BOND,	26	60
Edgarton MOTTE,	26	60	Martin COLE,	40	
Owen TYLOR,	26	60	Miles KNIGHT,	40	
James FLECKENS,	26	60	Samuel GARNER,	26	60
Benjamin SHARPE,	26	60	John GILL,	26	60
Charles WOOD,	26	60	James TUCKER,	26	60
Arthur MC DONALD,	26	60	William GRIFFIN,	26	60
Francis WILLIAMS,	26	60	Cornelius RYAN,	26	60
Edward KING,	26	60	James LEE,	26	60
Solomon WALTERS,	26	60	William SHEPARD,	26	60
William MC KINSEY,	26	60	John ROSIER,	26	60
John ETHERAGE,	26	60	Nathan BULLOCK,	26	60

(246) (Cont.)

NAMES	Dol.	90ths	NAMES	Dol.	90ths
William PRICE,	26	60	George KELLUM	26	60
William MC INTIRE,	26	60	Absalom LEGGETT,	26	60
Alexander MORRISON,	40		Peter ALIXON?,	26	60
Joseph JONES,	29	30	John BRADY,	26	60
James SMITH,	26	60	Miles HUDSON,	26	60
Anthony TONEY,	26	60	John FIELDS,	26	60
Luke BATES,	26	60	Hardy RASHIER,	26	60
James MC INTIRE,	40		Francis GRAHAM,	26	60
Enoch LAMBERTZ,	40		William ALBROOKS,	26	60
Robert HENDERSON,	40		Stephen WILLIAMS,	26	60
Parker ROGERS,	29	30	Samuel WEST,	26	60
Thomas HORREGTON,	29	30	James STANLEY,	26	60
Dempsey BENTON,	26	60	George SPEARMAN,	26	60
Joseph HAND,	26	60	John BRYANT,	26	60
John KELLUM,	26	60	William TYNER,	26	60
Frederick SHAVER,	26	60	James SYKES,	36	60
Willis WHITFIELD,	26	60	Giles HERRINGTON,	36	60
Jesse BUNN,	26	60	Robert SANDERLIN,	36	60
William HEATH,	26	60	James CRUMPTON,	26	60
Thomas SAVAGE,	26	60	Frederick JOHNSON,	26	60
William WALKER,	26	60	William MORTON,	40	
John COLLINS,	26	60	William ECCLES,	40	
William BATEMAN,	26	60	Andrew RICHARDSON,	40	
John DUE,	40		William OSTUN?,	26	60
Archibald COLDBATH,	40		Cason FULCHER,	26	60
John ROBERTSON,	29	30	David CLAY,	26	60
John BLAMER,	39	30	James MOORE,	26	60
John ROBESON,	29	30	William HENSLEY,	26	60
Peter ORDER,	36	60	Willoughby SHEPARD,	26	60
Thomas SCOTT,	26	60	Joseph ALLEN,	26	60
Abner PIERCE,	26	60	Alexander M'KINSEY,	36	60
Abraham SCOTT,	26	60	Moses BARNES,	36	60
Randolph GREEN,	26	60	Joshua TUCKER,	26	60
John TALBURT,	26	60	Isaac BROWN,	26	60
Anthony WHITEHOUSE,	26	60	William LANE,	26	60
Thomas ANGLE,	26	60	Jesse ROUNDTREE,	26	60
John NOBLES,	26	60	Martin BLACK,	36	60
Henry DECKERSON,	26	60	Anthony FRANCIS,	26	60
William TAYLOR,	26	60	Joshua RELL,	26	60
George FOWLER,	26	60	John PETTIE,	26	60
Elijah WARD,	26	60	James MOORE,	26	60
Stephen SMITH,	26	60	Simeon MOORE,	26	60
Nathan SCARBOROUGH,	26	60	Hezekiah SRINGER,	36	60
Nathan MORRIS,	26	60	Solomon PAGE,	26	60
John CHESTER,	36	60	William THURSTIN,	26	60
John SIMPKINS,	26	60	William MERRIDITH,	26	60
Jacob HUKMAN,	26	60	Edward WOODWARD,	26	60
Chosel DECKSON,	26	60	Ezekiel SMITH,	26	60
David WHITE,	26	60	John ABUTH,	26	60
Isaac CARTER,	26	60	Elisha PALMORE,	26	60
Willis WOOD,	26	60	Edward KING,	39	30
John LESLEY,	26	60	James LINDSEY,	39	30
Drury SCOTT,	26	60	Henry SANDERS,	39	30

(246) (Cont.)

NAMES	Dol.	90ths	NAMES	Dol.	90ths
Miles DURDON,	26	60	James HOLLIS,	29	30
Patrick LAREY,	26	60	Peter PETRICE,	26	60
Elijah MOORE,	26	60	John FULLER,	26	60
Daniel M'LARRIN,	26	60	Nathan SLADE,	26	60
Churchill WHITE,	26	60	Edward BALDWIN,	26	60
Joseph HURLEY,	40		Edward ADCOCK,	26	60
Thomas DODD,	40		William LILLETON	26	60
Michael DICKSON,	40		John M'ALISTER	26	60
Thomas PONDER	33	30	Thomas BAXTER,	26	60
Benjamin HARRIS,	26	60	Robert DAVIS,	26	60
William REYLEY,	26	60	James KELLY,	26	60
William DOBBINS,	29	30	Thomas CASON,	26	60
Hugh COMER,	29	30	William EMMERY,	26	60

(To be continued.)

(247) For Private Sale, Pursuant to the last will of Francis CLAYTON, Esq. deceased
That well known valuable plantation and parcel of land, called Rocky Point, on the
North-East river, in New-Hanover county, containing by the original grants, 1920
acres, with a large brick house and other buildings.. Also, the plantation and lands
on the Sound, where Mr. CLAYTON usually resided (formerly Mr. HARNETT's) containing
about 800 acres, with a commodious dwelling house... Proposals will be received in
Wilmington, by Archibald MACLAINE, Henry URQUHART, or Henry TOOMER, the acting Executors, to whom the lands are devised for sale... Wilmington, Oct. 14, 1790.

(248) p. 54 Wanted, Two smart, active Lads, one about 12, the other 15 years of
age, as apprentices to the Watch-Making and Jewellery Business. Apply to Peter
STRONG.. Cash given for Old and Cut Silver. Fayetteville, Oct. 25.

(No. 8, of Vol. II.) Monday, November 1, 1790. (Total No. 60.)

(249) p. 59 Fayetteville. Died-On Tuesday last, Mr. Samuel HAWLEY, of this town,
in the 25th year of his age, greatly lamented by all his acquaintance.

(250) Extract from the proceedings of Congress, Wednesday, July 21. Mr. WILLIAMSON
reported on the petition of H. E. LUTTERLOH that it would be proper to give him an
annuity, as a reward for his extraordinary merit and services.

(251) Abstract of specie due the non-commissioned officers and privates of the
North Carolina line, on account of their pay for..January, February, March and April,
1783, taken from Mr. Ebenezer JACKSON's settlement.

(Continued)

NAMES	Dol.	90ths	NAMES	Dol.	90ths
John THOMSON,	26	60	William MUCKLEYEA	26	60
Luke VICKORY,	26	60	Hezekiah HARGROVE	26	60
David EMLEN,	26	60	Vincent KING,	26	60
John WHITEHEAD,	26	60	Robert GILL,	26	60
William HENSON,	36	60	John GRINNAGE,	26	60
Henry CARTER,	26	60	John LAW,	26	60
Georg TIPPET,	26	60	William HADSWORTH,	26	60
Coleby JACKSON,	26	60	Hardy CARROL,	36	60
William PRIVET,	26	60	Nathan SYLVESTER,	26	60
William THOMSON,	26	60	Mathew WIGGINS,	26	60

NAMES	Dol.	90ths	NAMES	Dol.	90ths
Lewis LUDWICK,	26	60	Moses JONES,	26	60
Aaron PHILLIPS,	26	60	Dempsey STEWART?,	26	60
John SEAGRAVES,	26	60	Warren BROWN,	26	60
Isam AVERY,	26	60	Benjamin BROWN,	36	60
Abraham PARKER,	26	60	Arthur WIGGINS,	26	60
Lewis GEORGE,	26	60	William WOOD,	26	60
Moses CARTER,	26	60	William NICHOLS,	26	60
Charles HOOD,	26	60	John PATTEN,	26	60
Mordecai CONNOR,	26	60	Willis HUGHS,	26	60
Edward NEWTON,	26	60	James COLSON,	26	60
John ATWOOD,	26	60	p. 60 Richard ARCHDEACON	26	60
Jacob MELOTT,	26	60	William FORTUNE,	26	60
Hezekiah HIGHFIELD,	26	60	William CRAE?,	13	30
John GRANT,	26	60	Thomas RUTHERFORD,	9	30
Aaron SPRINGFIELD,	26	60	William RULEY,	26	60
William TRENT,	40		John LOLLER,	40	
Edward HARRIS,	26	60	Vachel JAMES,	40	
John FRALEY,	29	30	George MILLER,	26	60
John HALL,	29	30	Benjamin CONNOR,	26	60
Thomas ROMAN,	29	30	Ezekiel JONES	26	60
John THOMSON,	26	60	John GOOD,	26	60
Bird SHEPERD,	26	60	Joseph MASSEY	26	60
John WOWDLE	26	60	Benjamin HOLLINGSHEAD,	26	60
Robertson GOODIN,	36	60	Stephen GARRISON,	26	60
James WEST,	36	60	Samuel ADKINS,	26	60
Joseph WOBSON,	26	60	John COLLONS,	19	10
Jeremiah ADAMS,	26	60	Francis ALDRIDGE,	26	60
Thomas LOW,	26	60	Zachariah WINNE,	26	60
John SMITH,	26	60	John MELTZTEAR,	26	60
Angus CAMPBELL,	26	60	William COOKE,	26	60
John MOW,	26	60	Samuel GUENN?	26	60
Lawrence UNGER,	26	60	Francis AUDLER?,	26	60
John WILSON,	26	60	Ephraim HAWKINS,	26	60
Bazil HOLLAND,	26	60	Frederick MAINES,	26	60
Fer_inand WAGUNSALES,	26	60	David KEAN?,	26	60
Joseph SIMPKINS,	26	60	Philip MASSEY,	26	60
Michael YOUNG,	26	60	David SMITH,	26	60
John PROGER,	26	60	Thomas HOLLINGSHEAD,	26	60
Philip SAMBLY,	26	60	Will MORRIS,	26	60
Lew B ECTO ,	26	60	William WARD,	26	60
Peter STILLARD,	26	60	Jesse POLLOCK,	26	60
Charles GAZLEY,	26	60	Samuel SMITH,	26	60
Drury MARRETT?,	26	60	William JACKSON,	26	60
Thomas WILSON,	8	40	Charles STEWART,	26	60
George GINSINGS,	3	10	James PETTES,	26	60
Darling MADREY,	40		Willie GOODEN,	26	60
Isaac WOTY,	40		Joseph FULRALL,	26	60
Christopher MILLER,	40		Nathaniel WALTER,	26	60
Jacob VICK,	40		James DEPRUST,	26	60
Burrel SMITH,	8	60	Benjamin FLOOD,	26	60
Daniel POTTER,	29	30	William CONNOR,	26	60
Benjamin BOID,	29	30	William LEPARD,	36	60
Scon BARNETT,	29	30	William PARKS,	26	60

(251) (Cont.)

NAMES	Dol.	90ths	NAMES	Dol.	90ths
David WHEELOR,	29	30	Patrick LINDEN,	26	60
Lewis WEBB,	29	30	William MANDERS,	26	60
James ELLUMS,	29	30	Gabriel MARTIN,	26	60
John BRAGWELL,	26	60	William CUNNAGAN,	26	60
Elisha WAID,	26	60	Peter PILAND	26	60
Jacob SMITH,	26	60	Samuel HERRINGTON,	26	60
David COLWELL,	26	60	Cloid LILTON,	26	60
William THOMSON,	26	60	John WORREL,	26	60
Ewell WRIGHT,	26	60	William WILLIAMS,	26	60
John M'CLOUD,	26	60	Francis SUMNER,	26	60
Samson MOORE,	26	60	David VANCE	26	60
John KIDDS,	26	60	George BRASWELL,	26	60
John EDLOW,	26	60	Samuel HUGHS,	26	60
Richard CAIN,	26	60	David WOODWARD,	26	60
Shadrack COLLINS,	26	60	James PARKS,	26	60
Dennis SCOTT,	26	60	Micajah HICKS,	26	60
Worsey CONNOR,	26	60	John MANNING,	26	60
Philip JORDAN,	26	60	Abner MICHAEL,	26	60
Samuel HART,	26	60	James MONK,	26	60
Richard FURNIVAL,	3	60	Robert WHITAKER,	36	60
Lemvel VASSERE,	26	60	Benajah BAGA,	26	60
William MITCHELL,	26	60	William REAMS,	26	60
John BROWN,	26	60	Andrew HADDOCK,	26	60
Hugh KILPATRICK,	26	60			

(To be continued.)

(252) The subscriber begs leave to inform..that he has removed his shop next door below Mr. W____'s tavern, and opposite Mr. RITCHIE's store, where he carries on the business of Hair-Dressing and Shaving. He has for sale, Hair-Powder-Pomatum-Powder Bags and Puffs-Wash Balls-Shaving-Soap-Tooth-Powder in boxes... S. STAIERT. October 30, 1790.

(253) p. 61 For Sale, The famous Grist and Flaxseed Mill, at present possessed by Mr. John ECCLES. Also, 400 acres of land on the west side of Cape-Fear river, about five miles from Fayetteville, where Elias STONE lives..150 acres..104 acres on the east side of the river, near Mrs. TOMMY's, formerly D. PORTER's..640 acres..640 acres ..400 acres..640 acres..500 acres..640 acres..640 acres..200 acres on the drains of Cross-Creek, near John M'PHERSON's. 150 acres on the west side of the town, adjoining Haymount. Also, The House and Lot where Mr. RITCHIE lives, opposite Mr. ADAM's store.. Apply to James HOGG. Fayetteville, October 28.

(254) The co-partnership of Isaac and Samuel HAWLEY being dissolved by the death of the latter, the subscriber, surviving partner, requests..settlement... Isaac HAWLEY. Fayetteville, Nov. 1, 1790.

(255) Forty Shillings Reward. Whereas the subscriber's house was broken open on or about the middle of October instant, and..stolen from him..One note of hand from Neil M'CRANEY to Mathew Roan WHITE, for 22 pounds. One note from Efler (or Esler) KILLPATRICK to John KILLPATRICK, for 25 dollars specie. One note from Archibald M'BRIDE to Robert HODGE, for 12 gallons Rum. And one note from John KERBEEN to John BIBBIN, for 20 shillings, all of which were endorsed to the subscriber. This is..to caution all persons from negociating the above notes.. The..reward will be paid, and no questions asked, on their delivery to George TAYLOR. Elizabeth-town, Bladen co. October 30.

(256) Five Pounds Reward. Ran Away from the subscriber, living in Iredell county, North-Carolina, on the first day of July last, a negro fellow named FRANK: he is of a yellow complexion..about 5 feet 8 inches high... October 18, 1790. John WORK.

(257) Notice. The late proclamation of his excellency governor MARTIN shews that the treasurer of the United States has orders to pay out the cash for arrearages due to the officers and soldiers who have served a certain length of time in the continental army. In consequence..I have opened an office in Fayetteville, for the accomodation of the persons concerned... John PORTERFIELD. Fayetteville, October 27.

(258) This is to forewarn all persons from receiving, by any conveyance, a note of hand given by me to Benjamin BAGLEY, of Chatham for 36 pounds, payable the 25th day of December next, as I am determined not to pay the same, having been deceived by him in the purchase of a horse, for which said note was given. Ephraim COOK. Fayetteville, October 26.

(259) All persons having any demands against the estate of the late Mr. Samuel HAWLEY, deceased, are requested to render in their accounts..to Isaac HAWLEY, Adm'r. Elizabeth HAWLEY, Adm'x. Fayetteville, Nov. 1, 1790.

(No. 9, of Vol. II.) Monday, November 8, 1790. (Total No. 61.)

(260) p. 67 Fayetteville. Monday last both houses of the honourable the legislature of this state, met in this town, for the dispatch of public business. The hon. William LENOIR, esquire, is chosen speaker of the senate, and the hon. Stephen CABARRUS, esquire, speaker of the house of commons.

(261) Proceedings of the General Assembly. House of Commons, Monday, November 1, 1790. .. On motion, John HUNT, esquire, was chosen clerk, and John HAYWOOD, esq. assistant clerk to the house. House adjourned. Tuesday, November 2. .. Received from the senate the following message: Mr. Speaker and Gentlemen, We propose that the two houses ballot at 4 o'clock this evening, for three engrossing and committee clerks, and nominate Mr. Curtis IVY, Mr. Pleasant HENDERSON, Mr. John DIXON, and Mr. Richard FREAR.

(262) p. 68 On the last day of the supreme court at Salisbury, the grand jury appointed their foreman, William DENT, esquire, Major John CRUMP and Major Harry TERRELL, a committee to wait upon John STEELE, esquire, with the following address. Salisbury District, Superior Court, September Term, 1790. The grand jury,..return their thanks to the honorable John STEELE, esquire, for his spirited support, and faithful attention to the interest of this state, during the last session of congress ... William DENT, foreman. John CRUMP, Harry TERRELL. Joel LEWIS. William BETHELL. Thomas KING. James COTTON. John H___. Zachariah RAY. John T. LONGINO?. Walter BRALEY, Charles POLK. Obadiah W. BENGE. Joseph HAYDON. Jacob CLINARD. John M___

(263) State of North-Carolina, ss. By his excellency Alexander MARTIN, esq.. A Proclamation. Whereas, the..lieutenant governor of the commonwealth of Virginia, hath transmitted to me, his proclamation in council, offering a reward of 150 dollars for the apprehending a certain Benjamin WOODWARD, who, being charged on the confession of James ARTHUR, one of his accomplices, of having feloniously counterfeited and passed, certain certificates and public securities of that commonwealth, hath absconded from justice... Given under my hand..at Danbury, the first day of September, A. D. 1790, and 15th year of the independence of the United States of America.

(263) (Cont.) Alexander MARTIN. By his excellency's command. Thomas ROGERS, P. Sec. God Save The State.

(264) p. 71 Ran Away from the subscribers, last night, an indented servant, named William BOOTH; he is about 28 years of age, 5 feet 8 inches high, of a dark complexion ... Ten Pounds reward. Rob. & Wm. NORRISS. Fayetteville, Nov. 8, 1790.

(No. 10, of Vol. II.) Monday, November 15, 1790. (Total No. 62.)

(265) p. 74 European Intelligence. London, September 2. Paul JONES is in the highest favour with General FAYETTE, and is now under a spelling and reading master, in order to make him competent to deliver a speech to the national assembly, on the subject of liberty uncontroled by law.

(266) p. 75 Fayetteville. The following gentlemen are re-elected representatives in Congress..in the state of Virginia, Viz. James MADISON, Richard Mand? LEE, Alexander WHITE, John PAGE, Josiah PARKER, and Samuel GRIFFIN. ____ VENABLE is elected in the room of Isaac COLES, who declined offering.

(267) On Wednesday last was started for at the race course, a purse of 130 pounds, by General EATON's mare Eclipse and Mr. Paul JEFFERS's horse Nonparial.-First and second heats taken by Eclipse.

(268) p. 76 Proceedings of the General Assembly, House of Commons.. Friday, November 5. .. Mr. HAY presented a petition from Thomas OVERTON and Richard STREET, praying for a law for keeping Deep river open for a free passage of fish up the same-which..Mr. HAY presented a bill agreeable to the prayer of the petition. Saturday, November 6. The committee of privileges and elections, to whom was referred the petition of Thomas HASLIN, of the town of Newbern, reported..that the election for the town of Newbern was legal, and that Mr. GUION, the setting member, is entitled to a seat in the present general assembly. Mr. Alexander MEBANE presented a bill for building a court-house in the town of Hillsborough..read..passed, and sent to the senate. Mr. PERSON presented the petition of F. X. MARTIN.. Mr. PERSON presented the petition of John RAINEY...

(269) p. 78 Rob. & Wm. NORRISS, Saddlers and Harness-Makers, Have just received, directly from Glasgow, a general assortment of Saddlery and Harness Furniture... Fayetteville, Nov. 8, 1790.

(270) For Sale, Five hundred acres of Land on Lake Wacomaw, adjoining to Mr. DUPRE's Plantation, with a small house thereon. For terms, apply to the subscriber or to Mr. Severin ERICHSON in Wilmington. William MENG. Fayetteville, Nov. 15.

(271) The subscriber begs leave to inform..that he has opened a Vendue Store in this town... James BAKER. Fayetteville, Nov. 4, 1790.

(272) Ran Away from the subscriber, living in Salisbury, a likely Negro Fellow, named ABRAHAM, about 30 years old, about 5 feet 6 inches high of a yellow complexion... Conrod BREAM. Salisbury, Oct. 28, 1790.

(273) p. 80 Strayed or Stolen from the subscriber, a dark bay horse... James BURNSIDE. Fayetteville, Nov. 15.

(No. 11, of Vol. II.) Monday, November 22, 1790. (Total No. 63.)

(274) p. 83 Fayetteville. On Wednesday last the..general assembly..proceeded to the balloting..when his excellency Alexander MARTIN, esquire, was unanimously re-elected governor, and the honorable John HAYWOOD, esquire, public treasurer.

(275) Appointments. Samuel BENTON, colonel of the cavalry for Hillsborough, Robert SMITH, colonel of the cavalry for Salisbury district. Thomas HARVEY, major of the cavalry for Edenton district. The honorable Charles BRUCE, and Philemon HAWKINS, esquires, are chosen members of the governor's council.

(276) In the county of Chatham, in this state, there is a kid, belonging to Henry Lewis LUTTERLOH, esquire, of nearly the following description...

(277) The following is a copy of an address..to the President of the United States, from the Governor and Council of this state, at their last meeting.. Alexander MARTIN. Wyatt HAWKINS, President. Done in council unanimously, at the Rockingham Springs, June 26, 1790. By order, Thomas HENDERSON, C. C.

(278) p. 84 Proceedings of the General Assembly. House of Commons, Friday, November 12. Received from his excellency the governor a message, with the resignations of Wyatt HAWKINS, James TAYLOR, and Jesse FRANKLIN, esquires, as members of the council of this state. Saturday, November 13. Mr. CALDWELL presented the resignation of George DAVIDSON, lieutenant-colonel of Iredell county, read, accepted, and sent to the senate. Received from the senate..: We propose that the bill to make Cross-Creek navigable, together with the petition of Mark RUSSEL on that subject, be reported upon by a joint committee...

(279) State of North-Carolina, ss. By his Excellency Alexander MARTIN, esquire.. A Proclamation. Whereas frequent and atrocious robberies have been, and are daily committed in various parts of this state: and whereas Seth COLTER and John ABBOT are supposed to be the leaders of a gang of villains now infesting the neighbourhood of Fayetteville..do hereby offer a reward of 50 pounds, current money, for the apprehending each... Alexander MARTIN. By his excellency's command, J. GLASGOW, secretary.

(280) p. 85 At a meeting of the Episcopal Clergy and Laity of the state of North-Carolina, held at Tarborough, on the twelfth day of November, 1790: The Reverend Doctor MICKLEJOHN was unanimously chosen President. .. Resolved, That the reverend doctor MICKLEJOHN, the reverend Charles PETTIGREW, the reverend James L. WILSON, of the clergy; and John LEIGH, William MC. KENZIE and Joseph LEECH, esquires, of the laity..be, and are..appointed deputies to represent the clergy and laity of this state in the next general episcopal convention, to be held at New-York in September 1792.. Resolved, That the reverend doctors MICKLEJOHN and CUTTING; the reverend Messrs. BLOUNT, PETTIGREW, MC. DOUGAL, and WILSON, of the clergy, and Jonathan KIT-TERELL of Granville, James MILLS of Warren, Henry HILL of Franklin, William MC. KENZIE of Martin, esquires; doctors LEIGH of Tarborough, and DICKINSON of Edenton, and colonels LONG of Halifax, and LEECH of Newbern, of the laity, be appointed a standing committee of the episcopal church in this state... John NORWOOD, Sec. C. Tarborough, Nov. 13, 1790.

(281) Ran Away from the subscriber, living in Samson county,..a negro fellow, named PETER..he is a well made fellow, about 5 feet 10 inches high..10 pounds reward... Amos RUNNELS. November 20, 1790.

(282) p. 86 Strayed or stolen..a Dark Bay Horse.. Whoever will..deliver him to Dr. John UMSTEAD, in Orange county..shall be rewarded. Fayetteville, Nov. 22.

(283) p. 86 The book entitled "the office and authority of a Justice of the Peace, according to the laws of North-Carolina", being more than half completed, subscriptions will cease to be received on the first day of December next... F. X. MARTIN, Nov. 20, 1790.

(284) Ran Away from the subscriber in July, 1789, a negro fellow named LONDON, between 30 and 40 years old, 5 feet 8 inches high, between a black and yellow countenance, straight and slim made, very small sleepy eyes..short feet and thick ancles.. 10 pounds reward to..deliver him to me, in Mecklinburgh county, on Big Sugar Creek, near the old nation ford. Littleberry SMARTT. Nov. 20, 1790.

(285) Ran Away from the subscriber,..25th of September last, a negro fellow named BEN, about 19 years old, 5 feet 7 or 8 inches high..a very black countenance, thin lips..small mouth, and sharp nose, is left handed. I will give 10 pounds reward.. to deliver him to me in Bladen county. Daniel SHIPMAN. N. B. suspect he will endeavour to get to Northampton, near Halifax, as he was raised there. Nov. 20, 1790.

(No. 12, of Vol. II.) Monday, November 29, 1790. (Total No. 64.)

(286) p. 91 Fayetteville. Proceedings of the General Assembly. House of Commons. Thursday, November 18. Mr. TAYLOR from the joint balloting for a governor, treasurer, public printer..reported that his excellency Alexander MARTIN, esquire, was elected governor-John HAYWOOD, esquire, treasurer, and Messrs. HODGE & WILLS, printers.. Friday, November 19. The bill to establish the warehouses now building in Fayetteville by James RITCHIE and John WINSLOW, and to empower the court to appoint inspectors to the same, was read the third time and passes. Tuesday, November 23. The bill to incorporate the physicians and surgeons of this state, by the name of the North-Carolina Medical Society, which was read the second time, passed, and sent to the senate. p. 92 Wednesday, November 24. Mr. GAITHIER presented the resignation of Thomas FELPS, a justice of the peace for Rowan county, which being read, was accepted and sent to the senate. Mr. ANDERSON presented the resignation of Roger GRIFFITH, as colonel of Chatham county, which being read, was accepted and sent to the senate. Resolved, that this house resolve itself into a committee of the whole house to take under further consideration the propriety of giving instructions to Samuel JOHNSTON and Benjamin HAWKINS, esquires, senators of this state in the Congress of the United States.

(287) p. 93 Roger SHERMAN, Pierpoint EDWARDS, James HILLHOUSE, Jonathan STURGES, and Jonathan TRUMBULL, esquires, are elected representatives of the state of Connecticut, in the Congress of the United States.

(288) p. 93 Public Notice is hereby given, that the subscribers have taken that commodious and pleasantly situated house in this town, lately occupied by Mr. DORSEY, and improve the same as a Coffee-House and Tavern.. They also carry on their Vendue and Commission business as usual... JOCELIN & D'HERBE. Wilmington, November 22, 1790.

(289) Just Received, And for sale by the subscriber, at his store in old-street, opposite Messrs. PERRY & TARBE's, A variety of Woolens: Also,..European and West-India Goods... Alex. YOUNG.

(290) All persons indebted to the estate of William HOOPER, esquire, deceased, are requested to make..payment... Ann HOOPER, Executrix. William HOOPER, Executor. Hillsborough, Nov. 25.

(291) Was delivered at the landing, from on board Messrs. CLARK & M'LERAN's boat,

(291) (Cont.) among the goods of the subscriber, a bunch of Frying Pans. The owner, upon describing the property and paying the expence of this advertisement, shall have them on application to John WHIPPLE. Fayetteville, Nov. 29.

(292) p. 94 War Department. September 9, 1790. Information is hereby given to all the military invalids of the United States, that the sums to which they are annually entitled..due on the 4th of March ensuing, will be paid by the Commissioners of Loans.. H. KNOX, Secretary of the Department of War. General SKINNER is Commissioner of Loans for the state of North-Carolina.

(293) For Sale,..about three miles below Fayetteville, commonly known by the name of Spring Hill, now in the occupation of James BLOODWORTH, esquire, containing, with the lands adjoining, about 1500 acres..proposals will be received by John HAY, John INGRAM, or William Barry GROVE, esquires, in Fayetteville, or by me in Wilmington. A. MACLAINE. November 20, 1790.

(294) Whereas in the year 1771, I gave five obligations to Frederick GOBBLE, each ..seven pounds 10 shillings, Maryland currency, (dollars at 7s 6).. I have paid and taken up all but the last obligation..and being informed, that the said obligation was sent to this state..give public notice to whomsoever may have such obligation, to apply to Basil GATHIER, living in the Forks of the Yadkin rivers, in the county of Rowan, having requested him to discharge such obligation, as I am about removing to the state of Georgia. Christopher HOLMAN. November 29.

(No. 13, of Vol. II.) Monday, December 6, 1790. (Total No. 65.)

(295) p. 99 American Intelligence. Philadelphia, October 30. Extract of a letter from James STIMPSON, esquire, Russian Consul, at Gibraltar, August 30, 1790.. Inclosed I send you a list of the 14 surviving Americans at Algiers, on the 9th of last month; six I find died of the plague in 1787 and 1788.. "Prisoners names-Ship Dolphin-captain O'BRIAN, Andrew MONTGOMERY, Jacob JENAVIER, William PATERSON, Philip SLOAN, Peleg LORING, John ROBERTSON, James HALL. Schooner Mary-Captain STEPHENS. Alexander FORSYTH, James CHAIRTTA, George SMITH, John GREGORY, and James HERMETT."

(296) Fayetteville. Proceedings of the General Assembly. Friday, November 26. The committee, are of the opinion, that the emigration of artizans into this state will be of great public utility, and do therefore recommend a bill to authorise the said Henry Emanuel LUTTERLOH to carry into effect his intended plan.. Thomas PERSON, chairman. Mr. PERSON presented a bill to authorise Henry Emanuel LUTTERLOH, to raise by lottery, a sum of money to defray the expence of bringing into this state, a certain number of foreigners..read the first time, passed and sent to the senate.

The chairman of the committee on the judicial system, reported-That a change is necessary..and have adopted the one presented by Alfred MOORE, esquire, with some amendments. Benjamin SMITH, Chairman. Received from the senate the following bills, viz..A bill to enable Prudence DURPHIE to sell a tract of land in Iredell county, &c. Saturday, November 27. The committee to whom was referred the petition of Helen TYLER, reported.. A. MEBANE, chairman. p. 100 Monday, November 29. The speaker laid before the house, a letter from Abisha THOMAS, esquire, agent from this state to the United States.. Thursday, December 2. Received from the senate the bill for establishing an inspection of tobacco, at the ferry of Thomas EATON, on Roanoak river. The following gentlemen are chosen members of the governor's council, viz. Caleb PHIFER, Griffith RUTHERFORD, William LITTLE, Philemon HAWKINS, Charles BRUCE, John FAULCON, and William GOUDY, esquires.

(297) p. 101 To his excellency Alexander MARTIN, esquire, governor of the state of North-Carolina. Sir, The general assembly of the state of North-Carolina acknowledge the receipt of your several messages.. We return you our thanks for the same... W. LENOIR, S. S., S. CABARRUS, S. H. C.

(298) At a meeting of the Trustees of the University of..North Carolina, at Fayetteville, the 24th of November, 1790, it was..agreed, that the following resolution of thanks, be given to Benjamin SMITH, esquire: Whereas, Colonel Benjamin SMITH, of Belvidere, in the county of Brunswick,..North Carolina, was pleased benevolently to grant..the 18th day of December, 1789,..to the trustees of the university..certain valuable lands, amounting to 20,000 acres.. Resolved, That this board do accept the said grant of lands, and..entertain a proper impression of the public spirit and liberality manifested by Colonel SMITH, in this his early and valuable donation... Alex. MARTIN, President. By order, James TAYLOR, Secretary.

(299) Peter STRONG Pays Cash for Old and Cut Silver... Fayetteville, Dec. 6, 1790.

(300) Stolen from the subscriber..a dark Bay-Mare.. Any person who shall bring me said mare, shall have Five Pounds reward, and for the thief and mare, Ten Pounds. Archibald M'DUFFIE. Cumberland county, 4 miles above Fayetteville, Nov. 24.

(301) L. A. DORSEY, Respectfully informs..that he has removed from the house he occupied, belonging to Mr. TOOMER, to that convenient house belonging to Mr. HILL, in Market Street, opposite the Naval-Office... Wilmington, Dec. 1, 1790.

(302) To Be Leased, For the term of four years, from the first day of January next ensuing, A Platation, on the North west river, about six miles from Wilmington, late the residence of Robert SCHAW, esquire, deceased.. For terms, apply to the subscriber in Wilmington. Thomas WRIGHT. December 6, 17_0.

(303) Stolen or strayed from the subscriber..a Bay Horse... William COCHRAN. Fayetteville, Dec. 4, 1790.

(304) p. 102 Stolen from the subscriber, on the night of the 4th instant, from Col. L. DEKEYSER's stable, a horse, bridle, and saddle... Samuel SIMPSON. Fayetteville, Dec. 5, 1790.

(305) Alex. YOUNG, Has Just Received, A large assortment of European & West-India Goods... Fayetteville, Dec 6.

(306) p. 104 JORDAN & BURKE, At their store in Hay-Street, corner of the State House Square, and opposite Colonel THACKSTON's, offer for sale..an assortment of Fall Goods.

(No. 14, of Vol. II.) Monday, December 13, 1790. (Total No. 66.)

(307) p. 106 Fayetteville. General MARTIN..favoured (us) with the following account: That on the third of November last,..federal troops and militia, under..general HARMER, consisting of about 100 men, were attacked by a party of the Shawanoe tribe of Indians, on the river St. Joseph, and entirely defeated with the loss of 50 killed; after which the Indians attacked the main army, consisting of about 500, who were likewise defeated, with the loss of 130 killed and 260 wounded. Among the killed are Col. FOUNTAIN, General SCOTT's son, and Major WILLIS...

(308) The bill for regulating the Judiciary of this state, passed..which provides for an additional judge of the superior court and a solicitor-general, which officers

42

(308) (Cont.) were balloted for on Friday last, and were, For Judge-Spruce M'COY, esq. 97-John HAY, esquire, 32-Adlai OSBORN, esquire, 7-Waitsdell AVERY, esq. 7-John SETGREAVES, esquire, 1. For Solicitor.-John HAYWOOD, esq. 85-John Lewis TAYLOR, esq. 37-Col. DAVIE, 4-Mr. M'COY, 13-Mr. AVERY, 6.

(309) p. 107 Proceedings of the General Assembly. House of Commons. Saturday, December 4. .. Mr. HANDY presented the resignation of Arthur BRYAN, as colonel of Johnston county, which was accepted. Wednesday, December 8. p. 108 Ordered that the following message be sent to the senate: Mr. Speaker and Gentlemen, We have received information of the death of Mr. Richard GRIST, one of the members of this house, and propose that the members of both houses attend the corps to the place of interment, at four o'clock to-morrow evening. Received from the senate the bill for establishing an inspection of tobacco, on Dan river, on the lands of Thomas HARRISON, in Caswell county.

(310) Fayetteville, December 13, 1790. As Timothy BLOODWORTH, esquire, was last February elected a member of Congress of the United States..We, the subscribers, members of the general assembly from the counties of Onslow, New-Hanover, Duplin, Bladen, Brunswick, Sampson and Moore, in the Cape-Fear division,..do recommend to our constituents to re-elect him... Robert W. SNEAD, John SPICER, John A. CAMPBELL, John G. SCULL, Joseph DICKSON, Shadrach STALLINGS, Duncan STEWART, William E. LORD, Richard CLINTON, James THOMSON, Thomas TYSON.

(311) p. 109 To Be Sold, By Public Auction, on the fourth day of January next, before Mr. TOOMER's Vendue-Store, in Wilmington, the following Valuable Lands, 1251 acres, by three patents situate in Bladen county, on both sides of the north-west branch of Cape Fear river,..bounded on both sides of the river by lands belonging to Arthur HOWE, esquire, below, and by those of the estate of Goodwin ELLETSON, esquire, deceased, above. 1000 acres being in two patents of 500 each in Brunswick county, on Allegator branch, between the main road near Mrs. MILLS'? (on WOOD's creek) and the river.. 1568 acres, beginning on WOOD's creek, and running down the same and the north-west river, to the plantation formerly of William WATTERS, esq. but now belonging to the estate of Thomas NEALE, jun. and back for compliment. 350 acres on the north side of Black river.. Terms. One year's credit. Bond,..or receipts upon any allowed claim against the estate of John ROWAN, esquire, deceased... Mary ROWAN. Fayetteville, 9th December.

(312) To be Let, The Lot and Houses lately possessed by Mr. DEKEYSER, on Green-Street, immediately above Mrs. EMMET's. Apply to James HOGG. Fayetteville, Dec. 13.

(No. 15, of Vol. II.) Monday, December 20, 1790. (Total No. 67.)

(313) p. 114 Fayetteville. On Wednesday last both houses of the General Assembly of this state adjourned.. During the session the following acts were passed, viz.- to amend an act passed in Hillsborough, in April, 1784, entitled, an act to encourage Enoch SAWYER to make a road through Pasquatank river swamp, opposite to his plantation. to confirm unto Thomas Pool WILLIAMS, of Currituck an indefeasible title to two acres of land at Bellsville, in said county. to empower Etheldred RUFFIN, Thomas BRANTON, Williby WILLIAMS, and Hymeric HOOKER, the securities of Benjamin CASWELL, late sheriff of the county of Dobbs, to collect an account for the taxes due from the inhabitants of the said county, for the year 1789. to empower James CRAIGE, guardian of the orphans of David CRAIGE, of Rowan county, deceased, to sell and dispose of part of the real estate of the said David CRAIGE, for the payment of a debt due by him to the public. for vesting the property of certain negroes in the heirs of Mark NEWBY. to vest the property of certain lots of land,..in..Tarborough

(313) (Cont.) in Edmund HALL and his heirs. to authorise William M'CLELLAN, of the county of Rockingham, to extend a mill dam across Mayo river. to appoint commissioners to direct and establish a gap or slope on the mill dam of Samuel HIGH, at the falls of Nuse river, in Wake county.. p. 115 to establish the tobacco-warehouse now building by James RITCHIE and John WINSLOW, at Fayetteville.. to amend an act passed at Fayetteville, in 1788,..to authorise and enable John COLSON to return to this state .. to vest the title of a piece..of land lying in Granville county, in James FORSYTH and his heirs, in fee simple. for making conformable to the plan the second course of a tract of land lying in Jones county, formerly Craven, granted by patent to John RICHARDS, bearing date the 24th day of November, 1738, containing 300 acres on both sides of Trent river. to establish the titles of certain lands in Simon, David, William, Jonathan, and Polly TURNER. for the inspection of tobacco on Dan river, on the land of Thomas HARRISON, in Caswell county. for the relief of Thomas RIDGE.

(314) Whereas I gave my obligation to Philip ALSTON for 1550 pounds, to be paid in Negroes, cash, &c. for a certain piece of land on Deep-River, payable the 13th day of this month, at which time I tendered the negroes and cash and he would not receive the same, but wants to take an undue advantage thereof; this is therefor to forewarn any person from purchasing said bond, as the greatest part is paid... Thomas H. PERKINS. December 14, 1790. (p. 116)

(No. 16, of Vol. II.) Monday, December 27, 1790. (Total No. 68.)

(315) p. 122 Fayetteville. Proceedings of the General Assembly. House of Commons. Monday, December 13. The committee appointed to count and burn the ragged money in the treasury..burnt the sum of 5,464 pounds 18 shillings and threepence, ragged money. Matthew LOCK, Chairman. Resolved,..that Francis CHILD, the comptroller of public accounts..is hereby appointed to receive the accounts or pay rolls of the officers commanding..troops (of Davidson county). Tuesday, December 14. .. Therefore resolved, that the resignation of Mr. John HAYWOOD, as assistant clerk to this house be accepted, and that Mr. Pleasant HENDERSON be appointed..in his stead. Received from the senate..resolutions..directing the comptroller to issue a certificate to Joseph LEACH .. We the subscribers protest against the resolution for removing the loan-office of the United States. First-Because it is beneath the dignity of the legislature of North-Carolina to interfere with the servants of Congress. Second-Because the measure directed is inadvisable and impolitic. Edward JONES, John LEIGH, D. WITHERSPOON, John HAY, Lemuel CREECY, John HAMILTON, James TAYLOR. Received from the senate the following resolution for concurrence, viz. North-Carolina. In Senate, December, 1790. The judges of the superior courts of law and courts of equity..having refused a writ of certiorari, issued by the judges of the federal district of North-Carolina, relative to a suit..in which Robert MORRIS, John Alexander NESBITT and others are complainants, and Nathaniel ALLEN, Alexander BLACK, William SCOTT, and others are defendants... W. LENOIR, S. S.

(316) p. 124 Died-On Monday morning last, after a short illness, Mr. Joseph PATERSON, of this town, merchant; and on Tuesday his remains were interred by the Phoenix lodge of Free-Masons, with the usual solemnities. - Last week, James COUNCIL, esquire, of Bladen county. - In Wilmington, Archibald MACLAINE, esquire.

(317) Fayetteville, December 10, 1790. Copy of a letter from John STEELE, esquire, to William B. GROVE, esquire, in Fayetteville, dated at New-York, July 27, 1790... John STEELE. This may certify that the above letter..was delivered to me..and the newspapers enclosed..classed Mr. STEELE among the number who had voted against the assumption of the state debts, William B. GROVE.. Having resided in New-York during the last session of Congress..I am enabled to certify, that John STEELE, esquire, and

(317) (Cont.) his colleagues not only voted against the assumption of the state debts, but opposed the measure spiritedly in all its stages. Abishou THOMAS, Agent for settling the accounts of North-Carolina with the United States. It is well known that the funding bill never received the signature of the President until the 4th of August; and it can be made to appear by Spruce MACOY, esquire, that a copy of the law..and a letter from me were read publicly at Morgan superior court the first or second day of September-.. I defy the tongue of malice..to make it appear that I have on any occasion deserted or neglected the interests of my constituents. John STEELE.

(318) p. 125 Lost, on Monday last, a Tobacco Note, issued by POTTS and CAMPBELL to Thomas UBANKS, of the following description, viz. No. 1128 1263 193 1070. Whoever will deliver said note to the subscriber, in Chatham county, or Messrs. POTTS and CAMPBELL, Fayetteville, shall be handsomely rewarded. Thomas UBANKS. Fayetteville, Dec. 27.

(319) The commissioners of Fayetteville hereby publish an account of their receipts and expenditures for the present year... Paid John CAMPBELL, surveyor, for running the lines of the burial ground 16:0; Paid James MEARS for work done on Person-street 13 10 0 Paid William COCHRAN his account for work done on COCHRAN's bridge, 3 12 0; Paid Caleb D. HOWARD in part for printing tickets, 12 0 0 Paid James BLOODWORTH in part for work done at Campbellton landing, 5 11 0 Paid William ENGLAND, for lumber, hauling, and negro hire, for COCHRAN's bridge, 25 17 0... Published by order, R. MUMFORD, Clerk.

(320) p. 126 Whereas the town of Lumberton has improved far beyond the expectation of those who became adventurers in that lottery-the subscriber..would be glad that every person who is a holder of Lumberton lottery tickets, will file them in the clerk's office... John WILLIS. Lumberton, Robinson county, December 12, 1790.

(321) Made his escape from Wadesborough, in Anson county, on the 11th instant, a young man, named William WILLIAMS, who was taken up on suspicion of forgery. He is a resident of Pitt county-about 19 years of age, yellow hair-.. 20 pounds reward. Jesse GILBERT. Anson, Dec. 16, 1790.

1791 - All issues missing except for the following from North Carolina State Library -January 3 through March 7.

(No. 17, of Vol. II.) Monday, January 3, 1791. (Total No. 69.)

(322) p. 131 Fayetteville. On Saturday last, at the annual meeting of the inhabitants of this town for the choice of a magistrate of police, and commissioners of the town, the following gentlemen were elected-Magistrate of Police. James PORTERFIELD, Esquire. Town Commissioners. Robert ADAM, Duncan M'Auslan, William ARMSTRONG, Richard COCHRAN, Alexander M'IVER, James DICK, James MOORE.

(323) To the freeholders and freemen of Cape-Fear division. Gentlemen, The solicitations of a respectable number of my fellow-citizens, have induced me to offer myself a candidate for..representative for the Cape-Fear division, in the ensuing Congress of the United States.. I am, gentlemen, With respect, your very Humble servant, W. B. GROVE. Fayetteville, Dec. 24, 1790.

(324) On the first day of March ensuing, at the market-house in Hillsborough, will be let to the lowest bidder, the building of a court-house for the district of Hillsborough... J. HARPUR, A. TATOM, W. WATERS, Com's.

(325) Lost, on Friday last, between the Court-House and Mr. VAN's, in Fayetteville, a small bundle of papers, in which was cash,..of 42 or 43 shillings. The papers are of material consequence to the subscriber, who will give the money to the person who has found it, upon their delivering the papers to the printers hereof, or me in Richmond County. Duncan M'FARLAND. January 3, 1791.

(326) Notice is hereby given, that about the 8th..instant, there came to this neighbourhood, a negro man, who appears..to be the property of Mr. Robert LOWRAN, 12 miles from Petersburg, in Virginia. The fellow calls himself CHARLES; he is about 5 feet 5 or 6 inches high,..age of 20 years, well made, of a yellow complexion, speaks good English, and saith his former master was one BRADLEY, on black-river, South-Carolina. If the fellow be the property of Mr. LOWRAN, this friendly notice is given by the subscriber living in Iredell County, Catawba river, near the Island Ford. Tho. M'KAY, J. P. Dec. 28, 1790.

(327) p. 132 Died, on Monday the 22d of November, in Salisbury, of a lingering and painful illness, Mrs. Elizabeth STEELE, relict of Mr. William STEELE-mother of the hon. John STEELE, and Margaret MAC CORKLE, wife of the reverend Samuel MAC CORKLE.. She twice supported with dignity, the character of wife and Widow. Her character will be better understood by the following letter..date February 5, 1783, when her other son Robert GILLESPIE was living.. Elizabeth STEELE. .. Her first husband was murdered stript and barbarously mangled by the Indians, in the Cherokee war, that preceeding the last.-Her second husband died of a lingering illness...

(328) p. 134 Education. Gentlemen who wish to encourage literature in this part of the state, are hereby informed, that the Grove Academy in this county, will, on the second Monday in January, again open; where the Greek and Latin languages will be taught, and also the Sciences. .. By order of the trustees, Thomas ROUTLEDGE, Vice President. Duplin County, Dec. 24, 1790.

(329) p. 135 Whereas, the subscriber was robbed, in the night of the 10th of November last, of his pocket book, containing a note of hand against John COLEMAN, for 20 pounds (which he has since paid to me)-One other note against Thomas CHILES, for 50 pounds-And one other note against Nathan POWELL for four pounds nine shillings and four pence-I hereby forewarn all persons not to purchase..same... Charles ROBINSON. Dec. 28, 1790.

(No. 18, of Vol. II.) Monday, January 10, 1791. (Total No. 70.)

(330) p. 140 Philadelphia, December 4. The loaf sugar made from the maple sugar, and now exposed for sale by Messrs. Edward and Isaac PENNINGTON, has been pronounced by impartial judges to be equal to any loaf sugar of the same quality that ever was made from the West-India sugar-cane. We hear that a large Boiling House for..refining the maple sugar, will be erected during the present winter..near Cooper's town, under the direction of William COOPER, esquire...

(331) Fayetteville. Samuel STERETT, William PINCKNEY, Joshua SENEY, William Vans MURRAY, Philip KEY, and Upton SHEREDINE, esquires, are elected federal representatives of the state of Maryland.

(332) Died-On Friday last, after a short illness, Mrs. Ann HERO, of this town.-Lately, in Orange county, Jesse BENTON, esq. artorney at law.-In Boston, the honorable James BOWDOIN, esq., late governor of the commonwealth of Massachusetts.

(333) A state of the conduct of the Judges, referred to in a resolve of the General

46

(333) (Cont.) Assembly, published in the Fayetteville Gazette, of December 27.
Edenton, Nov. 19, 1790. Superior court of law..equity for the district of Edenton,
In the course of the term a writ of certiorari,..of the circuit court for the district of North-Carolina..commanding the judges of the court of equity for the district of Edenton, to certify an original bill of complaint..against Nathaniel ALLEN,
Alexander BLACK, William SCOTT, William BOYD, William BENNETT, Archibald BALL, Thomas COX, Christopher CLARKE, Charles JOHNSON, Josiah COLLINS, and James IREDELL, at
the suit of Robert MORRIS, John Alexander NESBIT, and David Hayfield CUNNINGHAM in
his own right, and as executor of the testament and last will of Redmond CUNNINGHAM,
deceased...

(334) p. 142 Five Tobacco Notes Lost. Lost or mislaid by Mess. George MORRISON &
Co., of Petersburg, the five following Tobacco Notes. to wit-No. 1896-..issued by
POTTS & CAMPBELL to Wm. HABLET. No. 26-..issued by POTTS & CAMPBELL to Richmond
PIERSON. No. 27-..to Richmond PIERSON. No. 568-..issued by LORD & DAVIS to Joseph
WINSTON. No. 53-..issued by LORD & DAVIS to John OVERTON. Any person who may have
found the same, and who will deliver them to Patric ST. LAWRENCE, esquire, in Chatham
county, or the subscriber in Fayetteville, shall be generously rewarded... W. BA-
CHOP. Fayetteville Jan. 5, 1791.

(335) p. 144 The printing-office is removed to the long room in the house belonging to Mr. HOGG, in Green-street, lately occupied by Col. DEKEYSER.

(336) To Be Let. The rooms under the new printing office. Apply to James HOGG.
January 10, 1791.

(No. 19, of Vol. II.) Monday, January 17, 1791. (Total No. 71.)

(337) p. 155 Stolen on the 12th of December last, about three miles from Fayetteville, a Bay Horse..and a Brown Mare.. Any person who will deliver them to the subscriber in Charlotte, Mecklinburg county..10 pounds reward. Evan SHELBY. Jan. 24,
1791.

(338) To Be Rented, For one or five years, from the 1st January last, The whole or
any part of the lower story of the State-House, in this town.. For terms apply to
Lewis BARGE, or Matthew LYLE. Fayetteville, Jan. 24, 1791.

(339) Feats of Activity!!! William Powers KNIGHT, Lately from Charleston, will per-
form on Thursday Evening, the 27th instant, at the State-House, the following feats
of activity... Tickets-At 5 s. each..at the Printing-Office, and of the performer,
at Colonel WILLIS's.

(340) p. 156 The honourable Beverley RANDOLPH, esq. is re-elected governour of
Virginia...

(341) p. 157 Congress of the United States. House of Representatives. Wednesday,
December 8. .. The petition of John CARLISLE, praying compensation for military
services was read and referred to the secretary of the treasury. p. 158 Thursday,
December 9. A message from the senate..that they have agreed..for the appointment
of two chaplains, and have on their part appointed the Right Reverend Bishop WHITE.

(342) Canal Company. (Fayetteville ?) The Directors are to meet on..Thursday next,
at colonel DEKEYSER's.. All persons who are desirous of undertaking all or any part
of the works, or who wish to furnish cypress and pine plank, also ton-timber,..are
desired to leave their proposals in writing with John WINSLOW, Sec.

(343) In the Court of Equity, Fayetteville District. Decem. Term, 1790. Martha HICKS, complainant, vs. Charles MEDLOCK, defendant. Ordered, That the defendant appear and file his answer, on or before..the 23d day of April next, or the bill will be taken pro confesso. R. MUMFORD, C. M. E. Jan. 24, 1791.

(344) p. 162 Albany, November 25. New-Baltimore, formerly known by the name of Prospect or VANDERZEE's-Landing, on the 14th instant received its name by a majority of the votes of its inhabitants, and the discharge of several cannon. New-Baltimore is situated on the west side of Hudson's river, 14 miles south of the city of Albany, 15 north of the city of Hudson, and three miles below CORYMAN's landing...

(345) Philadelphia, December 16. Yesterday evening the honorable Judge WILSON, law professor in the college of Philadelphia, delivered his introductory lecture in the p. 163 hall. After Mr. WILSON's lecture, a commencement was held for conferring doctors degrees in medicine. The..commencement was introduced by an address from doctor RUSH, professor of the theory and practice of medicine in the college. The candidates Isaac SAYRE, A. B. of New Jersey, and Moses BARTRAM, A. B. of Philadelphia were then examined on..their respective theses.. The degree of doctor of medicine was conferred on both by the provost; also the degree of doctor of laws on the hon. James WILSON, Francis HOPKINSON, and Edward SHIPPEN, esquires.

(346) Baltimore, December 10. On Tuesday last the ship Sampson, captain Thomas MOORE, arrived here from London.-In this vessel came passenger, the Right Reverend Doctor John CARROL, recently consecrated bishop of the catholic church in the United States. In the same vessel also came passenger (and was landed in Virginia) the Right Reverend Doctor James MADDISON, bishop of the episcopal church of Virginia, who was, on..20th September last, consecrated at Lambeth Chapel, London...

(347) Fayetteville. Report of the sub-committee of finance, of the last general assembly, on the sums of money due the public up to the year 1790... James TAYLOR, Chairman. On Thursday and Friday last, was held, the election for a representative in congress for Cape-Fear division-The ballots in this county, were-For Timothy BLOODWORTH, esq. 38-William Barry GROVE, esq. 866. The hon. John SITGREAVES, esq. is appointed judge of the district court for the district of North Carolina, in the room of the hon. John STOKES, Esq. deceased. William H. HILL, Esq. is appointed district attorney, in place of Mr. SITGREAVES. We are informed that Alfred MOORE, Esq. has resigned the appointment of attorney general of this state.

(348) Died-Lately at Wilmington, Mrs. HILL, consort of W. H. HILL, Esq.

(No. 21, of Vol. II.) Monday, January 31, 1791. (Total No. 73.)

(349) Congress of the United States. House of Representatives, Tuesday, December 14. .. Mr. BURKE presented a petition of Ann ROBERTS, widow of Owen ROBERTS, late colonel of artillery, who was wounded at Stono, South-Carolina, praying for seven years half pay as his widow, which was read and ordered to lie on the table. Wednesday, December 15. Mr. BLOODWORTH presented the petition of Henry E. LUTTERLOH, praying compensation for services, which was read. Mr. LAWRENCE presented a petition of Timothy MIX, serjeant of artillery, who lost his right hand at the battle at Fort Montgomery, praying the benefit of a pension as an invalid, was read and referred to the Secretary at War. The petition of Thomas RANDALL, of New York, merchant, praying compensation for the sails, rigging, &c. of a sloop taken for the public service, and for the Hull of sd. sloop destroyed, was read and referred to the secretary of the treasury.. Mr. FITZSIMONS presented a petition of John CHURCHMAN, praying the attention of congress to a petition formerly presented; especially to that part in.

(349) (Cont.) which he solicits Congress to fit out a vessel, in which he may proceed to Baffin's Bay, for the purpose of making discoveries, which was read and ordered to lie on the table. Mr. GILMAN presented a petition of Isaac MANSFIELD, praying compensation for services as chaplain in the late army of the United States, which was read and ordered to lie on the table. (p. 164)

(350) p. 166 For Sale, Several Likely Negroes. .. For terms, apply to WALKER & YOUNGER, in Wilmington, or in Fayetteville, to David ANDERSON. Jan. 31, 1791.

(No. 22, of Vol. II.) Monday, February 7, 1791. (Total No. 74.)

(351) p. 170 Fayetteville. The hon. Nathaniel MACON, esquire is elected member of Congress for the Centre division...

(352) This day the notorious horse-thief Seth COLTER, was brought to town, having been taken a few days since, by Mr. STOKES, of Chatham, and some others, near Lumberton, in Robinson county...

(353) p. 171 Died-Last week, Mrs. MAC ALLESTER, wife of colonel Alexander MAC ALLESTER, of Cumberland county.

(354) The Subscribers to the Fayetteville Races, who have not yet paid up their subscription, are requested to settle the same with the subscriber..on or before the last of the present week. James BROWNLOW. Feb. 7.

(355) p. 173 Congress of the United States. House of Representatives, Wednesday, December 22. Mr. LEE presented a petition from S. SUMMERS, an assistant quartermaster, who had received no compensation for his services last war. Referred to the secretary of the treasury. p. 174 Friday, December 24. Mr. MOORE presented the petition of Thomas NELSON, in behalf of the executors of sundry mariners who perished on board the frigate Randolph, which was blown up in..the last war. Monday, December 27. Mr. GOODHUE presented the petition of Isaac OSGOOD and others, praying the grant of a sum of money to enable him to carry on the brewery of malt liquors in an extensive manner...

(356) p. 175 Books. To begin selling at Public Auction, On the First Monday of March next, The whole Stock in Trade, Belonging to John CAMPBELL.. Any gentlemen sending their orders to John CAMPBELL or William NUTT, for any of the above..books ..may depend upon their being answered... Wilmington, Feb. 2, 1791.

No. 23, of Vol. II.) Monday, February 14, 1791. (Total No. 75.

(357) p. 181 Fayetteville. The honourable John STEELE, esquire, is re-elected representative in the congress of the United States, for the Yadkin division.

(358) The subscriber will give the Highest Price, In Cash, for any quantity of Whaet, under 3000 bushels, delivered at his mill in Fayetteville-He lodges at colonel DEKEYSER's. John GREEN. Fayetteville, Feb. 14, 1791.

(359) PERRY & TARBE, Have For Sale, at their Store, the corner of Green and Old-Streets, near COCHRAN's mill: Jamaica and New-England Rum, Gin..Madeira Wine..Molasses, Sugar and Coffee, Chocolate, Pepper and Allspice, Ginger,..Teas,,Salt, Powder and Lead. Also, A Complete Assortment of Dry Goods... Fayetteville, Feb. 14, 1791.

(360) BUFFEY (or BUSSEY) & SMITH, Have For Sale, at their Store, in Old-Street, West-India Rum..French Brandy, Sugar.. Also, A general assortment of European piece Goods, Hard Ware, &c. &c.

(361) Richard COCHRAN, Will Lease Several Lots, In Fayetteville, well situated, on Gillespie, Hay, Green, Old, and Maiden Lane Streets. Also, A Rice Plantation, on Cape-Fear river, two miles and an half below Fayetteville. Feb. 14, 1791.

(362) For Sale, A Tract of Land, on the waters of Brown Creek, in Anson county, adjoining Mr. LANCER's land, containing 400 acres. For particulars, enquire in Mecklinburg county, of Samuel HARRIS, or Barl LANIER. Feb. 14, 1791.

(363) p. 184 Copper Stills, And all kinds of Copper and Tin Ware, made and sold by the subscriber, in this town. John NAYLOR. Fayetteville, Feb. 7, 1791.

No. 24, of Vol. II.) Monday, February 21, 1791. (Total No. 76.

(364) p. 187 Congress of the United States. House of Representatives. Wednesday, December 29. The petition of Shubael SWAINE, a prisoner, confined in gaol for a breach of the revenue law, praying Congress to take his case into consideration, and remit his fine, was read.. Mr. FITZSIMONS presented the petition of Philip BUCK, praying compensation for disability occasioned by services on board one of the row gallies during the late war, and for a schooner lost.. Mr. HEISTER presented the petition of Anna Wilhelmina Elizabeth LONGCANNER, praying compensation for services rendered by her late husband, during the late war.. Mr. LAWRANCE presented the petition of Winthrop SARGENT, praying compensation for additional services whilst executing and performing the duties of governor of the western territory.. Mr. BOURNE presented the petition of Simeon THAYER, late a major in the continental army, praying to be placed on the list of pensioners, on account of disability occasioned whilst in service...

(365) p. 188 Albany, Jan. 14. XIV Pillar of our happy federal government! Yesterday morning, the pleasing intelligence of our sister state of Vermont having adopted the constitution, was received...

(366) New-York, Jan. 22. Sunday night last was lost in the snow storm, on EATON's Neck Reef, near Huntington, Long-Island, Brig Sally, captain Benjamin KEELER, belonging to Stanford, Connecticut, laden with molasses-vessel, cargo and people all lost; four dead bodies have been found.. There were either 10 or 11 persons on board.

(367) Fayetteville. To the Senate and House of Representatives of the United States in Congress assembled. The memorial of the college of physicians of the city of Philadelphia,.. p. 189 to impose such heavy duties upon all distilled spirits, as shall be effectual to restrain their intemperate use in our country. Signed by order of the college, John REDMAN, President.

(368) Died-At Hillsborough, 'rs. HAYWOOD, wife of John HAYWOOD, esquire, treasurer of this state. (p. 189)

(369) Married-in Bladen, on Saturday last, Capt. John STEWART, to Miss Charlotte Jeanett STEWART.

(370) Five Pounds Reward. Ran Away from the subscriber, on Monday the 14th inst. a Negro Man named HARPER nearly or quite six feet high, yellow complexion, and very likely; about 23 years old..speaks very good English, is country born and was bred

(370) (Cont.) some where about Roan-Oak. J. PORTERFIELD.

(371) For Sale, Seventy-Three and a half acres of Land, laying on VERNER's? Creek, in Chatham County, during the life time of my wife. For terms..Robert FERGUSON. Hillsborough, Feb. 18, 1791.

(372) All persons indebted to the estate of the late Col. John STOKES, are desired to come in prepared to settle.. Those persons having accounts with the estate, who reside in..Fayetteville may..exhibit them to me at that place..from the 21st to the 25th instant; and at any time afterwards at my house in the Forks of the Yadkin River. Rowan county. Richmond PEARSON, (Administrator.

(373) Lost, on Wednesday last, a paper, containing about 12 pounds in cash, and two Tobacco Notes..: No. 1746 1280 150 1130..issued Dec. 13, 1790, by LORD and DAVIS, to William THOMPSON. No. 2035 1660 120 1540..issued Feb. 16, 1791, by POTTS and CAMPBELL, to George HOLT... CALLENDER & DEAN.

(374) p. 19_ Encouraged by the assurances of some of the most respectable persons in Wilmington, the subscriber offers his services as a teacher of the English and Latin languages, also writing and arithmetic.. He has already opened school in that large..room over Messrs. JOCELIN and D'HERBE's vendue store. R. HARLEY. Wilmington, Feb. 5, 1790.

No. 25, of Vol. II.) Monday, February 28, 1791. (Total No. 77.

(375) p. 197 Fayetteville. Extract of a letter from the honorable Benjamin HAWKINS dated at Philadelphia, January 18, 1791...

(376) Extract of a letter from the honorable Timothy BLOODWORTH, to a friend in Fayetteville, dated Philadelphia the 13th January, 1791.. A bill has passed the senate to admit Kentucky in the union in June, 1792.

No. 26, of Vol. II.) Monday, March 7, 1791. (Total No. 78.

(377) p. 203 Congress of the United States. House of Representatives, Wednesday, January 19. .. p. 204 A petition from William DEWEES, and a petition from William BLACKLEDGE were referred to the secretary of the treasury,.. Thursday, January 20. A petition of Robert MEAD was presented by Mr. LAWRANCE, which was read.. A petition of C. and J. SANDS and W. LIVINGSTON, in behalf of themselves and associates, praying compensation for damages sustained by a contract for supplying the army with provisions.. Friday, January 21. Mr. MADISON presented the petition of W. C. WEBB and Conyers WHYTE..read and referred to the secretary of the treasury.

(378) A Receipt to make an excellent American Wine, communicated to the Burlington Society for promoting Agriculture and Domestic Manufactures by Joseph COOPER, esq. of Gloucester county, New Jersey...

1792 - All issues missing except for the following American Antiquarian Society-August 7; September 25; October 2, 9, 16, 23, 30; November 6, 27; December 11.

FAYETTEVILLE GAZETTE.
Printed by Alexander MARTIN, for John SIBLEY.
(Vol. I.) Tuesday, August 7, 1792. (Numb. 1.)

(379) Excise Act. Second Congress of the United States. At the first session,

(379) (Cont.) begun and held at the city of Philadelphia in the State of Pennsylvania, on Monday the twenty-fourth of October, one thousand seven hundred and ninety-one. An Act concerning the duties on spirits distilled within the United States... Jonathan TRUMBULL, Speaker of the House of Representatives. Richard Henry LEE, President pro. tem. of the Senate. Approved May 8th, 1791. George WASHINGTON, President of the United States.

(380) South-Carolina. At a meeting of the inhabitants of St. Bartholomew's Parish, July 8, 1792. Whereas, it has been a custom..in some of the states..to ship to this state, such of their slaves as have been condemned for crimes.. Resolved, 1st. That we do bind ourselves each to the other..that we will not buy, or sell..any slave or slaves, imported from any of the other states.. .. 5thly, That Paul HAMILTON, Esq. Dr. Robert PRINGLE, Daniel DOYLEY, O'Brien SMITH, Benjamin POSTELL, Esq. Colonel Peter YOUNGBLOOD, Dr. Matthew ODRISCOLL, Captain Alexander MURRY, and William M'CANTS Esq. be a committee for the support of and carrying into effect these resolutions.. Signed by the unanimous order of the meeting. Peter YOUNGBLOOD.

(381) Philadelphia, June 25. The Constitution of Kentucky was finally ratified by the Convention of Danville, on the 26th day of April last. The first legislature was to meet at Lexington, on the 4th instant. Isaac SHELBY, Esq. is elected Governor. John VINING, Esq., of Delaware..declines being re-elected..for member of Congress for that State.-John DICKINSON, Esq. has also notified that he declines serving as Governor, in case of appointment.

(382) Charleston, July 9. On Friday morning last arrived here the brig Charleston, Capt. GARMAN, in 15 days from Philadelphia. On the 5th instant,..arose a heavy squall of wind..with rain and severe thunder and lightning..which..killed a horse on deck belonging to the hon. W. SMITH..knocked down Mr. W. P. YOUNG, who lay for a considerable time deprived of his senses, and was very much scorched and otherwise hurt...

(383) Knoxville, May 5. The 5th of April as a Cherokee, with four squaws, was passing peaceable, near the house of James HUBBARD, on French-Broad, he had two guns discharged at him. One ball grazed his cheek; the other passed through his side, giving him a slight wound. This HUBBARD is one of those people who went down the Tenessee last spring to attempt a settlement at the Muscle Shoals; and there are strong reasons to suspect that the two guns were fired by his two sons, minors who live with him.

(384) Fayetteville. Tuesday, August 7. It is with much satisfaction we announce.. that by the timely exertions..of Mr. GROVE, there is a prospect of checking..the gang of daring Horse Thieves, who have so long infested..this place. A man of the name of William COOK had been seen lurking about the pasture..and a short time after one of them was stolen. Mr. G...pursued him almost to the frontiers of Georgia..took him.. he is now confined in goal.. John RICH and Simon HADLEY have been apprehended.. RICH assumed the name of George ROBERTSON. His Excellency the Governor..has ordered a Court of Oyer and Terminer to be held here about the 24th instant for the trial of the above named persons.

(Vol. I.) Tuesday, September 25, 1792. (Numb. 8.)

(385) As some of the Citizens of Upper and Lower Fayetteville continue to cut and carry away Timber off the subscriber's Land, about one mile below Town-He now gives notice,-For the last time-That he is resolved to prosecute..all such intruders... Wm. Barry GROVE, Fayetteville, September 3.

(386) To The Ladies who are Lovers of Literature. A Society of literary character established at Philadelphia, intend publishing.."The Ladies Magazine, and repository of entertaining knowledge".. Subscriptions received by Robert CAMBELL, Philadelphia, and by the principal booksellers in the United States. Philadelphia, Aug. 1.

(387) Henry E. LUTTERLOH, Begs leave to inform..that his first Lottery commenced Drawing the 16th of July, ult. and was compleated the 28th inst. at the Court-House in this town. The Prizes of the fortunate Tickets will be paid on the original bein; delivered at the Lottery Office. He also proposes the following Scheme of a Second Lottery, The Drawing of which will commence the 20th of November next, in Newbern... Newbern, Aug. 28.

(388) The Subscribers Have entered into Co-Partnership in order to furnish and supply the Market of Fayetteville, with Beef, Mutton &c... John WILLIS, William VANN, Jesse PEACOCK. Fayetteville, September 10, 1792.

(389) An Abstract Of the principal alterations in regard to the Revenue from distilled spirits, made by the Act of Congress of the eighth day of May, 1792... William POLK, Supervisor, District of North Carolina, Fayetteville, Sept. 17.

(390) Boston, August 30. The following account is transmitted us by a correspondent at Sanford,.Maine. Capt. William BROWN, of Hudson, in the state of New-York, just arrived here, informs..that on the 17th July, 2 P.M. in lat. 23,5, long. 64,37 being in the brig True Blue from St. Kitts, bound to New-York, was struck with lightning, and set fire; the blow was so severe, as that Capt. BROWN, his mate, and six hands, a cabin boy, with three passengers,..were knocked down..and..stunned..they remained motionless 13 or 15 minutes.. Capt SMITH..got his boat out and came to their relief. Capt. DEVEREAUX, in a ship from Norfolk, in Virginia, bound for Martinico..got out his boat..came up some time after Capt. SMITH's boat had returned to the schooner. The exertions of this Captain (aged 66) were great upon the occasion...

(391) An Address To The Citizens of Westmoreland, Washington, Fayette and Alleghany Counties, On The Revenue Law. By John NEVILLE, Esq. Inspector of the Revenue, Survey No. 4, District of Pennsylvania. Friends and Fellow-Citizens, The law you complain of is a clear exercise of a constitutional power...

(392) To the Public. The President and Fellows of the Medical Society of the state of Delaware..announce the following question, as a subject of prize dissertation, and..invite the ingenious and learned of all nations to the competition. Question-What is the origin and nature of the noxious power which prevails, especially in hot and moist climates, during summer and autumn, and produces intermittent and remittant fevers, and certain other diseases? By what means may this insalubrity of climate be corrected, and the diseases thence arising most successfully prevented and treated? .. The premium shall consist of Three Hundred Dollars... Published by order of the society, Edward MILLER, Sec.

(393) To The Editor of The Fayetteville Gazette. Sir, When we consider how much the reputation of William MATTHEWS has been wounded by some assertions emitted by William COOK, lately executed persuant to the sentence of the Hon. Court, &c. by which the morals and honesty of him, viz, MATTHEWS, were rendered very susceptible; as he stood thereby charged with having stole, or been accessary to stealing a horse, belonging to Mr. MOORE..W. COOK, did, on the morning before he was executed, declare solemnly, that, he himself stole the horse above described, the theft of which he had formerly charged against Mr. MATTHEWS... James KEDDIE, James LEONARD, The above sworn to before me, J. MOORE, J. P.

(394) By virtue of the power in me vested, I have appointed Duncan MACREA, Esq. Collector of the Revenue in the County of Cumberland.. The appointment of Collector: for the Counties of Sampson, Moore, Richmond and Anson are yet unmade.-Persons well recommended, will on application to Col. James READ, or myself, be commissioned. William POLK, Supervisor of the Revenue, District of North Carolina.

(395) To Be Sold on Credit, A Valuable Farm, Situate three miles from Pittsborough, in Chatham County, containing upwards of 300 acres..with a new dwelling House thereon 24 by 28 feet..also a Granary lately built, 36 feet square.. Also, One Tract, situate on LANDRAM's Creek, in said County of Chatham, containing 500 acres.. The terms may be known by applying to Mr. William GUTHERY, about four miles from Pittsburgh, or to the subscriber at Newbern. Benj. WILLIAMS.

(396) Five Pounds Reward. Ran-away from the Subscriber last night, Three Negroes. SAMPSON, a stout fellow, 24 years of age, black complexion, very active-TIM, 19 years of age..yellow complexion-SARAH, 23 years of age, yellow complexion... Phil. HODGES. Little-River, Sept. 10, 1792.

(397) Ran-away From the subscriber, a Negro Man, Named DOUGLAS purchased from Mr. William COOK, of Fayetteville..-he is a low, well made fellow... J. WILLIS. Lumberton, Sept. 15, 1792.

(398) Two Negroes Apprehended. Came to my Plantation on Cape-Fear river, one mile from this town, on the..5th of March, last, and now in my possession, a Negro Man and a Negro Woman, who say they have no master-that they have been strolling about ever since the British left Charleston, except four or five years, when they were in the service of a Mr. James CRAIGG, on LINCHE's Creek, in South-Carolina... James MORE. Fayetteville, September 11, 1792.

(399) All persons indebted to the estate of Joseph MOTT, deceased, are requested to make immediate payment to the Subscriber... Duncan M'AUSLAN. Administrator. August 17, 1792.

(400) Newspapers. To give facility to the conveyance of newspapers agreeably to the law of the United States, the Post-master General proposes... Timothy PICKERING. General Post-Office, Philadelphia, June 1st, 1792.

(401) Lands for Sale. To Be Sold at Public Vendue, in the Town of Wilmington, For Six Months Credit In the First Week of March, next The Following Tracts of Land, Belonging to the Estate of, Parker QUINCE, Esq. deceased. 1400 Acres on Town Creek in Brunswick County.. 650 Acres in Brunswick County, between LOCKWOOD's Folly and Cape Fear. 440 Acres on the North West Branch of Cape Fear River, in Bladen County, joining Virginia PORTER's Neck. 350 Acres on Town Creek formerly belonging to Mr. John POTTER. A Tract with a Mill Seat, formerly the property of William MOSELY, Esq. on Hollyshelter, containing 640 Acres. Two Vacant Lots of Land in the Town of Brunswick. 1140 Acres on the Hawfields, near Hillsborough. 400 Acres called Catfish on the North West Branch of Cape Fear River, about 8 miles from Wilmington. One Tract on the head of Elizabeth River, containing 640 Acres. At the Same Time and Place..For Ready Money 13 Prime Slaves, Belonging to the same Estate..terms by applying at Wilmington, to Thomas CALLENDER, Executor, Susannah QUINCE, Executrix. Or Richard QUINCE, jun. Wilmington, August 17, 1792.

(402) Peter STRONG, Informs the public, that he continues to carry on the Clock, Watch, and Jewellery Business, At his Old Stand In Fayetteville...

(403) Post-Office, Fayetteville. The Northern and Southern Mails arrive at this office every Monday, about 5 P. M.... John SIBLEY, P. M. August 7, 1792.

(404) For Sale at CALLENDER's Cash Store, One Door East of Messrs. URQUAHART and M'FARLANE...

(Vol. I.) Tuesday, Octobber 2, 1792. (Numb. 9

(405) State of North-Carolina. Wilmington, Superior Court, September Term. The Grand Jury..present..grievances.. And the Jury..request that their presentments may be published, and that a copy be sent to the next General Assembly. James WALKER, Foreman. J. M'KINZIE, W. E. LORD, Thomas WRIGHT, John LONDON, John ALLEN, Robert COUNCIL, John CLARK, John TULLWOOD, J. SHEPPARD, James PRICE, C. A. BELOAT, William STEPHENS, William JONES, David GREER, Richard QUINCE, John LIVINGSTON, William CAMP-BELL.

(406) Fayetteville. List of Letters Remaining in the Post-Office. Published agree-able to the Post-Office Law. Capt. Lion ALFERD,-Robinson, Abiah ADAMS,-No. Carolina, James BAKER,-Chatham, John BUIE-Near Fayetteville, John BIDDLE-Fayetteville, Mrs. BIDDLE-do., John BURK, merchant, do., Rev. Dougald CRAWFORD, 3 letters-Raft Swamp, Malcolm CURRIE,-do., Richard COCHRAN-Fayetteville, Jannet CLARK-Mecklenburg, The Secretary of the Society of Cincinnati of No. Carolina-Fayetteville, William CALDWELL care of Messrs. CLARK and M'LERAN,-Fayetteville, John DELRYMPLE-Moore, Joseph GALE, 2 letters, Fayetteville, John HARE, COX's Settlement, Deep River, James HOUTON, 2 letters, Iredel, Hugh HOUSTON, SMITH's Creek, Charles Howell SIMMONS, Rutherford, General Henry HARRINGTON, Richmond, Thomas HINCHY, Cane Creek, Thomas JARMAN, David LEGGETT, Fayetteville, William LOVE, BULLOCK's Creek, Archibald M'DUGALD, Fayette-ville, Donald M'LEOD, 2 letters, do., Archibald MAC KAY, Near Fayetteville, John MASK, Montgomery, Thomas MAC CALL, Heron Lake, Alexander MC CALL, 5 letters, Fayette-ville, John MAC LOCHLAN, Rockfish, William MC KERACHIN, Fayetteville, Peter MAC FAR-LANE, Shocheal, James MC MELLAN, do., William MATHEWS, Mecklenburg, Alexander MC ARTHUR, Cumberland, James MC IVER, care of James PATTERSON, Fayetteville, Alexander MUNROE, Cross Creek, John M'CALL, Fayetteville, Murdock MC INNES, do., Charles MC ALLESTER, Fayetteville, Hannah MORFITS, do., John NIEL, do., Peter NICHOLSON, Rich-mond, Samuel NIGHT, Lincoln, Hugh OCHELTREE, Cumberland, James PATTERSON, Esq. Chatham, Daniel ROSS, Anson, Robert STEEL, Montgomery, John WEBB, Long Bluff, John WILLIAMS, Esq., Chatham, Daniel WALSH, Fayetteville, Col. Benjamin WILLIAMS, Chatham, John YATES, Esq., Bladen. John SIBLEY, P. M. Fayetteville, October 1, 1792.

(407) For Sale, Or To Let,..In the Town of Pittsborough, Chatham County. A New, Two Story House, Compleatly finished, and well fitted for a Tavern,..on two adjacent Lots, containing one acre..within one mile of the Mineral Springs, which, tho' but lately discovered, are much frequented in the season...P. ST. LAWRENCE, Pittsborough, September 29, 1792.

(408) Advertisement. Notice is hereby given to all those who have had dealings with William BACHOP, or BACHOP and PATTERSON, late of this place..the Books and papers of both are in the hands of the subscribers... Rob. DONALDSON, A. FURGUSON, Executors. Fayetteville, Oct. 1, 1792.

(409) The subscriber begs leave to inform..that he has opened a Boarding House And Tavern, in that commodious House, belonging to James HOGG, Esq. in Green-Street, where the Printing-Office was lately kept... David DUDLEY. Fayetteville, Oct. 1.

(410) Run-Away From the subscriber's plantation about the 15th of August, Two Negroes

(410) (Cont.) A Man, named NATT, who is very black, and rather tall, well known by the name of Cooper NATT-A Woman, not quite so black as the man, of a low stature, lusty, of the name of LUSEY. They appear to be about 40 years of age, are country born, and speak good English.. NATT formerly belonged to William HILL, Esq. near Wilmington, and is well known there... James JACKSON. GRAY's Creek, 12 miles below Fayetteville.

(411) Came To My Mill, On the 24th ult. A Negro Boy, Appears to be about 20 years of age, and says his name is JIM, about 5 feet 6 inches high, country born, and sensible, says he belongs to Barth. BEARD, near Ninety-six, in South-Carolina... John SIMSON. Fayetteville, October 1.

(Vol. I.) Tuesday, October 9, 1792. (Numb. 10.

(412) A letter from Danville, Kentucky, Aug. 21, says-"Two men who were taken at ST. CLAIR's defeat, and who made their escape from an Indian town, inform That Major TRUEMAN, of the regular troops, who bore one of the flags, reached the Glaze River, where the chiefs of many nations of Indians were assembled to hold a grand council; that he delivered to them a belt and talk, which was read to them by an Englishman;.. a council was held which ended in a determination to reject every offer of peace, and to put to death every American that should fall into their hands; that accordingly Major TRUEMAN and his party were tomahawked, and their bodies thrown into the river. They also inform, that Col. HARDIN, one of the most valuable citizens of Pennsylvania ..was killed by the Wyandots..."

(413) Rutland, (Vermont) Aug. 20. On Thursday night the 9th instant, the dwelling house of Mr. Alexander PATTERSON, of Pittsford, was consumed by fire. It seems that Mr. PATTERSON had been missing for several weeks..the children escaped out of the door..a day or two after, as some children were searching for pewter amongst the rubbish, just under where the bed stood, they discovered a number of bones..adjudged to be human bones, the skull, teeth, &c. remaining in the natural form.-On information of this, a jury of inquest was summoned. It was the opinion of the jury..that murder had been committed there, but by whom could not be ascertained. Suspicions are strong against Mrs. P. who has been examined, and committed for trial.

(414) Norfolk, (Virg.) Sept. 12. On Friday last a murder was committed, near MOORE's Bridge, Princess Anne county,.. A negro man belonging to Thomas LAWSON, Esq. had stolen something out of the black-smith's shop in which he worked, for which Mr. IRONS (the master of the shop) told him as soon as he had finished a ploughshare, which he was then about, he would give him a flogging. While Mr. IRONS was stooping to finish some work at the bench, the negro took the ploughshare and struck him a violent blow on the back of his head, and he expired within ten minutes after. The negro did not attempt to make his escape, and was committed to goal.

(415) Fayetteville. Tuesday, October 9. (From a Boston paper.) To Mankind at large... Timothy DEXTER.

(416) Mr. James CAREY, late printer and proprietor of a Dublin paper entitled the rights of Irishmen, proposes publishing a daily paper in Richmond.

(417) The Supreme Executive of the State of Massachusetts, have granted a pardon to Joshua ABBOT mentioned in a late paper to have been convicted of murder in the county of York.

(418) Married)-At Warren, Mr. John WILLIS, of this town, to Miss Elizabeth PARKS.

56

(419) Died-In Paris, the celebrated John Paul JONES, in the utmost poverty. A Col. BLACKDEN was obliged to raise a small sum of money by way of subscription, in order to bury him...

(420) Samuel GREEN, Has For Sale, At His Store, In Fayetteville, Drugs and Medicines English and West-India Goods, Woman's Shoes-Saddles and Bridles-Stationary-Books... October 8, 1792.

(421) Irish Linens. Directly Imported From Ireland And For Sale, by the Subscriber, At Col. DEKEYSERs... James WAUGH. Fayetteville, October 9th, 1792.

(422) Just Published And For Sale, at the Printing-Office, Newbern. A Collection of the Statutes of the Parliament of Great-Britain, Which are now in force in the State of North-Carolina..Copies of which may be had of Messrs. William FARRIS, Washington; HODGE and WILLS, Edenton; Joseph ROSS, Tarborough; Stephen CAMBERLING, Greensville; B. STITH, Halifax; John HOGG, Hillsborough; Robert DONNELL, Wayne; PERRY and TARBE, Fayetteville; Montfort STOKES, Salisbury; Dr. J. KINGSBURY, Mattamuskeet; Mr. William FERRAND, Swansborough.

(423) The subscriber being now in possession of Messrs. NOYES and PORTER's Books and Papers.-All persons..are desired to render their accounts..make payment..to the subscriber only; who is appointed assignee for the creditors of NOYES and PORTER. Monday, the 29th Inst., Will be exposed, at Public Sale, At Mr. Lewis BARGE's house, Lately occupied by Col. WILLIS, A Quantity of Dry Goods and A Waggon and Team... John W. CHARLES. Fayetteville, October 8, 1792.

(424) The subscriber having removed to the shop lately occupied by Mr. MURCHISON, Taylor, continues to carry on the Gold Smith's and Jewellery Business... Philip OTT. Watches Cleaned and Repaired with care and dispatch. Fayetteville, Oct. 2.

(425) For Sale, About 100 acres of as good Up Land as any in Chatham County, all well timbered, and within three miles of an excellent spring, and about the same distance from Mr. ST. LAWRENCE's former residence, and adjoining the lands of Mr. William HENRY, deceased... Robert FERGUSON.

(426) To the Officers of the late Continental Line of the State of North Carolina ... H. MURFREE. Murfreesborough, Sept. 1792.

(427) Wilmington District, ss. In Equity. Sept. Term, 1792. Robert BARNES, versus Richard JONES. Ordered,..that unless answer be filed at, or before next March term, Complainants Bill will be taken pro confesso. Thomas DAVIS, C. & M. E. W. D.

(Vol. I.) Tuesday, October 16, 1792. (Numb. 11.

(428) Fayetteville. Tuesday, October 16. By an officer from the Rock Landing, arrived at Charleston, we are informed that Col. M'GILLIVRAY, having entirely lost the confidence of the Indians, has retired..to New Orleans, there to remain in a private station, by order of the Spanish Governor.

(429) By a letter to..the Governor of Virginia, we are authorized to announce.. (says the Virginia Gazette) that Col. HARDIN, with his companion, on a mission to the Indians respecting a treaty of peace..were..made prisoners and sentenced to be burnt as spies. Col. HARDIN saw his companion expire..and was..the next morning.. to have experienced the same fate-but was stolen from his confinement by eight young Wyandot warriors, who safely conducted him to Fort Washington.

(430) The Dashwood packet from England brought a Diploma from the university of Edinburgh, conferring the degree of doctor of laws on the hon. John JAY, chief justice of the United States.

(431) Married)-On Thursday evening last, by the Rev. Mr. KERR, Mr. James ELTING, Merchant, to Miss Sally DUDLEY.

(432) Died)-On Wednesday last, at Wilmington, Mr. Alexander S. URQUAHART, Merchant of that place.

(433) General Post Office, Philadelphia, Sept. 10, 1792. Proposals will be received at this Office..for carrying the mails of the United States... Timothy PICKERING, Post Master General.

(434) To Be Let,..The Houses and Lot, On the east side of Green Street, Where the Printing-Office was formerly Kept. It has six rooms with fireplaces, two of which are large Halls, a Kitchen, a Garden, and an excellent Cellar... James HOGG. Fayetteville, Oct. 1.

(435) Proposals from the Maryland Insurance Fire Company. For Insuring Houses, Buildings, Stores, Goods, Wares and Merchandize, from loss and damage by fire.. Published by order of the President and Directors, Jacob Franks LEVY, Register. Baltimore, June 8, 1792.

(436) Stephen GRAHAM, Taylor, from London. Begs leave to inform the Public, that he carries on the above business..in the House lately occupied by Mr. Jacob HARTMAN, next door to Mr. ADAM's Store... Fayetteville, October 16, 1692.

(437) By a request of a number of the Inhabitants, the Electors of Fayetteville are requested to meet at the State-House... James PORTERFIELD, Magistrate of Police.

(438) The Members of the Fayetteville Library, are requested to attend a quarterly meeting at the State House on Saturday next, precisely at 11 o'clock A. M. John SIBLEY, Librarian.

(Vol. I.) Tuesday, October 23, 1792. (Numb. 12.

(439) Fayetteville, Tuesday, October 23. Mr. HASWELL's Printing-Office, at Rutland, Vermont, with all its contents, was consumed by fire, on the 25th ult.

(440) Admiral Paul JONES did not die in poverty, as has been reported, it is said that he left more than 1000 l. sterling, to two sisters in the West of England.

(441) Mr. Benjamin JOHNSTON, of Lynn, Massachusetts, has shipped this year..20,604 pair of shoes, made by his workmen...

(442) On the 18th ult. the Rev. Dr. CLAGETT was consecrated Bishop for the State of Maryland in New-York, by the Right Reverend Dr. Samuel PROVOST.

(443). Federal Electioneering, From the Gazette of the U. States, Western Ticket. The following names for representatives to the next Congress appear on a list for the counties of Washington, Westmoreland, Fayette, and Alleghany, in the state of Pennsylvania.. William FINDLEY, John SMILIE, William MONTGOMERY, John M'CLAIN, Andrew GREGG, Moses M'CEIN, Robert WHITEHILL, John W. KITTERA, Daniel HEISTHER, Jonathan B. SMITH, Peter MUHLENBERG, Charles THOMSON, William SCOTT.

(444) Charles JORDAN Has For Sale, At His Stores in Wilmington and Fayetteville, A General Assortment of Fall Goods... October 23, 1792.

(Vol. I.) Tuesday, October 30, 1792. (Numb. 13.

(445) Whereas I am lawfully and rightfully possessed of certain negroes, viz. ROSE, EMILIA, SAM, HANNAH, NED and RHODEY, bequeathed to Becky, the daughter of Levi GLASS late of Bladen County, deceased, by virtue of my intermarriage with the said Becky, Now these are to forewarn all persons, not to have any dealings, or other else to do with the said negroes, or any of them... 22d October, 1792. John EAGAN.

(446) Came to my Plantation on Cape-Fear, five miles from Fayetteville, a Negro Fellow, who says his name is ISAAC, the property of a Mr. SOLOMONS, living at the Long-Bluff, on Pee Dee River, South-Carolina... Thomas PICKETT. October 30, 1792.

(447) Brought to my Platation on, on the 13th day of June last, by Mr. John MILLER, a Run-away Negro Fellow, who says his name is CHARLES, that his owner's name is William ROSS, moved from Lanchister county in Virginia, to Washington County in North-Carolina. He is about five feet four inches high, country born and sensible. When brought to me he was effected with the Venereal disease, and through humanity I employed a physician to cure him which cost six pounds.-He is now in my possession in Moore County. Jacob GASTER. October 30, 1792.

(448) Ran away from the subscriber's plantation, one mile from Fayetteville, Two Negroes, a man and a woman. They were lately advertised..as runaways, they have been in my possession since March last. James MORE. Fayetteville, October 30.

(449) Baltimore, October 12. Wednesday evening last arrived in this town from Mount Vernon..the President of the United States..early yesterday morning he proceeded..to Philadelphia; when the Artillery, commanded by Capt. David STODDARD, and the Light Infantry right wing commanded by Captain John MACHENHIMER, the left by Lieutenant Henry SPECK, all in uniform, paraded, and again saluted him.

(450) Winchester, October 8. Two traders..who have stores in the Territory of the United States south of the River Ohio, last week received letters from their agents there.. "Knoxville, Sept. 12, 1792..the celebrated John WATTS, has marched at the head of 500 warriors,..destination unknown.." French Broad, Sept. 19, 1792. "I am informed, that there are 600 Indians out against this part of the country, likewise, that they have killed two men, brothers, of the name of GILLESPY, who lived below Knoxville, which place I hear is evacuated."

(451) Fredericksburg, October 11. In the upper end of Culpepper, in the neighbourhood of the Ragged mountain, on Sunday evening last, was committed a most shocking and inhuman murder, by David YOWEL, on the body of Nancy CLARK, a young woman about 16 years of age...

(452) Petersburg, October 18. We are informed that Richard Henry LEE has resigned his office as a senator from this state to Congress. Col. John TAYLOR, of Caroline county, has been mentioned as a proper person to fill that important office.

(453) Fayetteville, Tuesday, October 30. Fire. On Tuesday evening last..the roof of the large House occupied by Col. DEKEYSER was in a blaze..a large store, occupied by Mr. DONALDSON..only 8 feet from the other appeared wrapt in flames. This house was about 100 feet long and 30 feet wide, and filled with goods to the third story, and with the other..was the property of Col. James PORTERFIELD.. It was only by

(453) (Cont.) very great exertions that Messrs. MAC AUSLAN and HOWAT's store and the row of houses from that corner to the state house square, were preserved. The fire..spread across the street next to COCHRAN's Mill, and Mr. PERRY's store was burning furiously-the engine was then turned upon the mill, and Mr. PERRY's store blown up..the mill was saved..the house of Mr. William COCHRAN, occupied by Mr. BRANTON, and the one on the opposite corner, occupied by Mr. DEBRUTZ, were on fire.. Mr. COCHRAN's house was blown up, and the engine brought to play upon Messrs. BUFFY and SMITH's store..there stopped. The exertions and activity of some gentlemen..cannot be reflected on but with the highest degree of gratitude... Mr. William NORRIS, Mr. David M'NIEL, and Mr. Barry STOKES...

(454) Died.)-on the 19th Inst. at the Shallow-ford, surry county, Mr. Isaac SESSIONS. Merchant of that place.

(Vol. I.) Tuesday, November 6, 1792. (Numb. 14.

(455) Philadelphia, October 10. The following is extracted from a letter received lately from Charleston: "Captain Robert MAXWELL and a Mr. SPEARS, an Indian trader, are arrived here with dispatches from Gen. PICKENS and Col. ANDERSON.. A body of the Cherokees, Creeks and Shanese, in all about 500 men.. An old trader by the name of RAMSAY, hath been killed in the Creek nation, and a Mr. SHAW, an agent from Congress, narrowly escaped the same fate."

(456) Fayetteville, Tuesday, November 6. Since the late fire in this town, a laboring man, by the name of William CRAWFORD, who has a wife and family in town, has been missing: Several persons recollected to have seen him in Col. DEKEYSER's house, apparently intoxicated, but a few minutes before the roof fell in..Wednesday last, as some persons were clearing the cellar where Col. DEKEYSER's house stood, they found a human scull and some remains of most of the bones of a human body, which puts it out of all doubt that he perished in the flames.

(457) At the close of the Poll for a member of Congress, in Anne-Arundel county, Col. MERCER had a Majority of 147 votes. In the counties of Kent, Caecil, and Hartford, Gabriel CHRISTIE, Esq. had a Majority of 954.

(458) Occurrence. On the 31st ult. was experienced here one of the most violent gales of wind, that has been known for many years.. A house at the Flatts, on Mr. William CAMPBELL's wharf, was taken off its foundation which drifted some miles up the river, with two negroes on the roof, who were saved. J. MUMFORD, D. Collector.

(459) The subscriber hereby informs..that the House he lately occupied being burned, he has again opened a House of Entertainment, And Boarding, in the large house where he formerly lived, on the other side of the Bridge, belonging to Mr. HOGG... Lee DEKEYSER.

(460) Wanted, From 100 to 400 Tons squared Yellow Pine Timber..not less than 25 tons ... J. BURGWIN. He has for sale, A few barrels Brown Sugar... Wilmington, Nov. 1, 1792.

(461) LORD & GALE, Inform the Public, that they carry on the Watch Making, Gold Smith, and Jeweller's Business, At the shop lately improved by Mr. MOORE, Hatter, opposite to Mrs. EMETT's... Fayetteville, Nov. 5.

(462) The subscriber has lost the 4th Vol. of the American edition of Blackstone's Commentaries. He will reward any person that will inform him of it, or leave it with the Printer. S. GREEN.

(463) The Public is hereby informed, that the Co-Partnership of NOYES and PORTER is dissolved. J. NOYES.

(464) This Is To Give Notice, That Henry DELAMOTHE, has a Note given by me..for 24 pounds. I therefore forewarn all persons from taking an assignment on said note, as I am determined not to pay it unless compelled by law. Isaac PATTERSON. The above Note was granted..for six months rent of a house which I then occupied, but which was burned in the late fire, in six weeks from my first occupancy. Fayette-ville, October 5.

(465) Run away from the jail in Fayetteville, on the night of the 30th ult. two negroes, CHARLES and JEM. CHARLES is of a yellow complexion-has bushy hair-is about six feet high, well made, of an indolent disposition, of few words, and about 35 years of age. This fellow is the property of Mr. Levi SOLOMONS, Merchant, Black Creek, near George Town, S. Carolina. JEM is a very black fellow, country-born, about 5 feet 4 inches high, stout made, and belongs to Bart. BEARD, near Ninety-Six, South-Carolina... William VANN, Jailer.

(Vol. I.) Tuesday, November 27, 1792. (No. 17)

(466) Fayetteville. Tuesday-November 27, 1792. From Newbern-To The Editor. Nov-ember 17.-"The assembly meet here, on Thursday last, agreeably to the Governor's Proclamation..the Hon. William LENOIR, Esq. Was chosen Speaker of the Senate, and Hon. Stephen CABARRUS, Esq. Speaker of the House of Representatives, Montfort STOKES, Esq. Clerk of the Senate, John HUNT, and Pleasant HENDERSON, Esqrs. Clerks of the House of Representatives.. The House appointed two of the members from each dis-trict to report what public bills are necessary to be passed this session. John Lewis TAYLOR, and William WOOD, Esqrs. are for Fayetteville district."

(467) On the 2d instant was executed in Hillsborough, Samuel FULLER, of Granville county, for the horrid and unnatural murder of his own son. Mr. FULLER, until..a few years past, has conducted himself as a good and respectable citizen, has raised a family in good repute..and..had acquired considerable property. .. A man near three score years of age, unworthily takes to his bed an abandoned woman, and keeps her in defiance of a faithful wife, and a number of children.. On the morning of the fatal catastrophe, this son went..to drive her off; when high words ensued, and soon after a gun was discharged by the father at the son..which killed him instantly.

(468) To The Public. The large Lottery proposed, is by desire put into a division of 200 tickets, at One Dollar and a half, silver each ticket... E. H. LUTTERLOH, Proprietor of the lottery. Edward SIMSON, Treasurer of do.

(469) Whereas the Books and Bonds of Aulay MAC NAUGHTON and Company..of..the store in the Upper Town of Fayetteville which..since the death of Mr. Aulay MAC NAUGHTON, were under the charge and keeping of the subscriber, and have been lately secretly conveyed away from the Company's house at Campbleton..as it is believed with an im-proper intention of collecting the balances due.. The several debtors are hereby forewarned not to pay the same until further notice... Duncan MAC ASLAN. Fayette-ville, November 19, 1792.

(470) The subscriber having received full power and authority, on account of the Heirs of the late Aulay MACNAUGHTON, and of Messrs. COLQUHON and RITCHIE, of Glasgow, Merchants..of the late House of Aulay MACNAUGHTON, and Co. of this state, and the only surviving partners thereof-which Powers have been..proven before the Honorable Samuel ASHE, Esq. one of the Judges of the Superior Court.. Public Notice is here-

(470) (Cont.) by given to all persons..indebted to the concern of Aulay MACNAUGHTON, and Co..that the subscriber is alone authorized to receive the said debts.. And whereas in the management of the said company concerns, since the death of Mr. MAC-NAUGHTON, Duncan MAC ASLAN, formerly a clerk to the..company, hath assumed to himself a power to interfere in the said business without any authority... James RITCHIE. Fayetteville, November 26, 1792.

(471) Whereas the undersigned William FALKENER, of Warrenton, and Joshua CARMAN, of Fayetteville, both in the State of North-Carolina, did, on the third day of May, 1790, enter into an agreement, and contract with John WILCOX, of Chatham County..for the purchase of sundry Tracts of Land..in Cumberland County, and on account of which they gave their joint obligations to the said John WILCOX..which..hath brought suits against the subscribers in the Superior Court of Law and equity in Hillsborough. Now be it known unto all persons, that the said John WILCOX did fail to fulfil his en-gagement for which the said..notes were given.-This is therefore to..forewarn.. against..giving value for the said obligations, as they will not..be paid... Willm. FALKENER, Joshua CARMAN. October 16, 1792. (Copy of notes.-Dated 3d May, 1790, and witnessed by Dolphin DAVIS and G. DUDLEY.)

(472) Strayed or Stolen, From the subscriber..a bay Horse... Lewis BOWELL. Fayette-ville, November 19, 1792.

(473) Fayetteville District, ss. In the Court of Equity. Octo. Term 1792. Thomas BRANTON versus Thomas DICKSON, Ordered, That Defendant file his answer, on or Before the first day of the ensuing term, or the Bill to be taken pro confesso. R. MUMFORD, C. M. E.

(474) Fayetteville District, ss. In the Court of Equity. Octo. Term. 1792. Mary DOWD, versus John BECK, Ordered, That Defendant file his answer, on or Before the first day of the ensuing term, or the Bill to be taken pro confesso. R. MUMFORD, C. M. E.

(475) A Child Left. I Left my child, named Margret HOGAN, aged about four years, last spring with a certain Nicholas WILLIAMS, a Frenchman, then living near Liberty-town, for him to take care of until I returned from Philadelphia to which place I was then going on business-And now on my return, find that said WILLIAMS is moved away, with my child, to some place that all my vigilence has failed in finding out. Therefore any person who can give account where..WILLIAMS..resides or can be found.. convey such intelligence to the Printer in HAGER's town, will..confer a most lasting obligation on a poor disconsolate mother..who has no reward to offer dher than Grat-itude. Mary HOGAN. N. B. Said WILLIAMS is a silversmith but mostly follows ped-dling; and I am told, that he and his wife (who is an Irish woman) call the child their own.

(Vol. I.) Tuesday, December 11, 1792. (No. 19)

(476) To Be Sold-at Public Vendue, In the town of Wilmington. At the Superior Court, the first week in March next, unless disposed of before at private sale. Five valu-able Lots in the said town..on the north side of Dock-street, from the corner to the river, with a good Wharf, two commodious three story Dwelling Houses with stores and cellars; a large Ware House, Blacksmith's shop, stable, and every necessary outbuild-ing... E. DEWEY.

(477) Congress. House of Representatives Of the United States, in Senate, April 4, 1792. The committee, to whom the subject of weights and measures was referred, report

(477) (Cont.) that it is their opinion.. 4. The standard rod..shall be divided
into five equal parts, one of which, to be called a foot, shall be the unit of measures of length for the United States: That the foot shall be divided into 10
inches; the inch into 10 lines; the line into 10 points; and that 10 feet make a
decade; 10 decades a rood; 10 roods a furlong; and 10 furlongs a mile..through the
agency of Samuel MEREDITH, Treasurer of the united states, in Philadelphia, and
William SEATON in New-York, the amount of public securities purchased is 1,495,457
dollars and 89 cents...

(478) Indian Affairs. Extract of a letter published in a late Kentucke Gazette.
"Official accounts say, that the five lower towns of the Cherokees, have declared
war, and that 300 Cherokees and 100 Creek Indians, were to march the 7th instant..
expected..against Cumberland.. The LITTLE TURKEY is an Indian, and I well remember
the conduct of the HANGING MAW in the year 1786, when KEANNA and his party decoyed
and murdered READ and BISHOP.. KEANNA, by an unexpected event, fell into our hands,
and was fortunately shot through the head by Col. OUTLAW. Last year John WATTS was
our beloved confident. We now learn that he is commander of the army which is march-
ing against us."

(479) Richmond, (Virginia) November 26. On Sunday the 4th instant, there arrived
at Knoxville, eight Indians from the Cherokee nation; three..were principal chiefs,
viz. the STANDING TURKEY, the WARRIOR's SON of Estanaula, and the HANGING MAW, from
the beloved town of Chota. The object..was to hold a talk with governor BLOUNT, to
assure him of the pacific disposition of their nation, and to request that they
might..hunt without molestation. On Saturday the 10th they were safely conducted
to the bank of the river, opposite to the town of Coyatee, on their return home, by
major George FARROGOOD, and a party of gentlemen. The eighth, a party of Indians
stole eight horses from GAMBLE's Station, about 12 miles from Knoxville. On Friday
the ninth, two regiments of territorial troops, under..Col. CARTER and Col. CHRISTIAN,
marched from Knoxville, to guard the frontiers, and to build forts and stations between the Papo Ford and the junction of the Clinch and Tenesee. On Saturday the
tenth, General SEVIER pursued his route from Knoxville, escorted by a troop of horse
raised in Greene County, and commanded by Capt. RICHARDSON, to take command of the
frontier army, now..12 to 15 hundred men.. On Monday the twelfth, the house of
Ebenezer BYRAM, on Beaver Creek seven miles from Knoxville, was attacked..by..about
15 Cherokee Indians.. Mr. BYRAM and Mr. JEFFERIES, the only two men in the house,
fired at the two Indians..at the window..both fell..the Indian party..fled.. It
deserves to be noted, that Mr. BYRAM is upwards of 60 years of age.

(480) Charleston, November 27. We are informed, that about three weeks ago, one
M'CLOSKEY, at the head of about 80 men, set out from Franklin county in Georgia, on
a hostile expedition against one of the Cherokee towns.. A letter from Franklin
County says, "John WATTS at the head of about 400 Creeks, and 100 Cherokees was
lately defeated in an attack on Cumberland, with the loss of 150 warriors, and himself mortally wounded through each thigh."

(481) Fayetteville, Tuesday-December 11, 1792. North Carolina, November 16, 1792.
The following gentlemen have been chosen Electors of the President and Vice-Presi-
dent of the United States, for their respective districts. Morgan and Salisbury
Districts-William PORTER, Matthew LOCK, and James TAYLOR, Esqrs. Hillsborough and
Halifax-Joel LANE, John MACON and John B. BENFORD, Esqrs. Edenton and Newbern-
Richard Dobbs SPAIGHT, Stephen CABARRUS, and Peter DAUGE, Esqrs. Fayetteville and
Wilmington-J. L. TAYLOR, A. MOORE, & B. SMITH, Esqrs.

(482) Having observed an advertisement in the Fayetteville Gazette, signed John

(482) (Cont.) EAGAN, in which he asserts a right to certain 6 negroes.. The subscriber conceives it a duty incumbent on him to prevent any unlawful purchases..
The negroes which Mr. EAGAN says were "bequeathed to his wife by her father", were
by myself purchased at Sheriff's sales in Robeson County, as belonging to GLASS's
estate..previous to the death of Levi GLASS, a judgment was obtained against him,
for a note of hand..and after his death those negroes were sold to satisfy said judgment. So far from being "lawful", the possession which Mr. EAGAN now holds I shall
prove to be illegal, for they were taken, and are now held without my consent.. I..
forewarn..from purchasing said negroes, viz. ROSE, EMILIA, SAM, HANNAH, NED and RHO-
DEY... Thomas WHITE.

(483) Stolen from the subscriber at Wake-Court-House..a bright bay Horse..stolen by
a free mulatto man of the name of THOMAS BOWSER, a blacksmith.. Any person apprehending the thief, and recovering the horse, by leaving him with the subscriber, at Col.
J. LANE's at Wake Court-House... Peter BIRD.

(484) To Be Let, To the Lowest Bidder, On the second Thursday in January next, at
LEWIS's Bridge, on New-Hope, in Orange County, The Building of a Bridge on New-Hope
creek, where LEWIS's bridge now stands, on the road leading from the seat of government to the place fixed for building the University... George DANIEL. Charles COL-
LIER. Commissioners.

(485) The subscriber, though derogatory to his feelings, finds himself necessitated,
from some unfortunate domestic circumstances, to forewarn the public from trusting
Eliza GRAHAM, once the partner in his cares, on his account she having, without any
just provocation absented herself from the embraces, bed and board of an ever fond
and indulgent husband... Alexr. GRAHAM. Burke County, near Little River.

(486) The subscribers request all persons who have any demands against them to bring
in their accounts..as the term of their partner ship is expired... D. JORDAN. J.
BURKE. Fayetteville, November 28.

1793 - All issues missing except for the following from American Antiquarian Society-
January 2; March 5, 12; May 21, 28; June 4; November 19.From University of North Carolina Library-April 30; June 11, 18, 25; July 2, 9, 16, 23, 30; August 6.

(Vol. I.) Tuesday, January 2, 1792. (1793) (No. 22.)

(487) To The Public, In vindication of my character unjustly Set forth by Mr. James
RITCHIE of Fayetteville, I am constrained to represent my conduct respecting my in-
terference in the business of A. MACNAUGHTON and Co. I was employed by Mr. A. MAC-
NAUGHTON, deceased, as Factor and Clerk..in Fayetteville..these six years past, and
continued..until the time Mr. MACNAUGHTON died intestate, without having a settlement
of my accounts or being discharged. I have no doubt but Mr. RITCHIE may be vested
with the full power and authority he sets forth.. I am sorry he has so willfully and
glaringly misrepresented facts..before the County Court of Cumberland at the time
Letters of Administration were granted to myself, in conjunction with Mr. James RIT-
CHIE and Joseph MILNE, on the estate of the deceased Mr. MACNAUGHTON.. After administration was granted..Mr. Joseph MILNE, with Mr. Henry URQUAHART, both of Wilmington,
applied to the County Court of New-Hanover, for a second administration..which was
set aside, and the former administration permitted to continue. When we could not
agree on the mode of conducting the Company's business, we mutually agreed to refer
the same to the arbitration of two gentlemen of respectability.. After due consideration, they gave it as their opinion, that I should manage the business at the Fayetteville and Campbleton department, with the benefit of an assistant, and that Mr.

(487) (Cont.) MILNE should transact the business at Wilmington, with the help of another... Duncan MACAUSLAN.

(488) To The Public. In order further to embellish the injustice of the "rightfull and lawfull possession" which Mr. EAGAN advertises to "certain six negroes"..the following circumstances were omitted, thro' mistake, in my former advertisement, by its being verbally delivered to the Printer: About 18 months since, I exchanged two of the negroes mentioned by EAGAN, viz. EMELIA and HANNAH, with a Mr. Cader HATHORN, of Robeson County, and took in return..a fellow named JACK. Of the means which EAGAN made use of to possess himself of the negroes from HATHORN, I cannot positive-ly say..HATHORN..and his father, in my absence, stole the fellow from my yard. For this theft, I have entered a complaint to the Attorney-General... T. WHITE.

(489) Strayed or Stolen, From the subscriber..a sorrell Horse..reward of five pounds, and if stolen, the thief detected and brought to justice..a reward of 20 pounds... W. LESLIE. N. B. The said Horse was purchased by Mr. K. MURCHISON, of this place from Col. BRENAN, five miles from Salisbury.

(490) The subscribers having been appointed a committee of the Board of the Trust-ees of the University of North-Carolina... David STONE, Sam. M'CORKLE, Samuel ASHE, A. MOORE, John HAY.

(491) To be hired in Fayetteville, For 12 months from the 13th of January next, Two Mulatto Fellows, House Carpenters. For terms apply to Thomas SEWELL.

(492) A valuable Lot for sale, On the North-West side of Messrs. LANGDON and WARD's store... R. ROWAN, jun. Fayetteville, Jan. 1.

(493) Augusta, Nov. 17. On Monday last the Circuit Court of the United States was opened by the Hon. Thomas JOHNSON, one of the Associate Justices of the Supreme Court of the United States, and the Hon. Nathaniel PENDLETON, District Judge of this district. Four persons, who sailed from Boston to the island of Martinique, and from thence to Savannah in May last, were indicted and tried for stealing..a number of Negroes, belonging to inhabitants of that island. Samuel SKINNER, of Boston.. supercargo of the vessel..was found guilty by the Jury on his own confession..and was sentenced to receive 39 lashes, to pay a fine of 1000 dollars, all lawful charges of the prosecution, and to stand committed till the sentence was complied with. The other three prisoners..Nathaniel HICKMAN, Robert WATTS, and Nathaniel RIDGEWAY, were acquitted...

(494) T. & J. BEGGS, At their shop on Hay-Mount, Fayetteville, make and sell, Rid-ing chairs..Chair-Wheels..Windsor Chairs..Spinning Wheels, Bedsteads, with short posts, turned.. A couple New Sulkies, and a few Windsor Chairs, which may be seen at Mr. BEBEE's Paint Shop.

(495) Fresh Goods. The subscriber begs leave to inform..that he is just returned from New-York with a neat and extensive assortment of Dry Goods... John JOHNSTON. He at the same time requests all those that are indebted to the late firm of John JOHNSTON and Co...to exert themselves to pay the same... Wilmington, December 1792.

(496) The subscribers being about to leave this state, request all..accounts.. and indebted to them to make payment. KELLY & KING.

(Vol. I.) Tuesday, March 5, 1793. (No. 32.)

(497) Miscellany. Mr. Samuel FENNO, alias, Philip St. Francis DE BABBAS, Historical and Allegorical writer to the Fayetteville Gazette, &c. &c. &c. (letter).."Slander, the worst of poisons, ever finds An easy entrance in ignoble minds. On eagle's wings immortal slanders fly, While virtuous actions are but born and die." I am, dread Sir, Yours as you demean yourself., David MACNEILL, March 4, 1793.

(498) Fayetteville. Tuesday-March 5. Elections. The following gentlemen, we hear are appointed Representatives to Congress, for their several districts, viz. No. 4-Gen. Thomas MEBANE. No. 5-Nathaniel MACON. No. 8-Wm. Johnston DAWSON. No. 9-Thomas BLOUNT, Esqrs. No. 2-Gen. Matthew LOCK. No. 3-Joseph WINSTON, Esq.

(499) Indian Affairs. Knoxville, January 12. On the 23d instant, returned to this town from captivity with the Cherokees Capt. Samuel HANLY, to the joy of his friends and country. In the course of the present week arrived in town, John THOMPSON, one of the interpreters of the United States in the Cherokee nation, and Arthur COODY, late one of the British interpreters.. On Thursday the 22d instant John PATES was killed by Indians on Crooked creek, about 16 miles from this place, and four scalps taken off him; by what party not yet discovered.

(500) Died.)-A few days since, at his Plantation near this town, Mr. Edward HOWARD. -At Edenton in the 56th year of his age, Thomas BENBURY, Esq. Collector of the port of Edenton, a gentleman not less esteemed for the benevolence of his disposition than for the goodness of his heart.-Mr. Matthew MALLEY, for many years an inhabitant of that town. (Note: State Gazette of North-Carolina, published in Edenton, North Carolina, Vol. VIII., Saturday, March 30, 1793., Numb. 376., shows Myles O'MALLEY as administrator to the estate of Matthew O'MALLEY, deceased, dated Edenton, March 29, 1793.)

(501) Notice, That contrary to my contract with Mr. MC NICOLL, in his lifetime-Mr. MC FARLANE requested of me a bond for a balance of money due the concern on which my contract was established. This is..to forewarn..all..not to trade for the same-Because I can prove by the face of the account..as well as from the testimony of Major James ANDERSON (living on Deep River, Chatham) That it is fraudulently obtained... Philip TAYLOR.

(502) In order to defray the debts of James WHITE, late of Bladen county-Will Be Sold, At the place on South-River, where the said WHITE formerly lived on the 10th April next. All the perishable property of said estate agreeable to Law. W. H. BEATTY, Administrator.

(503) A Bargain. 2250 Acres Land-For Sale: ... A Body of Land, scituate in Burnswick-County, on the Sea-Shore, between Little-River and Shallow Inlets, adjoining Lands of Mr. Needham GAUZE, and Mr. Peter ALSTON... Alex. M. FORSTER.

(Vol. I.) Tuesday, March 12, 1793. (No. 33.)

(504) Fayetteville, Tuesday-March 12. At a late meeting of the inhabitants of this town, the following gentlemen were elected Town Officers for the ensuing year, viz. Magistrate of Police, Col. James PORTERFIELD, Commissioners-Robert ROWAN, John INGRAM, Jesse POTTS, James DICK, John WINSLOW, David ANDERSON, and John SIBLEY, Esquires.

(505) Dancing Assembly.. The fifth Dancing Assembly will be on Friday evening next at Col. DUDLEY's-Cool-Spring. J. PORTERFIELD, R. DONALDSON. Managers.

(506) Public Notice To All Persons Indebted To The Concern of Aulay MACNAUGHTON and

(506)(Cont.) Company.. That I am alone authorised to receive said debts..in this Gazette, Duncan MACAUSLAN appeared..as administrator on the private estate of Mr. MACNAUGHTON, and also under an award..by John BURGWIN, George HOOPER and John HAY, Esquires.. But how far I have been warranted in the assertion "that he had..left the Company's service" will appear from annexed affidavits of Mr. John WILLIAMSON and Mr. Henry URQUAHART, as well as by an extract of a letter from Mr. MACNAUGHTON to Richard KENNON, Esq. Chatham County.. Mr. MACAUSLAN still withholds from me Bonds and Notes..as also a quantity of..Tobacco part of which appears..to have been shipped by Messrs. Robert DONALDSON and MACAUSLAN and HOWAT... James RITCHIE. (Affidavits and letter).. "I have therefore concluded to do business for myself, in conjunction with Mr. James HOWAT." (Signed) John WILLIAMSON. Sworn to before me this 5th day of February, 1793. Mar. R. WILKINS, J. P...

(507) For the purpose of raising a sum of money to repair the State-House. To-Morrow evening, at the State-House, The Gentlemen of Fayetteville will present, Mr. MOORE's excellent Tragedy, The Gamester.. Tickets, at seven Shillings and six-pence each, may be had of Dr. INGRAM and Mr. CLARK.

(508) The Subscriber intends to open a School at Lumberton..in April, where he engages to teach..English..Arithmetic..Geometry, Trigonometry, Altometry, Langimitry, Surveying, Navigation, Geography and Astronomy: together with Algebra and the sciences to which it is applicable viz. Optics and Prespectives; and the method of applying it to Hydraulics, Hyarostatics, according to the Newtonian Mathesis... Joseph PRINDLE.

(509) Laurel-Hill Fair, Established by an Act of Assembly, Will commence on the second Tuesdays of May and November, and continue four days, at the Fair-Plains in Richmond County... Duncan M'FARLANE.

(510) Congress. House of Representatives of the United States. Tuesday, Feb. 7. .. Mr. SMITH of Vermont, presented the petition of Gideon BROWNSON, praying compensation for military services, during the British war; he was wounded, captured, &c. Friday, Feb. 8. On Motion of Mr. CLARKE, the committee was discharged to whom had been referred the petition of John ROGERS, praying to be granted a tract of land by way of compensation for services performed as an Indian interpreter..referred to the secretary of state.

(511) By the Commissioners appointed to prepare the Public Buildings, &c. within the City of Washington, for the reception of Congress and for their permanent residence after the year 1800. A Lottery, For The Improvement of The Federal City.. Prizes- 1 Superb Hotel.. Tickets may be had of Col. Wm. DICKENS, City Treasurer at Washington; of messrs. James WEST and Co., Baltimore; of Mr. Peter GILMAN, Boston. One Hundred Dollars, Will be given for the best Plan of an elegant Hotel or Inn.. S. BLODGET, Agent for the affairs of the city.

(Vol. I.) Tuesday, April 30, 1793. (No. 38.)

(512) Fayetteville. Tuesday-April 30. Indian Affairs. Winchester, April 1. A list of murders and depredations committed in Mero district, between the 16th and 33d of January. Jan. 16. Colonel Hugh TININ was fired on, near Clarksville, on the north side of Cumberland, and badly wounded. Jan. 18. Major Evan SHELBY, James HARRY, and a negro belonging to Moses SHELBY, killed..on the north side of Cumberland. near the mouth of Red river. Jan. 19. Two boys of the name of DAVIDSON, were fired on in a canoe, near Clarksville. Jan. 22. Captain OVERALL and ___ BURNELL, killed on the truce from Kentucky, to the Dripping Spring.. Jan. 24. A salt boat from

(512) (Cont.) Kentucky,..was fired on at the mouth of Half Pone, on the cumberland..
Malachiah GASKINS and David CROW killed-Robert WELLS and John MELUGEN wounded. St.
Clair PRUIT shot thro' the knee, since dead. Jan 26, Thomas HEATON, and Anthoney
BLEDSOE (son of Col. Anthoney BLEDSOE fired on near Nashville, on the north side of
Cumberland, and both shot through the body: they are yet living.

(513) A gang of coiners have lately been detected at Hallowell, in the county of
Lincoln, Virginia.. Several of the gang are now secured in Pownalborough jail, and
the implements dies &c. are in the possession of Joseph NORTH Esq.

(514) Died.)-At his seat in Anson-county, on the 20th ult. the Honorable Samuel
SPENCER, L. L. D. and one of the Judges of the Superior Court of this State. "His
honor's health had been declining for about two years, but he performed the last circuit, three months since; and we understand, intended to have left his home in a few
days, for this town, where the Superior court is now sitting, had it not been for the
following unfortunate accident, which, it is thought, hastened his death: -He was
sitting in his piazza with a red cap on his head, when a large cock turkey passing,
the Judge being sleepy began to nod; when the turkey mistaking the nodding and the
red cap for a challenge, made so violent and unexpected an attack on his honor, that
he threw him out of his chair on the floor; and before he could get any assistance,
so beat and bruised him, that he died within a few days after."

(515) For the purpose of raising a sum of money to complete the State-House. On
Thursday evening next, will be presented at the Theatre. Mr. HOME's Tragedy of
Douglas; To which will be added, the humourous Comedy of Love A la Mode.. Tickets,
at 7s6 each, may be had of Dr. INGRAM, and Mr. A. CLARK.

(516) To the Public. In the year 1781, I contracted with Lewis BALLARD for a Class
Bond, which was given to William SIFFIN (or SISSIN), in the troublesome times, by
John POWERS, Robert CALLIER, James WOOD and others;.. As I have paid up my bond,
which I gave to Lewis BALLARD, for the class bond, ..I hereby forewarn all persons..
not to purchase such Bond or note, given to said BALLARD by me, at any time, as I
have discharged it. William MERRITT. April 30.

(517) The Lands, In Brunswick-County, lately offered for sale, will now be disposed
of, by Samuel BRAILSFORD, Esq. of Charleston, South Carolina; to whom they have been
conveyed, in fee, by A. M. FOSTER, Esq. The subscriber, in Wilmington, is authorised
to treat and agree with any person desirous of purchasing... J. N. GAUTIER. Wilmington, April, 1793.

(518) E. CALLENDER, has just Received, at his Store, Sundry Goods which he will Sell
Extremely Low... March 19, 1793.

(519) Great Bargain And Easy Terms of Payment. The subscriber has it in contempla-
tion to leave this country as soon as ____ and ____ is established in France (next
two lines illegible.) disposing of all his property, consisting of several Valuable
Mill-Seats, Near the center of this town and within 200 yards of the Court-House.-
Also Several valuable Town Lotts, Convenient to the ____ navigation of Cross Creek:
____ of the Court House on Rowan Steet, and on the west end of said street, a Saw and
Grist-Mill, Lately erected, with Timber Lands adjoining.. -Also near the Mills, A
large Rice Field.. He will also hire out, At Public Auction, on the first day of May
next..A number of Negro Fellows and Wenches... James GROSS. At the same time, will
be sold as above, All the wearing apparel, Gold watches, Jewels and House Linen, of
the late Mrs. GROSS... Fayetteville, March 20.

(520) Taken up, on Friday morning last by Mr. WILSON, and committed to goal, a stout young Negro Boy, appears to be from 12 to 15 years of age;-Says his name is GABRIEL, belonging to Col. Benjamin SMITH, near Wilmington... William VANN, Jailor. Fayetteville, April 2, 1793.

(521) The Subscriber hereby informs all those indebted to Aulay MACNAUGHTON and Co. that he will be under the disagreeable necessity of commencing suits against them, without distinction, unless they make payments, or..close their accounts.. He forwarns all..from paying the same, unless to Mr. John WILLIAMSON or Mr. John WATSON, of Fayetteville, or to Mr. Joseph MILNE, of Wilmington..in his absence from either place. James RITCHIE. Fayetteville, April 18, 1792.

(522) Edenton District, Court of Equity, October term, 1792. Aaron LASSITER, Complainant, against Aaron and William HILL, Executors of Ezekiel LASSITER, Defendants. This is to give notice, that, unless the above Defendant, Aaron HILL, put in his answer to the above bill of complaint, on or before the first day of next term..in.. Edenton, on the 18th..of April next, the said bill will be taken pro confesso; and judgment go against him... Thomas IREDELL, C. M. E. E. D.

(523) List of Letters, Remaining in the Post-Office, Fayetteville, on first day of April, 1793. BETHUNE, Mordecai. CAMPBELL, Farquar, Esq. Cumberland; CAMPBELL, Arthur, Col. FORESYTH, John, 2 letters, FAUX, Joseph. GIBSON, Stephen, Esq. Robinson; Trustees of the University of N. Carolina; JACKSON, James, Esq. Cumberland. KERR, William, Esq. N. Carolina; KIRWIN, Capt. do. KING, Edward. LEE, William, Randolph; LAMMON, Malcolm, Robinson. MC PHERSON, William, MAC DONALD, John, MC KENSIE, Andrew, MC INTOSH, Adam, MC BRYDE, Alexander, Little River; MC MILIN, Renal, MENDINALL, Elisha, Randolph; MC MALIAN, Dugald, Brown Marsh, MORSE, Elisha, Dr. Bladen; MC INTYRE, Andrew, MAC CALL, John, 2 letters; MURPHY, Edward, MAC LERRAN, Duncan, MAC LEOD, Donald, MC ALLESTER, Charles, MOORE, George, Capt., Robinson; MAC LEOD, John. OVERTON, Thomas, Col. 3 letters. RALLY, Hanson. STEWART, William, SMITH, John. TOTTEN, Joseph. WINGATE, Joseph, WINGATE, Cornelious, WATSON, John. Those names with no towns affixed to them, are for Fayetteville. John SIBLEY, Post-Master.

(524) The subscriber having been appointed..to collect the tax on all Produce sent from Cumberland-County, down the North-west branch of Cape Fear River... Duncan MC REA. March 26, 1793.

(525) Strayed from the Subscriber's Plantation, near Elizabeth Town, Bladen County ..A Dun Coloured Horse.. Whoever..will deliver him to Mr. Samuel MURLEY, in Fayetteville, shall receive a satisfactory reward... John B. WADDELL. Bladen, April 5, 1793.

(Vol. I.) Tuesday, May 21, 1793. (No. 41.)

(526) Indian Affairs. From Augusta, May 4. On the 7th instant, in Washington county, a son of Col. Francis PUGH was killed, and..double scalped.. Franklin county, 17th ult. A party of Cherokees killed and scalped a man of the name of TOWERY, on Chawgee-creek, between Tugalo and Kiokee, and..desperately wounded William FLEMMING, on Grove-fork of broad river..though he made his escape, we are informed he is since dead. This murder was committed by the Cherokee Indians on or near the frontiers of South-Carolina..on the Oconee river on the 22d ultimo. The Indians 37 in number, came to the house of Mr. Richard THRESHER..and killed Mr. THRESHER 2 children and a negro woman; Mrs. THRESHER..fled with an infant of about 5 or 6 months old in her arms, and leeped, into the river-the Indians pursued, shot her.. Mrs.

(526) (Cont.) THRESHER was about 25 years of age, of a respectable family, an elegant person, and possessed an uncommon education. .. General M'GILLIAVARY died
about two months since at Pensacola.

(527) 25 Dollars Reward! Broke Jail, On Thursday night last, the following prisoners, viz. Richard GRIFFIN, of Anson-County-he is near six feet high, thin visage,
has short back hair, and appears to be near 40 years of age. James HINDS, a lad,
between 19 and 20 years old, pale complexion, but very dark under the eyes, light
hair, and long narrow chin.. ___ MABERRY, a pale looking fellow..for GRIFFIN, 20
dollars, and HINDS, five dollars. Wm. VANN, Jailor. Fayetteville, May 21, 1792.

(528) Ran Away, From the subscriber, on Tuesday last week, a likely young Negro Man,
Named JAME-stout-built, of a dark copper-color, about 21 years of age.. It is supposed he is gone towards the Moravian Towns, or to his mother's in Salisbury.-He
speaks the Dutch and English languages plainly.. W. MACNAUGHTON. Fayetteville, May
3.

(Vol. I.) Tuesday, May 28, 1793. (No. 42.)

(529) Vermont. Bennington, April 12..in Sunderland-The wife of Mr. Isaac LEWIS, of
the southeast part of that town, left her house about ten o'clock on Tuesday morning
last..she did not return..the disconsolate husband thinks he traced her steps..to
the edge of the roaring Branch, so called where he fears she must have fallen in.

(530) Pennsylvania. Philadelphia, May 7. The ship Hope, of Charleston, Captain A.
TRUSDEL, from Cape-Francois, was chased by a schooner, the Capes of Virginia...

(531) Fayetteville, Tuesday-May 28. Married. Mr. Robert NORRISS, Saddler of this
town, with Miss Christian STANTON.

(532) Indian Affairs. From Knoxville, April 20. On Sunday the 30th ultimo, a party
of seven or eight Indians killed and scalped William MASSEY and Adam GREENE, at the
gap of POWELL's mountain, on Clinch, about 20 miles from Hawkins court-house. On
Monday the 8th instant, a party of Creek Indians, headed by young LASLEY..burnt a
house belonging to James GALLAGHER, on the south side of Holston, 20 miles from this
place. .. A detachment of mounted infantry followed them across the Tenessee,
though encouraged to pursue still further by the HANGING MAW..the company were obliged
to swim their horses in re-crossing the Tenessee, in attempting which, Mr. John M'
CULLOH a very worthy young man, was drowned. On Thursday the 11th inst. the house of
    BLACKBURN, on the north side of Holston, 14 miles from this place, was burnt by
Indians.. On the 15th instant, a party of Lieut. TEDFORD's rangers..killed one; who
proved to be the NOON DAY, a Cherokee of Toquo.

(533) A Tribute to Patriotism. Inscribed on the Tomb-Stone of Col. John BUTTRICK,
in Concord, Massachusetts. In memory of Colonel John BUTTRICK, who Commanded the
Militia Companies which made the first attack upon the British Troops at Concord,
north Bridge, on the 29th April, 1775. Having with patriotic firmness, shared in the
dangers which led to American Independence, He lived to enjoy the blessings of it,
and Died, May 26, 1791, Æ 60 years. Having laid down the Sword, with honor, he assumed the Plough with industry: By the latter to maintain what the former had won.-
The virtues of the Parent, Citizen and Christian, adorned his life. And his worth
was acknowledged by the grief and respect of all ranks At His Death.

(534) Notice. The members of the Board of Trustees of the University of North-Carolina..have not contracted for the buildings, further than by engaging Bricks and

(534) (Cont.) part of the Lumber... A. MORE, for the Trustees.

(Vol. I.) Tuesday, June 4, 1793. (No. 43.)

(535) Vermont. Bennington, April 19. Advices from Sunderland state that Mrs. LEWIS of that town who wandered from her family on Thursday morning, the 6th inst. ..was found in the woods..by her anxious neighbors, and tenderly conveyed to her joyful family.

(536) Virginia. Winchester, May 6. On Monday evening last..murder was committed, in the county of Berkeley, near Mr. Robert RUTHERFORD's Mill, on a poor laboring man of the name of JOHNSTONE. James CONOWAY and _____ M'CABE went to JOHNSTONE's house.. used abusive language (to JOHNSTONE's wife) M'CABE drew a pistol..which M'CABE instantly discharged..the deceased expired in a few minutes. M'CABE..re-loaded the pistol, took to the woods.. He is supposed to be about 5 feet 6 inches high, near 40 years of age..and is an ill-looking villain. CONOWAY is taken, committed to Martinburg gaol.. JOHNSTONE has left behind a wife and seven children in poverty and distress.

(537) District of North-Carolina.. The following are the gentlemen to whom distillers must apply, for the Entry of Stills, and payment of Excise. Craven-James BRYAN, Jones and Lenoar-Benajah WHITE. Wayne-William GREEN. Jonston-Lewis TINER. Glasgow-Samuel HALLIDAY. Brunswick, New Hanover, Onslow-Jonathan ROBISON. Duplin, Sampson and Bladen-Thomas SEWEL. Cumberland-Duncan M'RAE. Robeson-John STORM. Moore-John GILCHRIST. Richmond-Robert S. SEALE?. Anson-Isaac L NEIR. William POLK, Supervisor, District North-Carolina.

(538) New Invention. The subscribers hereby inform the Public, that they have invented an easy and cheap method of Carrying Boats Against the Current, so that, with the help of certain machinery, Three hands may work a Boat, which, in the usual way, requires Ten; the expense of which machinery will not exceed 80 dollars, for a boat that will carry 250 barrels. The inventors are now living in Averysburg, on Cape Fear river, are lately from Virginia... William DOLBY, William ROBINS. Averysburg, May 24.

(Vol. I.) Tuesday, June 11, 1793. (No. 45.)

(539) Philadelphia, May 16?. Yesterday afternoon, the citizens of Philadelphia.. attended a meeting in the State-house garden. An address congratulating Mr. GENET on his arrival was read, and unanimously adopted-To Edmund Charles GENET, Minister Plenipotentiary from the Republic of France to the United States.. Signed by order of the meeting. Charles BIDDLE, Chairman. Philadelphia, 17th May, 1793. Attest. Robert Henry DUNKIN, Secretary.

(540) New-York, May 8. The supreme court of the state of New-York..finished the tedious business which came before them during the session on the 4th instant.. Joel Sawyer WHITE, indicted for forging a bank bill of the United States, found guilty, and sentence of death passed on him, to be executed on the 13th June next. Jos. WEEB, (Alias Josiah STILES) and Isaac Storr HUTCHINSON, presumed accomplices of WHITE, in passing branch bank bills..are not yet tried.

(541) Pennsylvania. Philadelphia, May 23. Saturday afternoon..Mr. Samuel PORTER, aged 23 years, a son of Mr. R. PORTER of this city, fell from the upper part of Messrs. MORRIS's and MERKIN's sugar house which was five stories high..and died Monday morning about three o'clock.

(542) Virginia. Extraordinary instance of longevity in the County of Prince Edward. Petersburg, May 10. "There now resides in the neighborhood of prince Edward court house, a person of the name of John HOLLOWAY.. He left England in the year 1714, the day after the coronation of George the first, and arrived in Virginia a few weeks after that event. From these circumstances, he is at this time 124 years of age, appears to enjoy good spirits, and sings a song with strength of voice and distinct articulation. This man's life also furnishes an extraordinary trait; at the age of 67, he married a person aged 44, by whom he had issue a son now alive, aged 54, and where the father now lives."

(543) Fayetteville, Tuesday, June 11. Augusta, May 25. General Order. The brigadiers or officers commanding brigades are directed to cause the third and first class of the militia..to hold themselves prepared to act as circumstances may require... By order of the Commander in Chief, J. MERIWETHER, A. D. C.

(544) Died. On the 2d. ult.-At Charleston, S. C. Nathaniel H. CHURCHILL, Esq. attorney at Law. But a few days before his death, he was taken with a violent fever, which terminated in a delirium, he conceived the purpose, which he shortly after executed, of putting an end to his existence.

(545) State of North-Carolina, New Hanover County, May Term 1793. Notice is hereby given..to all the creditors of Isaac GOLDING, late of Wilmington, merchant, deceased, also to those of GOLDING and STODARD, That the said Isaac GOLDING is dead, and the subscribers have been qualified as Executors to his last Will and Testament, at the above term... Samuel LOWDER, Henry HOSKINS, Exec'rs.

(546) Strayed or Stolen From Fayetteville..a Bay Mare & roan Horse... J. ELTING.

(547) All persons are forbid trusting, purchasing from, or having any dealings with the subscriber's negroes... Robert COCHRAN.

(Vol. I.) Tuesday, June 18, 1793. (No. 45.)

(548) Department of State, to Wit: I Hereby Certify all whom it may Concern, that I have received an Official Communication of the form adopted For Letters of Marque by the French Republic.. Given under my Hand and Seal of Office, this 24th day of May 1793. Thomas JEFFERSON.

(549) Fayetteville, Tuesday, June 18. Married On Sunday evening, Mr. Edmund COOK, with Miss Polly GEE.

(550) South Carolina. Charleston, May 17. We hear that a party of the same villainous outcasts of society by whom the late doctor ST. JOHN was murdered, have added to their bloody catalogue the name of Charles GREENE, Esq. of Beech Hill, who on Tuesday last was also murdered...

(551) Taken up, by Mr. Stephen GILMOUR, and committed to jail in Fayetteville-a Mulatto Man, About 5 feet 7 inches high, well built..he says his name is PLYMOUTH;..a cooper by trade; about 23 or 24 years old; and that his Master's name is Anthony WHITE, living in South-Carolina, on Black-Mingo. Wm. VANN, Jailor. June 16, 1793.

(Vol. I.) Tuesday, June 25, 1793. (No. 46.)

(552) Domestic Articles. Pennsylvania. A Contrast. Philadelphia, June 4. .. The master of the brig Four Brothers (one of the prizes to the Embuscade) capt. Alexander

(552) (Cont.) ROBB, having a large family to maintain, and but little fortune, was part owner of the cargo of the vessel he commanded, Citizen GENET informed the crew of the frigate of his circumstances, and proposed to them to give up their claim to that part of the capture. The proposal was immediately and unanimously agreed to.

(553) Winchester, June 3. Sunday night John SWAIN, a soldier received a cut with a hatchet in the left arm, from one Henry BENNET, of NEFF's town, which occasioned his death. BENNET was imprisoned, and tried before a special court convened here on Friday last, who acquitted him...

(554) Fayetteville, Tuesday, June 25. Married. At Little River, Cumberland County, on Tuesday last, Mr. Angus M'DUGALD to the amiable Miss Mary BUIE, of that place.

(555) Those of the inhabitants of Fayetteville who wish to celebrate the anniversary of American Independence, are requested to leave their names with Mr. M'GUIRE, by Saturday the 29th of June. Col. PORTERFIELD, Col. OVERTON, Hon. Mr. GROVE, J. L. TAYLOR, Esq. Messrs. M'GUIRE, SIBLEY, and HOWARD, are appointed a Committee to arrange and regulate the ceremony of the day.

(556) Indian Affairs. Knoxville, May 4. On the 18th ultimo, on Little Pigeon, Jefferson county, 30 miles from this place, Joshua TIPTON and ___ MATTHEW were Killed, and ___ SIBELUS wounded, by Indians, as they were watering their horses from the plough.

(557) Savannah, June 6. Mr. SEAGROVE has received an answer to the talk he sent into the Creek Nation from the Cossiah King, the Mad Dog of the Tuckabatchees, the whit's Liutenant, and John RINNARD dated Hitchets Town, May 16, wherein they say they were much surprized on receiving the account of Mr. FLEMING and some others being killed at St. Mary's.

(558) Agreeable News. From the Bennington paper of 10th ult. We hear from Niagara, by Mr. HATHAWAY, who left there on the 23d of April, that the Indians had set in grand council for a number of days..the FARMER'S BROTHER, a Seneca chief spoke almost three hours in one language...

(559) To the Public. Whereas a certain John MUNROE, of Moore County, and James WATSON, of Richmond County, have reported that "I had Stolen from the stable of Mr. Daniel RAY, of Fayetteville, a Mare, belonging to a certain Duncan GRAHAM: which mare I had secreted several days, in James BURNSIDE's stable-That I afterwards sold her to Mr. James BRENAN, Merchant of Fayetteville, and that he sold her to John BURGWIN, Esq. of Wilmington." The whole of which report has been proved to be an infamous, malicious falsehood, invented and spread by the said MUNROE and WATSON, with a design to injure my character-in contradiction of which, the following depositions are annexed. Daniel M'LOCHLAN. Richmond County, June 20. State of North Carolina, Cumberland County. James BRENAN came before me and made oath on the Holy Evangelists of almighty God, that he never purchased of Daniel M'LOCHLAN any horse or mare, neither did he ever know..any man by the name of Daniel M'LOCHLAN. State of North-Carolina, Cumberland County. This day James BURNSIDES appeared before me, one of the justices for the said county, and made oath on the holy Evangelists of almighty God, that he never knew Daniel M'LOCHLAN of Richmond County to put or have horse or mare in his stable. James BURNSIDES. Sworn to before me, this 21st June, 1793. J. WINSLOW, J. P.

(560) The Subscribers Beg leave to inform the merchants of Fayetteville, that they have put their wheat Mills and Flax-Seed Warehouses in the most complete order...

(560) (Cont.) ECCLES and BROADFOOT. MACAUSLAN and HOWAT. Fayetteville, June 25.

(561) Public Notice is hereby given, That the Building of the Goai in Bladen County, ..will be let to the Lowest Bidder, on the second day of next August Court.. A plan of the building..may be seen by applying to Joseph SINGLETARY, Esq... T. BROWNE, J. SINGLETARY, J. BRADLEY, Commissirs.

(Vol. I.) Tuesday, July 2, 1793. (No. 47.)

(562) Fayetteville, Tuesday, July 2. The Subscriber-once more-gives Notice, to those of the inhabitants, of Fayetteville who have not paid their Town Tax for the year 1792-that unless the same is discharged before the 20th instant, the law will be enforced. Duncan M'RAE, Collector. July 2, 1793.

(563) Fayetteville Jail, July 1, 1793. Run-Aways. The following fellows are in my custody, viz. GEORGE, a black sensible negro..about 6 feet high, he reads and writes, and says he belongs to a Mr. HENDRICKSON, a Dutch carpenter, Society street, Charleston-and ISAAC, a small fellow, well made..is a carpenter by trade and says he also belongs to Mr. HENDRICKSON, carpenter aforesaid. Wm. VANN, Jailor.

(564) Public Vendue At Wilmington. Agreeable to an ordinance of the Board of the Trustees, of the University of North Carolina, Will Be Offered For Sale, On the third day of the ensuing Term of the Superior Court, for Wilmington District-at Wilmington ..Land situate in the County of New-Hanover-viz. 640 Acres, situate on the west side of the north east branch of Cape Fear River, back of Nathaniel JOHN's, John WILLIAMS's and Mr. WALKER's lines; granted by patent, dated Nov. 15, 1753, to Alexander SINGLE-TON, and by deed of..sale conveyed by him on the 5th of May, 1764, to Solomon HEWETT, deceased, who left no lawful heirs. 640 Acres,..on the east side of Black river, granted by patent..October 24, 1767, to the said HEWETT. 560 Acres, situate on the drains of Long Creek, and the widow MOORE's Creek, including the Cypress Savannah and the fork of the road, on the head of the Beaver-dam Branch, beginning at Arthur SLUCKEY's corner; granted the said HEWETT by patent dated July 21st, 1774. 100 Acres, situate on the west side of Long Creek, near James PORTIVIRNT's and granted by patent dated November 25, 1771, to Anthony du BOISE, and on the 26th day of March, 1778, conveyed by Jacob du BOISE,..to the said HEWETT. 300 Acres on the west side of Long Creek, granted by patent, April 20th, 1745, to Joseph PORTIVIEET, and conveyed by him to Anthony du BOISE who conveyed the same to Thomas CORBET, who, with his wife, conveyed the same by deed, dated October 2d, 1762, to the said HEWETT, and to one Nicholas TOURTEL, whose moiety..was afterwards sold upon execution, and purchased by the said HEWETT. 300 Acres on the west side of Long Creek, between Indian Bluff, and the above described 300 acres granted..September 27, 1756, to Anthony du BOISE, and by him and his wife..conveyed to the said HEWETT and to the said TOURTEL, whose moiety..was sold ..by the sheriff of New-Hanover, to Solomon HEWETT, aforesaid.

The aforesaid Lands having become escheat, were granted by the Legislature of this state, to the Trustees of the University... W. H. HILL, Attorney for the Board of Trustees. Wilmington. June 20, 1793.

(565) To Be Let-and Possession given, at a few days notice, The Houses and Lot, on the North side of the Court House square, now occupied by Mr. PEACOCK... Apply to James HOGG. July 2.

(Vol. I.) Tuesday, July 9, 1793. (No. 48.)

(566) Indian Affairs. Knoxville, May 18. Last Saturday James DONELSON arrived in

(566) (Cont.) town express, from Cumberland Mero district.. Among the many murders and depredations lately committed, by Indians in that district..between the 9th and 28th of April.. April 9. Colonel Isaac BLEDSOE, killed in his field near his own house.. 11. John HARMAN and ____ DOWDY were killed near the mouth of Sycamore, in Tennessee county. 14. Henery HOWDESHAL and PHARR killed near general RUTHERFORD's. 18. John BENTON killed on the road between captain REESE's and Colonel WINCHESTER's mill.. 29. Richard SHAFLER and ____ GAMBRELL were killed, and James DEAN wounded. 27. A party of Indians,..believed to be 200, attacked the stations at Greenfield and killed John JERVIS, and a negro fellow belonging to Mrs. PARKER-this station was saved by the single bravery of William NEELY, William WILSON, and William HALL.. 28. Francis RAMER was killed near the dripping Spring, on the trace between Cumberland and Kentucky. Last Tuesday week, two horses were stolen by Indians, James BOYD and Stephen GRAVES, at M'TEAR's station, 12 miles from this place:-and on Saturday night last, 15 horses were stolen from Mathew BISHOP's, eight miles from this place.. Killed by Indians, on Saturday last, Thomas GILLUM, and his son James GILLUM, on Bull Run, 18 miles from this place. The main camp of this marauding party is supposed to be in Cumberland mountain, in search of which the Governor has ordered out Capt. John BEARD, of Knox county, with 50 mounted infantry.

(567) Fayetteville, Tuesday, July 9. Fayetteville Canal Company. At a general meeting of the Canal company, at Col. DEKEYSER's on Wednesday last: Resolved... D. M'RAE. Fayetteville, Tuesday June 9.

(568) Chatham Races. To be run near Pittsburgh, on the last Wednesday and Thursday in September... Geo. LUCAS, Z. HERMAN, J. HENDERSON. Commissioners. Pittsburgh, July 4.

(569) Five Dollars Reward. Ran-Away from the subscriber, on Sunday, 30th June last, a Negro Man Named CHARLES-he has a yellow complexion, bushy hair, is about 6 feet high, well made..about 35 years of age, he was purchased last fall from a Mr. SOLOMONS, Black creek, S. Carolina... James BRENAN, Fayetteville, July 8, 1793.

(570) United States of America, North-Carolina District. Circuit Court, June Term 1793. Walter Ewing MACLAE, vs. Duncan M'AUSLAN. Equity. On motion of the Complainant's Counsel, and upon hearing the bill and exhibits of said complainant, and affidavit of John WILLIAMSON read-it is Ordered, That James RITCHIE, of Fayetteville, Merchant, be appointed particular Receiver, agreeable to the prayer of the Complainant's Bill, and that the Defendant do deliver over on the application of the said receiver, all the Book, Bonds, Notes, papers..of or belonging to the surviving partners of the late company of Aulay M'NAUGHTON and Company, merchants, or of and belonging to the said Walter Ewing MACLAE, sequestrator, &c... That, before the said James RITCHIE enters upon his office as receiver, he give security in the sum of 20,000 Dollars, with James M'KINLAY and John DEVEREAUS, securities... Attest, Abner NEALE, Clerk.

(571) Applications having been made by direction of the receiver..and Duncan MACAUSLAN having refused to deliver up the evidences and assurances of Debts therein expressed-The same is now advertised as a further caution to the concerned, to make no payments..due to the late houses of Aulay MACNAUGHTON, and Co. but to the subscriber or his order. James RITCHIE. Fayetteville, July 3d, 1793.

(Vol. I.) Tuesday, July 16, 1793. (No. 49.)

(572) LA FAYETTE Dead. Ghent, April 9. It was this morning reported, that the Marquis de LA FAYETTE Died, on the 12th inst. in the old prison at Berlin...

(573) Fayetteville, Tuesday, July 16. On the 20th ult. His excellency the Go
Convened the council of State at Newbern..appointing a Judge of the Superior Court,
to fill the vacancy occasioned by the death of the Hon. Judge SPENCER, when John HAY-
WOOD Esq. the late Attorney General was chosen-and John L. TAYLOR, Esq. appointed Attorney General in place of Mr. HAYWOOD.

(574) Notice is hereby given-That The Co-Partnership of PERRY and TARBE Is This Day
Dissolved. All indebted by bonds or notes, are requested to make payment by the first
day of September next.. P. PERRY, P. A. TARBE. The Business, in future, will be
continued by P. PERRY, as usual, at the same store-house... Fayetteville July 10,1793.

(575) All persons are forbid trusting, purchasing from, or having any dealings with
the subscriber's negroes... Joseph THEAMS.

(Vol. I.) Tuesday, July 23, 1793. (No. 50.)

(576) From the State Gazette. American Independence. Charleston, July 6, 1793. ..
The battalion of artillery and the Cadet corps were active in their salutes.. The
Cincinnati a band of brothers who have fought with success..went in procession to St.
Philips amidst the applauses of the surrounding citizens.. Their anniversary oration
is addressed to us. Col. Stephen DRAYTON was their orator...

(577) The Gazette. Fayetteville. Tuesday, July 23. We are authorised to assure
the public, that John Louis TAYLOR, esq. declines accepting the suffrages of his fellow citizens, as a representative to the next assembly, at the approaching election.
David MACNEILL, esq. of Fayetteville, has been appointed, by the Marshall of North
Carolina District, a Deputy-Marshal, for this district.

(578) The Anniversary Meeting of the Fayetteville Library Society will be held at
the State-House on Saturday next; where, it is hoped, there will be a general attendance. J. SIBLEY, Lib'___

(579) Letters, Remaining in the Post-Office, on the 20th instant-which, if not taken
out agreeable to Law, will be sent to the General Post-Office as Dead Letters. John
ANTHONY, John BUCHANNAN, Benjamin BRYAN, Luke BOWEN, Elisha CAIN, John CAMBELL, Joseph DEAN, 2. John ELLIOT, Edward ELTING, Joseph FAUX, Stephen GIBSON, William B.
GROVE, James GLASGOW, Esq'rs., Joel HAMMOND, 5-Isaac HAWLEY, James JACKSON, Esq. Tho-
mas KELLEN, William KER, esq. Edward KING, Capt. KIRWIN, John KELLER. Absolem LEG-
GET, William LEE, Edward MURPHEY, Andrew MC KINZEE, Elisha MENDINALL, Duncan MC ECH-
RAN, Dugald MC MILLAN, Murdock MC INNES, Robert MAC KAY, 2, William MATTHEW, Archi-
bald MC DUGALD, Murdock MC REA, Archibal MACKEY, John MC CALL, 2, James MC DONALD,
Adam MC INTOSH, Richard NALL. John PARKER, Richard POWELL, Joseph PYNE, James PAT-
TERSON. Walter RAND, John REX, Hanson RALLY. James STEVENS, William SHAW, Robert
SMITH, Sheriff of Cumberland county, John SMITH, William STEWART, Daniel SMITH, John
WILLIAMS, of Wake. J. SIBLEY, P. M. Fayetteville, July 23.

(580) Ran-Away, from the Subscriber..a Negro Fellow Named FRANK, of a very black
complection, about 30 years of age, 5 feet 9 or 10 inches high, and well made-he
lately belonged to MACNAUGHTON and Co. of Wilmington... John KENNEDY. The person
apprehending the above fellow, will be entitled to a liberal reward, on giving notice
to J. MC FEDRIAN. Fayetteville, July 23.

(Vol. I.) Tuesday, July 30, 1793. (No. 51.)

(581) Pennsylvania. Philadelphia, July 10. On Monday morning last died, Mr. Ben-

(581) (Cont.) jamin TOWNE, many years a printer in this city. His remains were interred yesterday evening attended by a respectable numbers of citizens; and most of
the typographical profession in Philadelphia.

(582) N. Carolina. Halifax, July 17. At the Federal District Court..at Wilmington,
on the 1st inst. a libel was exhibited in behalf of the owners of a British vessel
which had been taken by a privateer, commanded by a Captain HERVIEUX,..the libellants
..suggested that the privateer was heretofore an American bottom, and had..cleared
out at Charleston as an American vessel on a trading voyage, and had afterwards put
into Georgetown, and provided herself with arms, having..in quality of mate, a certain Gideon OLMSTEAD, an American citizen, who was active in capturing the prize:
Consequently..illegally taken and no prize. The Court..determined that the libel
should not be admitted,..not being cognizable in that Court.

(583) Cape Francois.. The brig Boon, Nathaniel BROWN, of New-York, sailed from
Port au Prince for Philadelphia the 29th of May last, and on the 1st June, about 7
o'clock, A. M. was brought to by the Joseph and Mary British privateer, David HARRIS
commander, owned by Messers. ALLEN, WHITE, and Co. of Kingston, Jamaica...

(584) Massachusetts. Salem, June 25. The supreme Judicial Court was held at Ipswich on Tuesday last. At this Court the noted Josiah ABBOT was found guilty of
knowingly passing a forged and a State note; and sentenced to pay a fine of 400 1.
in 20 days; and if not then paid, to be set in the pillory. The same person was
found guilty of a fraud in stealing a summons, after it had been left by an officer,
by which he recovered a judgment by default; and was sentenced to pay a fine of 150
1. in 20 days; if not then paid, to be whipped.

(585) Maryland. Baltimore, July 11. Yesterday, the committee appointed to examine
the situation of the French fleet arrived in this harbor, and to ascertain the number of passengers and the relief necessary to be given them, made..report.. Resolved
That a committee be also appointed to call on the inhabitants of the town, to request
them to give accommodation to the unhappy people, above mentioned, in such numbers
as is convenient to each family.. The above resolutions were unanimously agreed to
by a large number of citizens, assembled on the Exchange, and the following gentlemen appointed to carry the last into execution: Robert GILMOR, Philip ROGERS, Geo.
PRESSTMAN, Samuel HOLLINGSWORTH, Jeremiah YELLOTT, James CAREY, Thomas M'ELDERY,
Stephen WILSON, John O'DONNELL, Adam FONERDEN, Thomas COULSON.

(Vol. I.) Tuesday, August 6, 1793. (No. 52.)

(586) Fayetteville, Tuesday, Aug. 6. Printing-Office, Aug. 6. The Editor, To Subscribers. This paper (No. 52) completes one year, since its appearance.. The
Printer, Having an engagement to the Southward which renders his personal attendance
indispensable, the Gazette..must, after the next number, be Discontinued, for a few
weeks...

(587) From a New-York Paper. Major EUSTACE.. His services and knowlede of mankind
and things..extensive for his years, being born at Flushing on Long-Island, in the
state of New-York, on the 10th day of August, 1761; a liberal classical scholar at
William and Mary college in 1775, and confessed to be a genius of the first magni-
tude for earning; was Aid-de-Camp to general LEE in October 1776, and thereafter to
General SULLIVAN; and by his spirit and address made Col. BARTON prisoner in the
Jersies; and Congress in November 1777, resolved "that Mr. John Skey EUSTACE, who
had served with honor, fidelity and bravery, as Aid-de-Camp to General LEE and SUL-
LIVAN, have the commission of a Major in the service of the United States;" contin-

(587) (Cont.) ued for one or two years, resigned and then repaired to Georgia, where he was a Colonel and Adjutant-General, and other military and civil appointments, and admitted to the practice of the law in the Supreme Courts of that state, and with reputation; went abroad to the West-Indies, Spanish Main, Havanna, Ireland, London, Portugal, Court of Madrid, and four or five years residence in Bourdeaux; perfectly acquiring the language of those countries.

(588) The subscriber wishes to settle his accounts, therefore, all persons who have any demands against him, shall be Paid immediately, by applying to Jesse POTTS, Fayetteville, August 4, 1793.

(589) Lands For Sale. The well known Plantation, Spring-Hill, With the adjoining Plantation The Den, Situate on the North-west river of Cape-Fear, within three miles of Fayetteville; containing about 1600 acres.. Applications to be made..to George HOOPER, Esq., Wilmington. John HAY, Esq. Fayetteville.

(590) Notice is hereby given, That I have in my possession a Mortgage for the above Lands, known by the name of Spring-Hill, and the Den..containing 1600 or 1700 acres. Any person..on paying the amount of the Mortgage, with the interest due thereon to me, may have a title..but not otherwise. Thomas SEWELL. Sampson County, July 29, 1793.

(591) Mr. SIBLEY, To undeceive the public, and do justice to Mr. ATKINS; I beg the favor of you to publish the following.. I am, &c. W. J. "Raleigh, July 29, 1793. Sir, When I left Halifax town about 10 days ago, there were many reports circulating injurious to Mr. ATKINS, the undertaker of the State-House at this place.-Since I came here, I have inspected the work he has already done..in all probability the brickwork will be completed by the last of October, or middle of November..." Willie JONES.

(592) Just Opened, By the Subscriber-at Lumberton. A fresh assortment of Dry Goods ... J. RHODES. Lumberton, August 5, 1793.

(593) Was committed to the public jail of this county, on the 27th July a Negro Man Slave, about 25 years of age. He says, the man who now lays claim to him is named Joel WINFIELD, living upon Pee Dee, (and from the fellows account, it is likely in South Carolina) but also says, that he belonged to Benjamin HICKS, who lately died, that said HICKS brought him in Virginia, last summer, and brought him out to Pee Dee and had his residence near to a place called the Hill, and that after HICKS died WINFIELD claimed him for his property and took him into possession... David MURDOCH, Jailor. Duplin County, July 26th, 1793.

(594) Having been informed, that the Sheriff of Cumberland County, has advertised a certain piece of Land, on Deep-river road, about four miles from Fayetteville, (including the noted Cool-Spring) as the property of Duncan OCHELTREE?, lately deceased, This is to give notice..that the said land is my property, and has been held by my father and myself, as his heir, these 30 years, I therefore forwarn the said sheriff, and all other persons from selling, or middling with said premises. John M'CONNELL. Rowan County, July 25, 1793.

THE FAYETTEVILLE GAZETTE.
A Town and Country Paper; Printed every Tuesday, By Lancelot A. MULLIN, For John SIBLEY. (Vol. II.) Tuesday, November 19, 1793. (No. 65.)

(595) Letters remaining in the Post-Office Fayetteville, Nov. 5, 17_3. John ANTHONY,

(595) (Cont.) Martin county, Joseph ANDERSON, Esq. Nole-Chucky, Jefferson county, Alexander AVERIA, Averiaborough. B.-John ___ AN, Fayetteville. Samuel BALDING, Cape-Fare, Mess. JORDAN and BURK, Fayetteville. C.-Matthew CLARK, Fayetteville. D.-Charles DUCKETT, MACKAY's ferry, James O'DONNALD, Sullivan county, Gabriel DER-BUNTZ, Fayetteville, Joseph DEAN 2. E.-Edward ELTING, care of PERRY and TARBE, John ELLIOTT, Cumberland county, George ELLIOTT, Little-River, Jacob EDY, Fayetteville. F.-Francis FARRALL, Chat. county. G.-James GROSEE?, John GILLCHRIST, Raft-Swamp, Ann GATEWELL, Fayetteville, James GLASGOW, Fayetteville. H.-John HADDOCK, Orange county, Isaac HAWLEY, Fayetteville, John HENNANT, Bladen county. J.-Nathaniel JONES, Esquire, Wake county, Elias JONES, Duplin county, Mr. JACKSON, sen. Fayetteville, Samuel JOHNSTON, Esq. Martin county, John JAMES, Stokes county. K.-Edward KING, Fayetteville, Hanson KELLY, Bladen county, William KERR, Esq. care of John REA, Captain KERVIN, Big Stony-Run. L.-William LEE, Randolph county, Joseph LILLIBRIDGE; Swansborough. M.-Duncan M'FARLAND, Richmond county, Archibald M'BRIDE 2, Moore county, Mrs.? MOORE, Caswell county, Gilbert M'KINSEE, Robeson county, Captain Lewis MUNROE, martin county, Robert M'KAY 2, Iredel county, Rev. Angus MC DEARMID, Fayetteville, Jas. M'MILLAN 2, Robeson county, John M'NEIL, care of Daniel RAY, Murdo M'QUEEN, Chatham county, Captain Archibald M'KAY 2, Fayetteville, Patrick M'AUTHUR, Fayetteville, Hector M'QUEEN, Fayetteville, Alexander MACALSTER, Esq. Cumberland county, Andrew M'KINZEE, Rowan county, Malcolm M'PHERSON, Fayetteville, John M'LEOD, Fayetteville, Adam M'INTOSH, Fayetteville, Dr. Archibald M'DONALD, Fayetteville, John M'FEDRAN, Fayetteville, Daniel M'KAY, Richmond county, Ronald M'PHERSON, Buckhorn Swamp, Stephen MERRITT, Colesbridge. N.-Richard NALL, Wake county, Alexander NEILSON, Onslow county. O.-Col. Thos. OVERTON, Fayetteville. P.-Burrill PERRY, Franklin county, Joseph PYNE, Fayetteville, James PATTERSON 2, Chatham, Jesse POTTS, Cambelton, Richard POWELL 3, Lumberton. R.-Walter RAND, Fayetteville. S.-Wm. STEWART, Davidson county, Stephen SMITH, Duplin county, Robert SMITH, Moore county, James STEVEN, Fayetteville, Benjamin SMITH, Blue-Banks, John SMITH, Black River, Return STRONG, Little Pedee. W.-Robert WISTLAY, Erelin county. Sarah WILLIS 2, Cumberland county, William WILLSON, Fayetteville, Arthur WALKER, Yesdell county, Benjamin WALKER, Rowan county, John WILLIAMS, Wake county, Joseph WHITE, Cumberland county, Henry WESTLEY, Elegan county. J. SIBLEY, P. M.

(596) (Doctor RUSH's letter concluded.) ... Your sincere Friend, and former Preceptor in Medicine, Benjamin RUSH. Philadelphia, October 3.

(597) Fayetteville, November 19. Cornelius WINGATE Humbly informs the public, that he has taken the house called the Five corner'd House, near the Court-House in Fayetteville, where he has opened a House of Entertainment and Boarding... Fayetteville, Nov. 16, 1793.

(598) The subscriber uses this method to inform the public, that he has taken that commodious house at the Cool Spring, and intends to keep Boarding & Entertainment during the ensuing Assembly... G. DUDLEY. Fayetteville, Nov. 12, 1793.

(599) One Dollar Reward. Lost, on Thursday evening last, at the upper end of this town, A Jack-Screw. Any person delivering the same at Mr. ADAM's or Mr. ANDERSON's Stores shall receive the above reward. John ANDREW. November 15, 1793.

(600) To be Let, for any term of time, between one and five years, the Large.. House the Subscriber now lives in, near the Court-House in Fayetteville.. James MOORE. Fayetteville, August 27.

(601) The subscriber..finds it necessary in future to confine his sales to prompt payment..cannot open any further accounts upon the terms heretofore agreed upon,

(601) (Cont.) except in the article of Medicine, which he will continue to supply as usual. Marshal R. WILLKINGS. Wilmington, 13th November.

(602) All persons indebted to the estate of Alexander M'IVER, Deceased, are requested to make immediate payment... John MC KOY, T. ARMSTRONG. Adm'rs.

(603) The Lots in the village lay'd off at the seat of the University in Orange County, will be sold..at public Vendue, on Saturday the 12th of October next... W. R. DAVIE, A. MOORE, A. MEBANE, T. BLOUNT, Commissioners, July 22, 1793.

(604) To the Curious. The Subscriber having just compleated his Orrery, informs the trustees of seminaries of learning, who may wish for machinery of the kind for..their students..may be supplied on application to him. This machine will shew..the solar and lunar eclipses..day of the month and date of the year, leap years... William THOMAS. Ast. Richmond county, Sept. 16.

(605) For Sale, Those noted Saw-Mills on BLUNT's creek, including nearly 2000 Acres of Land, part..within the limits of the town of Fayetteville, and the Mills stand within three quarters of a mile from the State-House.. Price 750 1.-Also several valuable Lots in upper and lower Fayetteville.-Likewise, a House and Lot in the town of Pitsore, and several pieces of..Land in Chatham county.. For Terms please apply to the Subscriber at the seat of the University of North-Carolina, and at Fayetteville from the 16th to the 20th of December 1793, at William ARMSTRONG's Tavern. James PATTERSON.

(606) For Sale, by the Subscriber, about 1160 Acres of Land In Bladen County on the east side of the White Marsh.. For terms apply to Dr. John SIBLEY in Fayetteville, Mr. Richard HALLETT in Elizabeth-Town, and to Mr. George GIBBS or the Subscriber, on Black River. J. GIBBS. September 12th, 1793.

(607) Leather. The subscriber, at his store and Tanyard, near the State-House, Fayetteville has..a compleat assortment of Leather, for Shoes, Saddles, Harness Bridles &c... Samuel MURLEY. Fayetteville, Aug. 13, 1793.

(608) Take Notice! As James ANDERSON has advertised his Land for Sale on Deep-River, known by the name of RIGDON's ferry, also, the land the north side of the river fronting his, that was called James WILLIAMS's property, taken by execution for debt, and sold as James WILLIAMS's property, which was a combined piece of roguishness of Stephen RIGDON and James WILLIAMS, in getting a right and claim to this said land. As I, the said Reuben CLANTON, purchased this..land of one John RHODES and William WILLIAMS, that was entered and surveyed in the year 1762, and held peaceable and quiet possession till the year 1778, and paying up due taxes for this said land, till the Land-Office came to be opened again, as no old pattern was made out, and as I entered the said land over again agreeable to an Act of Assembly-Therefore, I would caution any stranger to become a purchaser... Reuben CLANTON. October 6th, 1793.

1795 - All issues missing except for the following from Harvard University Library-July 25; August 8, 15, 29.

THE NORTH-CAROLINA CENTINEL AND FAYETTEVILLE GAZETTE
(2 Dols. & an half per Ann.)
Saturday, July 25, 1795. (Number IX.)

(609) Fayetteville: Printed on Saturday, by Thomas CONNOLY, & Co. in the State-House, where Advertisements, Essays, articles of intelligence, &c. will be thankfully received and carefully inserted.

(610) The subscriber has for sale a valuable..House and Lot opposite the Masons-Hall-Likewise a very convenient dwelling house he at present lives in nearly opposite the Mill belonging to Robert COCHRAN, esquire, and opposite Mr. PERRY's brick building-he has also a very good Waggon and Team, and House-hold Furniture will be disposed of... Michael BUTLER. Fayetteville, July 18, 1795.

(611) For Sale. Two valuable Tracts of Land in Orange County; two or three miles from the University, one of 300 acres, the other of about 700 acres... Samuel PARKE. Randolph County, July 22, 1795.

(612) Wanted by the subscriber a Journeyman Hatter, one who can work both furr and wool.. Also as Apprentices, two lads from 14 to 16 years of age. John MORE. Fayetteville, July 25, 1795.

(613) Ten Dollars Reward. Will be paid to any person who will deliver to the subscriber in Georgetown, a mustie Servant Woman, named Nancy OXINDINE, she is a stout wench, of a light complexion..about 30 years of age.. It is supposed she has been entic'd away by her brother and sister..the latter lives in Fayetteville... James DUFFEL. Georgetown, South-Carolina, June 4, 1795.

(614) To Be Sold. Several valuable Tracts of Land..also some Lots improved in Fayetteville... F. SPILLER. Fayetteville, June 7, 1795.

(615) The Subscriber cautions all persons against receiving an assignment of a note he gave to John STROUD, 16th October 1794-For the sum of 100 guineas. The above note was deposited in the hands of John COPELAND, and was to become due on the event of a Race; but was prematurely delivered up, as the race has not been run. The subscriber will only pay it, in case the law so decides. Joshua BARFIELD. Little Pedee, South Carolina.

(616) Forty Shillings Reward. Strayed or Stolen from the subscriber,..a small Sorrel Mare... George BARGE.

(617) Philadelphia, Sept. 5, 1795. (Letter) Sir,... (signed) Thomas JEFFERSON. (To) Geo. HAMMOND, Esq.

(618) Black Lead for Sale. The subscriber having observed in some of the periodical publications of the Northern states-Black Lead recommended for painting the roofs of houses on account of its repelling influence against Fire.. Specimens of the Article may be seen..by applying to Messrs. Ebenezer STOTT, & Co. of Petersburg, Virginia, Robert DONALDSON, & Co. of Fayetteville, John MACAUSLAN, of Wilmington, or the Subscriber at Pittsborough, Chatham county, N. Carolina. John HENDERSON. June 20, 1795.

Saturday, August 8, 1795. (Number XI.)

(619) Philadelphia, July 21.. By a gentleman who left New-York on Sunday evening we have..the following account of the Town Meeting. The intelligence of the Town Meeting at Boston, which had entered into certain resolutions, disapproving of the treaty lately negociated with Great-Britain..reached this city..and a similar meeting would speedily be had here. On Friday evening a number of merchants met at the Tontine Coffee-house, and agreed upon an address to the citizens..signed by their chairman, James WATSON.. A proposition was made for appointing a chairman-Col. Wm. SMITH, and Commodore NICHOLSON, were named-the first was appointed, and took the chair. .. The person who took the lead..on the side of those who advocated an im-

(619) (Cont.) mediate condemnation of the treaty, were Mr. Brockholst LIVINGSTON, Mr. Peter LIVINGSTON, and Mr. Maturn LIVINGSTON; on the other side appeared Mr. HAMILTON, and.. Mr. KING.. A member (not thro' the medium of the Chair) then named 15 citizens as a committee, to whom the subject should be referred.. The persons..were Mr. B. LIVINGSTON, Mr. I. CLASON, Col. H. RUTGERS, Mr. F. NIXON, M. VARICK, Mr. I. R. LIVINGSTON, Mr. Jno. BROOME, Mr. SIMPSON, Mr. ELTING, Mr. DENNING, Mr. OSGOOD, Mr. GELSTON, Mr. W. W. GILBERT, Mr. BROWER, and Mr. Gurden MUNFORD...

(620) Messrs. CONNOLY, & Co. Gentlemen, For the information of the good citizens of the county of Robeson, you will please to insert in your impartial gazette, the enclosed copy of a letter addressed to me by.. John WILLIS, of Lumberton, Robeson county; also the copy of a letter which I have forwarded to Jacob RHODES, esq. of Lumberton.. George JAMES.

Raleigh, 8th February, 1795. Mr. JAMES, Sir, I Have understood that you have.. a large amount in the certificates issued by the state of North-Carolina..to vest in entering vacant lands.. I will undertake to furnish one million of acres, if you will furnish the bounty to the state. The fees to surveyors, &c..about 500 pounds.. John WILLIS. The above proposition was acceded to, at Raleigh, 8th February 1795. Geo. JAMES. Fayetteville, August 6, 1795. Sir, A few days ago I was in the County of Richmond, the surveyor of that County informed me that he did not believe there could be 10,000 acres of vacant land found in that county since the large surveys made last summer...

(621) The subscriber begs leave to inform..that he is carrying on the Baking Business in Hay street, opposite James SPILLER, Esq... Jacob HARTMAN. Fayetteville, August 8, 1795.

(622) A Certain John PYBURN, horse thief, was committed to goal in Fayetteville the 20th inst. who was taken on the south side of great Pedee, near Mares Bluff-and had ..a large bay Mare... William COOK. July 28.

(623) To be Sold, or Rented.-The commodious Dwelling and Bake-house, where the subscriber now lives in Hay-street, Fayetteville... John ELLIS. August 4.

(624) To be Rented..That well known commodious House called POWELL's Tavern.. The dwelling house 32 by 22, three story high, with an excellent kitchen, underneath the hall there is a ball room 22 by 24 feet, 7 windows, calculated to receive genteel societies. Two lodging rooms on the middle floor, a piazza, hall and two chambers, also one store and ware house, 24 by 32, a compting room and large loft.. One other house 36 by 14 feet devided into two rooms for the reception of a family..a stable 32 by 24 feet with a large loft..a plantation two miles and a quarter from town of 181 acres..the whole may be leased together, or in part..apply to Richard POWELL on the premises. Lumberton, August 7, 1795.

(625) Five Pounds Reward. Run-Away from the Subscriber on the 27th of June last, a small negro man named CUFF, about 40 years of age, five feet high..is remarkably dark ..speaks broken language, he drinks no spirits... Joshua CARTER. N. B. He has a wife near the mouth of Cape-Fear... Montgomery, Aug. 6, 1795.

(626) Llewellyn L. WALL, engages to teach Ladies and Gentlemen to play on the Guitar ... Fayetteville, July 4, 1795.

(627) The subscriber begs leave to inform..that he intends carrying on the Bolstering Business,..he will make Mattresses & Cushions of all kinds... C. B. MILLER. Fayetteville, July 4, 1795,

(628) Taken up by the subscriber at the plantation of John CARRAWAY deceased late of Cumberland county, a Small Black Fellow named CUFF..he is about five feet eight inches high and says he belongs to Joshua CARTER near the Narrows of the Atkin river ... William CARRAWAY.

(629) Just received and for sale by the subscriber in Wilmington,..Goods..Irish Linens..Plattilles or Dutch-Linens, Raven's Duck..fowling pieces..Holland Gin..apple Brandy..Queens Ware..Glass... Jeremiah DONOVAN. Wilmington, June 28, 1795.

(630) New York, July 20. Town Meeting.. On Friday evening there was a small meeting of the merchants, at the Tontine Hall, with Mr. HAMILTON, and Mr. Rufus KING at their head, who harrangued them. Mr. James WATSON in the chair..a very numerous body of citizens collected at 12 o'clock on Saturday, at the Federal Hall..a Chairman.. Col. William S. SMITH was nominated, appointed and took his stand upon the balcony of Federal Hall. Mr. Peter R. LIVINGSTON attempted to state the business of the meeting ..but the confusion was so great, that he could not be heard.. In the meantime Mr. HAMILTON..urging the necessity of a full discussion..was..opposed by Mr. Brockholst LIVINGSTON..the treaty..was in the hands of every one.. The question was then moved and carried, for the appointment of a committee of 15, to draft Resolutions, "expressive of their disapprobation of the treaty", and the following gentlemen were appointed..F. R. LIVINGSTON, John BROOME, Henry RUTGERS, David GELSTON, Brockholst LIVINGSTON, Theophilus COWER, Solomon SIMPSON, Abraham VARICK, Samuel OSGOOD, Isaac CLASON, Elias NIXON, William DENNING, William W. GILBERT, Peter ESTING, Gurdon MUN-FORD.

(631) Agreeable to an Order of the county court of Cumberland. On the 20th day of August next, will be exposed to public sale, at the plantation of William KIRKPATRICK, deceased, at the mouth of Rockfish creek-all the perishable property of said dec. Consisting of Horses and Cattle,..three yoke of Oxen..household furniture, a Waggon and Cart, a four oared Boat, a riding Chair..Seine.. At the same time & place will be rented a..Saw-Mill on Rockfish..there is navigation for rafts,..into Cape-Fear river ..not more than a mile from the said Saw mill... Joseph THAMES, Adm'r. Elizabeth KIRKPATRICK, Adm'x. July 16, 1795.

Saturday, August 15, 1795. (Number XII.)

(632) Town Meeting In Petersburg, August 4, 1795. On Saturday last..a considerable number of the inhabitants of this town and the counties adjacent, met in the..courthouse, for the purpose of expressing their opinions on the Treaty now depending between the United States and Great Britain. General Joseph JONES was..chosen chairman, and Mr. William WHITLOCK, Secretary. Mr. George R.? TAYLOR opened the debate... Mr. J. THOMSON followed Mr. TAYLOR...

(633) Charleston, Thursday, July 16. At a numerous meeting of the citizens of Charleston, held this day in St. Michael's church-John MATHEWS, Esq. was called to the chair.. Resolved, "That an election..be held at the Exchange..on the 17th, to choose 15 gentlemen as a committee to take into consideration the impending Treaty of Amity, Commerce and Navigation..and to report..to a meeting of the citizens..on Wednesday next.." Thomas HALL, John MITCHELL, Joseph RAMSAY and James SIMONS were appointed to receive the ballots.. Saturday the 19th of July, 1795. Thomas HALL reported; That 821 citizens..had balloted for the..committee of 15 and that the following gentlemen were duly elected, viz. Christopher GADSDEN, John RUTLEDGE, David RAMSAY, Edward RUTLEDGE, Charles Cotesworth PINCKNEY, Thomas Tudor TUCKER, Ædanus BURKE, William WASHINGTON, John MATHEWS, Thomas JONES, William JOHNSTON, John Bee HOLMES, John RUTLEDGE, jun., John Julis PRINGLE. Wednesday, July 22d 1795..meeting

(633) (Cont.) assembled in St. Michael's.. On motion resolved, That John Standford DART, be appointed secretary to the meeting...

(634) On the 11th of July, 1795, I was warranted by O. SPEAR, of this place, he has never yet appeared on trial, the reason of which can be easily determined by all who have an idea of the laws of this country. I should be sorry to cast any reflection on a Magistrate of this county, were it not for his ungentlemanlike treatment to me ..he has more than once violated the duties of his office... Geo. THOMPSON. Fayetteville, Aug. 1795.

(635) Lumberton, August 8, 1795. I Have in general a great aversion to newspaper altercation..it is absolutely necessary to my reputation, that the public should be informed of a transaction..between myself and..George JAMES on the 8th day of February last..at Raleigh.. I was then engaged in the land business..if he would furnish the bounty to the state, I would enter the lands and have them surveyed..he agreed and the money was to be forwarded in three weeks from that date,..we had not time to enter into articles of agreement, but agreed..it should be sufficient to exchange letters..while we both sat at the same table.. Upon the reception of this letter, I came home with the fullest expectation of carrying this business into effect-I communicated it to Major OGG and Mr. Jacob RHODES who were equally interested with me.. Mr. JAMES arrived here on the 16th of April; I then told him it was too late; I had made other arrangements, a great part of the land was entered... John WILLIS.

(636) Mess. CONNOLY, & Co. Gentlemen...I thought it my duty to display Mr. WILLIS's conduct to me..and I do still consider him an infamous liar and a common swindler.. a dam'd scoundrel, and destitute of the principles of a gentleman. George JAMES.

Saturday, August 29, 1795. (Number XIV.)

(637) Fayetteville: Printed on Saturday, by J. V. LEWIS & T. CONNOLY, in the State-House...

(638) Lumberton, Aug. 18, 1795. Messrs. Printers,..Mr. JAMES confessed to me, he had sold the lands, before he left New-York, and that he had now to pay on the wantage one shilling per acre, that he was ruined in property, and reputation.. I now believe that I shall take my leave of the subject forever, and the public decide as they may think proper. John WILLIS.

(639) New-York, July 28. Last evening arrived the schooner Dolphin, Capt. Wm. CUNNINGHAM, in 42 days from Havre-de-Grace.

(640) Savannah, August 13. The Honorable and Right Worshipful Brother William SMITH jun. was last evening installed Deputy Grand Master of Masons in this state. The ship Diana, of Kennebeck, from Jamaica, bound to Norfolk, put into Charleston the 5th instant in distress. Capt. COFFIN and three of his men died about 10 days before.

(641) Fayetteville, Aug. 29. Extract of a letter from Capt. James ART, at Martinique, July 9th 1795, to a merchant in Philadelphia...

(642) A public Caution. Whereas there have been several white people lately caught purchasing produce from my negroes, & in the mean time secreting their villainous designs from me-I think proper to forwarn all persons from purchasing any property in future from any negro slave I have..at their peril, as the law will be rigorously put in force against them. Wm. VANN. Fayetteville, Aug. 20, 1795.

(643) The Subscriber informs..that he has a New Livery Stable, just finished for the reception of Horses.. He still continues keeping the Fayetteville Hotel, to receive Boarders and gentlemen Travellers... S. STAIERT. Fayetteville, August 22, 1795.

HILLSBOROUGH

1785 - All issues missing except for the following from the University of North Carolina Library-October 6.

THE NORTH CAROLINA GAZETTE
1785. Thursday, Oct. 6. (No. 704.

(644) For Sale, The four following tracts of land lying in the county of Granville, viz. 640 acres on Tar-River, near Gen. PERSON's' 500 acres a little below Harrisburg whereon James JETT now lives; 200 acres near Granville court-house; 200 acres near Ransom SOUTHERLAND's-The above lands formerly belonged to Archibald HAMILTON, and Co. but now the property of the subscriber... Richard MOORE. Oct. 1, 1785.

(645) On Saturday the 22d day of November, Will be sold at the subscriber's house in Orange County, Ten likely country born Negroes... Lewis KIRK. Hillsboro', Oct. 3, 1785.

(646) For Sale, A Valuable plantation on the North West Branch of Cape-Fear river, 36 miles from Wilmington, known by the name of Indian Wells, containing 1320 acres, 500 of which are good low ground.. For terms apply to George LUCAS. Oct. 3, 1785.

(647) The subscriber wants a considerable quantity of Cow Hides &c. raw or dry, to be delivered in Hillsborough... John ALLISON. Oct. 3, 1785.

(648) Wanted Immediately, A Journeyman Goldsmith and Jeweller.. By Roswell HUNTINGTON. Hillsborough, Oct. 3, 1785.

(649) For Sale. A Very valuable plantation in Bladen county, late the property of Mr. Joseph WHITE, dec. known by the name of DONNOHOE's Bluff, on the South side of the N. W. branch of Cape Fear..containing 800 acres, about 40 acres..cleared, with a dwelling house and sundry out houses..within 35 miles of Wilmington..for terms apply to the proprietor at Fayetteville. Edward WINSLOW. Any person having demands against the estate of Mr. Joseph WHITE, dec. are desired to make them known to Edward WINSLOW, Ex. Fayetteville, Sep. 15, 1785.

(650) Bees-Wax. Michael SAMPSON wants a quantity for exportation, for which he gives the highest price in ready money or goods. Hillsborough, Sept. 14, 1785.

1786 - All issues missing except for the following from the University of North Carolina Library-February 16.

1786. Thursday, Feb. 16. (Number torn off.)

(651) Joseph STUBBINS, Currier and Tanner, late from Connecticut, Takes this method to inform..that he intends carrying on the Tanning and Currying Business in Hillsborough.. He likewise carries on the boot and shoe making Business. Hillsborough, Jan. 9, 1786.

(652) The subscriber having been by the last general assembly appointed commis-

(652) (Cont.) sioner for purchasing tobacco in the town of Fayette-Ville, for the use of the public, takes this method of informing the inhabitants of the districts of Salisbury, Hillsborough, and Morgan, of his said appointment... Robert ROWAN, Commissioner. Fayette-Ville, Jan. 2, 1786.

(653) For Sale, Two valuable Tracts of Land in Caswell, one containing 340 acres, well known by the name of the CHAPLE Tract, on the Country Line; the other is on the Country Line road, 18 miles from Hillsborough, containing 1000 acres. For terms apply to MUMFORD and MALLETS, at Fayette-Ville, or to Robinson MUMFORD, Hawfields.

(654) The subscriber hereby requests all those who are indebted to him in accounts, for the last year, to come and make immediate payment, as no further indulgence will be given. William JACKSON. Hillsboro', Feb. 16, 1786.

(655) Such Hibernian Gentlemen as intend celebrating the Anniversary of their titular Saint, on Friday the 17th of March next, are requested to leave their names at the bar of John TAYLOR, Esq. Hillsboro', Feb. 16, 1786.

(656) For Sale, A Likely young Negro, who has been bred a waiter..terms by applying to Col. EMMET of Fayette-Ville. Lois DE JUSSY. Feb. 5, 1786.

(657) The subscribers request all those indebted to them to discharge their accounts by the 1st of March... COURTNEY and WATTS. Hillsboro', Feb. 16, 1786.

(658) Agreeable to an act of Assembly of the State of North-Carolina, will be offered for sale, at the Court-House in Hillsborough, on the second Monday in May next, the following confiscated property in the county of Orange, viz. 3560 acres..on the waters of TRAVER's creek and Gun creek,adjoining the lands of Anthony COBLE, Michael CHARLES and Robert M'CULLOCH; 450 acres..on the waters of Stinking Quarter, adjoining the lands of Thomas M'CULLOCH and Peter HILTON; 525 acres on ULIAS's creek; 100 acres on the waters (Seven lines at top of column are torn off.) Henry COOKE lives; 200 on the waters of Enoe, adjoining the lands of William JOHNSTON; 300 on the Great Alamance, called HOUSMAN's Place; 200 on Little river, the above late the property of Henry Eustace M'CULLOCH; On the waters of Enoe 150 acres, late the property of James MILNER-A Tract of Land lying on the north side of Hillsborough, and adjoining, late the property of YOUNG, MILLER, and Co. One part of the lot No. 25; 3-4ths of the lot No. 35; Three lots No. 21 22 and 23; Four lots No. 31, 32, 33 and 34; Two lots No.   and 15 improved; 300 on Enoe, the west of Hillsborough adjoining, late the property of Edmund FANNING. 4200 acres on Saxapahaw river, entered by and granted to John LOVICK, Esq. in Nov. 1728.-Also 2,425 acres..to Robert FOSTER, in Nov. 1728.-As also 4,200 acres on..Saxapahaw river and Back Creek, entered by and conveyed to William LITTLE, Esq. in Nov. 1728.

And will be offered for sale at Randolph Court-House, On the first Monday in May next, 2500 acres of land called the rich lands of Uharee; 150 acres known by the name of the Three Forks; 4766 acres lying on the Caraway on Uharee..late the property of H. Eustace M'CULLOCH-500 acres on Stinking Quarter, adjoining or near the lands of Thomas BARTON; and 2250 acres on Stinking Quarter-this land has been sold by John COLLIER, Esq. late sheriff of Randolph to John BARTON, and reconveyed from BARTON to COLLIER; but as the sale was after return day of the execution, the sale and conveyance are void.. All confiscated and directed to be sold for the use of the state... Archibald LYTLE, Commissioner. Feb. 2, 1786.

(659) Michael SAMPSON Has authorized the subscriber to settle all his outstanding debts immediately..he is resolved to remove his store from this place. James PARKINSON. Hillsborough, Jan. 19, 1786.

(660) To be sold at private Sale, A Tract of land, about seven miles from Hillsborough, containing 400 acres,..on the road leading to the Country Line, and joining the lands of Thomas TAYLOR, Carnes TINNEN?, Frances WILKINSON, and Thomas LAPS-
LEY's,... Robert M'ENTIRE. Hillsboro', Feb. 6, 1786.

(661) COURTNEY and WATTS Have just opened for sale, at their Store in Hillsborough,
an assortment of Goods... Jan. 10, 1786.

(662) All persons who are indebted to the subscriber are desired to call and pay
of their respective accounts.. He has a valuable Plantation within four miles of
this town for sale... J. ESTIS. Hillsboro'. Jan. 19, 1786.

(663) By the United States in Congress assembled, New-York November 2, 1785. On
a report of the Board of Treasury to whom was referred a letter of the 24th of
October, from John PIERCE, Esquire, Commissioner of army accounts... Charles THOM-
SON, Sec.

(664) All those entitled to lands as Commissioners, Surveyors, Guards, Chain-Carri-
ers and Hunters, employed in running the line for the military claims, are desired
to apply at Col. ARMSTRONG's office, Hillsborough, for warrants which will be given
them by George DOHERTY, on their producing certificates authenticated as the law
directs. Jan. 5, 1786.

(665) Any person that will dispose of their Front Teeth (slaves excepted) may receive Two Guineas for each, by calling on Doctor LAYMEUR...

(666) Hillsborough: Printed by Robert FERGUSON for Thomas DAVIS, at the Printing-
Office adjoining the Court-House...

ABBOT, John 279
  Joshua 417
  Josiah 584
ABORN, John Anthony 210
ABUTH, John 246
ACADEMY, Grove 328
ACKEN, Gideon 246
ADAM, ___ 192,253,436,599
  Robert 114,322
ADAMS, Abiah 406
  Jeremiah 25.
  John 24,69,123,162,187
ADCOCK, Edward 246
ADKINS, ___ 192
  Samuel 251
AITKIN, R. 1
ALBERTSON, William 95
ALBROOKS, William 246
ALDRIDGE, Francis 251
ALFERD, Lion 406
ALIXON?, Peter 246
ALLEN, ___ 219, 583
  Jamima 46
  John 405
  Joseph 246
  Nathaniel 89,315,333
ALLISON, David 30,31
  John 647
ALSTON, Peter 503
  Philip 138,314
ALVES, Walter 188
AMBROSE, David 246
AMIS, Thomas 8
ANDERSON, ___ 286,455,599
  David 163,350,504
  James 501,608
  Joseph 595
ANDREW, John 599
ANDREWS, John 19
  Loring 128
ANGLE, Thomas 246
ANTHONY, John 579,595
ARANTZ, James 194

ARCHBELL, Nathan 85
ARCHDEACON, Richard 251
ARCHER, Abraham 116
ARCHIBALD, ___ 95,96
  Robert p. 8,p. 10
ARMISTEAD, Robert 41
  Sarah 41
  William 41
ARMSTRONG, ___ 664
  John 106,238
  T. 602
  William 322,605
ARNOLD, John 129
  Thomas 210
  William 117
ART, James 641
ARTHUR, James 263
ASH, Samuel 169
ASHE, Samuel 470,490
ATKINS, ___ 591
ATKINSON, Benjamin 50
ATWOOD, John 251
AUDLER?, Francis 251
AUSTIN, Samuel 1
AVERIA, Alexander 595
AVERY, ___ 27
  Isam 251
  Waitsdell 308
B ECTO , Lew 251
BACHELOR, ___ 30
BACHOP, ___ 217,408
  W. 334
  William 408
BAGA, Benajah 251
BAGGE, Traugott 207
BAGLEY, Benjamin 258
BAILEY, John 246
BAKER, James 50,271,406
  Mormaduke 92
BALDING, Samuel 595
BALDWIN, A. 1
  Edward 246
BALL, Archibald 333

BALLARD, ___ 79
  Lewis 516
  Robert 116
BANKS, Thomas 117
BANNING, Jeremiah 116
BARCLAY, Thomas 151
BARFIELD, Joshua 615
BARGE, George 616
  Lewis 201,338,423
BARKO, Leyman 246
BARNES, ___ 212
  Moses 246
  Robert 427
BARNETT, Scon 251
BARNUM, Moses 229
BARRON, James 103
BARTON, ___ 587
  John 658
  Thomas 658
BARTRAM, Moses 345
BATCHELOR, Josiah 116
BATEMAN, Levy 50
  William 246
BATES, Luke 246
BATTERSHALL, Benj. 20
BAXTER, Samuel 246
  Thomas 246
BEALE, ___ 82
BEARD, Bart. 465
  Barth. 411
  John 566
BEASLEY, John 45
  Joseph p. 10, p. 15
BEATTY, W. H. 502
BEATY, William H. 206
BEBEE, ___ 494
BECK, Henry 30
  John 474
BECKLEY, John 119
BEDINGER, Daniel 116
BEERNAN, Robert 71
BEGGS, J. 494
  T. 494

BELL, Malachi 212
BELOAT, C. A. 405
BENBURY, Thomas 500
BENFORD, John B. 481
BENGE, Obadiah W. 262
BENHAM, Drury 246
BENNET, Henry 553
BENNETT, William 333
BENTON, Dempsey 246
  Jesse 332
  John 566
  Samuel 275
BERRIAN, John 116
BETHELL, William 262
BETHUNE, Mordecai 523
BIBBIN, John 255
BIDDLE, Charles 539
  John 406
BINGHAM, Roswell 71
BIRD, Peter 483
BISCO?, George 116
BISHOP, ___ 478
  Mathew 566
BISSELL, Thomas 40
BIXTY, Joseph 92
BLACK, Alex. 8
  Alexander 315,333
  David 92
  Martin 246
BLACKBURN, ___ 532
BLACKDEN, ___ 419
BLACKLEDGE, William 55,377
BLAKELEY, John 216
BLAMER, John 246
BLANCHARD, Tho. 102
BLEDSOE, Anthoney 512
  Isaac 566
BLEWFORT, ___ 239
BLODGET, S. 511
BLOODWORTH, ___ 349
  James 293,319
  Timothy 310,347,376
BLOUNT, ___ 280,479
  Chas. 50
  Edmund 117
  Frederick 246
  J. 59
  James 61
  John Gray 96
  T. 603
  Thomas 498
BLUNT, ___ 605
BOID, Benjamin 251
BOND, ___ 50
  James 246

BOND (Cont.)
  John 184
BOOTH, William 264
BORDEN, William 212
BOSOROUN, Francis 225
BOURNE, ___ 364
  Benjamin 232
BOWDOIN, James 332
BOWELL, Lewis 472
BOWEN, Luke 579
BOWERS, Giles 246
BOWNE, Thomas 116
BOYCE, James 35
BOYD, ___ 230
  James 566
  William 333
BOYS, Joseph 197
BRADLEY, ___ 326
  J. 561
BRADY, John 246
BRAGWELL, John 251
BRAILSFORD, Samuel 517
BRALEY, Walter 262
BRANTON, ___ 453
  Thomas 313,473
BRASWELL, George 251
BREAM, Conrod 272
BRENAN, ___ 489
  James 559,569
BRIGHAM, Paul 81
BRIGHT, Charles 246
BRIOLS, ___ 92
  F. 38
BRITT, Thomas 92
BROADFOOT, ___ 560
BROCKET, John 36
BROOME, John 630
  Jno. 619
BROTHERS, ___ 51
BROUGH, Robert 35
BROWER, ___ 619
BROWN, Benjamin 251
  Ddm. 92
  H. 212
  Isaac 246
  John 92,117,167,251
  Joseph 246
  Nathaniel 109,583
  Thomas 193,246
  Warren 251
  William 170,246,390
BROWNE, T. 561
BROWNLOW, James 354
BROWNSON, Gideon 510
BRUCE, Charles 275,296

BRUER, William 97
BRUSH, Ebenezer 210
BRYAN, ___ 106
  Arthur 309
  Benjamin 579
  James 537
  Joseph 113
BRYANT, Dempsey 246
  John 246
BRYER, Benjamin 4
BUCHANNAN, John 579
BUCK, Philip 364
BUFFEY, ___ 360
BUFFY, ___ 453
BUIE, John 406
  Mary 554
BULL, James 92
BULLOCK, ___ 406
  Nathan 246
BUNN, Jesse 246
BURGWIN, J. 460
BURGWIN, J?. 208
BURGWIN, John 190,506,559
BURK, ___ 595
  John 406
BURKE, ___ 306,349
  AEdanus 633
  J. 486
BURNELL, ___ 512
BURNETT, William 246
BURNSIDE, James 140,273,
  559
BURTON, James 92
BUSH, George 116
BUSSEY, ___ 360
BUTLER, Michael 610
  Samuel 48
BUTTRICK, John 533
BUTTS, Archibald 246
BYRAM, Ebenezer 479
CABARRUS, S. 297
  Stephen 89,117,212,260,
  466,481
CAIN, ___ 188
  Elisha 579
  Richard 251
CALDWELL, ___ 278
  William 406
CALLENDER, ___ 373,404
  E. 518
  Thomas 401
CALLIER, Robert 516
CAMBELL, John 579
  Robert 386
CAMBERLING, Stephen 422

90

CAMPBELL,   50,51,141,
  142,318,334,373
  Angus 251
  Arthur 523
  Farquar 523
  James 4,171
  John 92,319,355
  John A. 310
  William 405,458
CAMPEN, John 246
CAPRON,   29
CAREY, James 416,585
CARLISLE, John 341
CARMAN, Joshua 471
CARRAWAY, James 31
  John 628
  William 628
CARROL, Hardy 251
  John 346
  Thomas 20
CARTER,   479
  Henry 251
  Isaac 246
  John 246
  Joshua 625,628
  Moses 251
CARVER, Job 37
CASEY, John 50
CASON, Thomas 246
CASU 85
CASWELL,   143
  Benjamin 313
CATTLETT, George 116
CHAIRTTA, James 295
CHAMPLIN, George 108
CHAMPNEY,   82
CHANDLER, James 20
CHAPLE,   653
CHARLES, John W. 423
  Michael 658
CHASE,   52
CHEEK, Amos 142
CHESLEY, Robert 116
CHESSON, Samuel 117,212
CHESTER, David 246
  John 246
CHILD, Francis 315
CHILES, Thomas 329
CHRISTIAN,   479
CHRISTIE, Gabriel 457
CHURCHILL, Nathaniel H.
  544
CHURCHMAN, John 349
CICATY, Austin 181
CLAGETT,   442

CLANTON, Reuben 608
CLARK,   1,291,406,507
  A. 515
  Christopher 92
  Isaac 246
  Jannet 406
  John 405
  Matthew 595
  Nancy 451
  Richard 50
CLARKE,   510
  Christopher 333
CLASON, I. 619
  Isaac 630
CLAY, David 246
  Joseph 1
CLAYTON, Francis 247
CLEARY, Patrick 234
CLINARD, Jacob 262
CLINTON, George 156
  Richard 310
COAKLEY, Benj. 92
COATES, Samuel 102
COBLE, Anthony 658
COCHRAN,   120,359,453
  Richard 322,361,406
  Robert 547,610
  Thomas 4
  William 303,319,453
COCKDELL, John 116
COFFIN,   640
COLDBATH, Archibald 246
COLE, Martin 246
  William 246
COLEMAN, John 329
COLES, Isaac 266
COLLEGES
  Philadelphia, of 345
  William and Mary 587
COLLIER, Charles 484
  John 658
COLLIN, Nicholas 115
COLLINS, Cornelius 116
  J., Sr. 59
  John 246
  Josiah 4,333
  Josiah the Elder 89
  Shadrack 251
COLLONS, John 251
COLQUOHON,   470
COLSON, James 251
  John 313
COLTER, Ezekiel 240
  Levy 246
  Seth 279,352

COLWELL, David 251
COMER, Hugh 246
COMSTOCK, Job 210
CONNOLY,   620,636
  T. 637
  Thomas 609
CONNOR, Benjamin 251
  Mordecai 251
  William 251
  Worsey 251
CONOWAY, James 536
COODY, Arthur 499
COOK, Edmund 549
  Ephraim 258
  Francis 116
  Jacob 56
  William 241,384,393,
    397,622
COOKE, Henry 658
  William 251
COOPER, Joseph 378
  William 230,330
COPELAND, John 615
CORBET, Thomas 564
CORBETT, Thomas 195
CORNELL, Joseph 227
CORYMAN,   344
COSTER,   51
COTTON, Henry 106
  James 262
COULSON, Thomas 585
COUNCIL, James 316
  Robert 405
COURTNEY,   657,661
COWER, Theophilus 630
COX,   406
  Thomas 63,333
CRAE?, William 251
CRAIGE, David 313
  James 313
CRAIGG, James 398
CRATZBURGH,   82
CRAWFORD, D. 214
  Dougald 406
  William 456
CREECY, Lemuel 117,212,
  315
CROSS, Stephen 116
CROUCH, William H. 226
CROW, David 512
  James 237
CRUMP, John 117,262
CRUMPTON, James 246
CUNNAGAN, William 251
CUNNINGHAM, David Hayfield
  333

CUNNINGHAM (Cont.)
  John 26,32
  Peggy 26,32
  Redmond 333
  Wm. 639
CURRIE, Malcolm 406
CUTTING, ___ 280
D'ESTAING, ___ 225
D'GAMBLE, ___ 225
D'HERBE, ___ 288,374
DANIEL, George 484
DART, John Standford 633
DAUGE, Peter 212,481
DAVIDSON, ___ 512
  George 278
  John 116
DAVIE, ___ 308
  W. R. 199,603
  William 210
DAVIS, ___ 334,373
  Aaron 31
  Devotion 117
  Dolphin 118,471
  James 213
  Oliver 108
  Robert 246
  Stage 116
  Thomas 427,666
DAWSON, William J. 110, 117
  Wm. Johnston 498
DE BABBAS, Philip St. Francis 497
DE JUSSY, Lois 656
DES LA DENNIER, Lewis F. 116
DE LA MONTAGUE, ___ 71
DEAL, Jacob 86
DEAN, ___ 373
  J. 28
  James 566
  Joseph 579,595
  Philip 246
DEBERRY, Henry 157,161
DEBRUTZ, ___ 453
DECKERSON, Henry 246
DECKSON, Chosel 246
DEKEYSER, ___ 312,335, 342,358,421,453,456, 567
  L. 220,304
  Lee 459
DELAMOTHE, Henry 464
DELANY, Sharp 116
DELIHUNTER, Samuel 30

DELRYMPLE, John 406
DEMORE, Jacob 92
DENNING, ___ 619
  William 630
DENT, William 262
DEPRUST, James 251
DERBUNTZ, Gabriel 595
DEVEREAUS, John 570
DEVEREAUX, ___ 390
DEWEES, William 377
DEWEY, E. 476
DEXTER, Timothy 415
DICK, James 322,504
DICKENS, Wm. 511
DICKINSON, ___ 280
  John 381
  S. 90
  Samuel 89
DICKSON, Joseph 310
  Michael 246
  Thomas 473
DIXON, John 261
DOBBINS, William 246
DODD, Thomas 246
DOHERTY, George 664
DOLBY, William 538
DONALDSON, ___ 453
  R. 505
  Rob. 408
  Robert 506,618
DONELSON, James 566
DONNELL, Robert 422
DONNOHOE, ___ 649
DONOVAN, Jeremiah 629
DORSEY, ___ 288
  L. A. 301
DOTY, Lemuel 31
DOUGHTY, ___ 29
DOUGLASS, William 246
DOWD, Mary 474
DOWDY, ___ 566
DOWNS, Nathaniel 92
DOYLEY, Daniel 380
DRAYTON, Stephen 576
  William 195
DREW, Dolphin 87
DROWN, Peter 7
DU BOISE, Anthony 564
  Jacob 564
DUAR, Sylvanus 20
DUBOIS, A. 30
  Margaret 92
DUCKETT, Charles 595
  Christopher 50
DUDLEY, ___ 505

DUDLEY (Cont.)
  David 409
  G. 471,598
  Guilford 114,121
  Sally 431
DUE, John 246
DUFFEL, James 613
DUGAN, Thomas 117
DUNKIN, Robert Henry 539
DUNNAVANT, Elijah T. 53, 54
DUPRE, ___ 270
DURDON, Miles 246
DURPHIE, Prudence 296
EAGAN, ___ 488
  Becky (GLASS) 445
  John 445,482
EASTERLING, William 106
EATON, ___ 267,366
  Thomas 296
ECCLES, ___ 560
  John 192,253
  William 246
EDLOW, George 251
EDWARDS, Pierpoint 287
EDY, Jacob 595
ELBERT, ___ 235
ELLETSON, Goodwin 311
ELLIOT, John 579
ELLIOTT, George 595
  John 595
ELLIS, John 246,623
ELLUMS, James 251
ELTING, ___ 619
  Edward 579,595
  J. 546
  James 431
EMETT, ___ 461
EMLEN, David 251
EMMERY, William 246
EMMET, ___ 312,656
ENGLAND, William 319
ERICHSON, Severin 134,270
ESTING, Peter 630
ESTIS, J. 662
ETHERAGE, John 246
EUSTACE, John Skey 587
EVANS, Thomas 238
EVELEIGH, Nicholas 125
EVERAGIN, Edward 117
EVERAIGN, ___ 212
EVERHART, John 52
EVERTON, John 50
EYREMAN, Jacob 52
FAGAN, Hugh 50

FAITHFULL, William 246
FALKENER, William 471
FANNING, Edmund 658
FARRALL, Francis 595
FARRIS, William 422
FARROGOOD, George 479
FAULCON, John 296
FAULKS, James 246
FAUX, ___ 139
  Joseph 523,579
FAYETTE, ___ 265
FELPS, Thomas 286
FENNEL, M. 105
FENNO, ___ 190
  John Ward 23
  Samuel 497
FERGU___, Alexander 50
FERGUSON, A. 167
  Robert 371,425,666
FERRAND, William 422
FIELD, John 62
FIELDS, John 246
FINDLEY, William 443
FINNEY, Thomas 13
FISK, James 58,92
FITCH, Ephraim 71
FITT, Thomas 29
FITZSIMONS, ___ 349,364
FLECKENS, James 246
FLEMING, ___ 557
FLEMMING, William 526
FLOOD, Benjamin 251
FLURY, H. 75
FONERDEN, Adam 585
FONTAINE, Francis 181
FORBES, Caleb 36
FORESYTH, John 523
FORSTER, Alex. M. 503
FORSYTH, Alexander 295
  James 313
FORTUNE, William 251
FOSDICK, N. F. 116
FOSTER, ___ 50
  A. M. 517
  Robert 658
  Seth 102
FOUNTAIN, ___ 307
FOWLER, Abraham 246
  George 246
FRALEY, John 251
FRANCIS, Anthony 246
FRANKFORD, John 92
FRANKLIN, ___ 179
  B. 135
  Benjamin 168,174

FRANKLIN (Cont.)
  Jesse 278
  John 179
FRANKS, David S. 151
FRAZIER, Jeremiah 117
FREAR, Richard 261
FRIES, John 52
FUHARD, John 212
FULCHER, Cason 246
FULLER, John 246
  Samuel 467
FULRALL, Joseph 251
FURGUSON, A. 408
FURNIVAL, Richard 251
GABLE, Daniel 52
  Jacob 52
  Peter 52
GADSDEN, ___ 82
  Christopher 633
GAGE, Thos. 92
GAITHIER, ___ 286
GALE, ___ 461
  Joseph 406
GALLAGHER, James 532
GALLOP, Ann 42
  Jeremiah 42
GAMBLE, ___ 479
GAMBRELL, ___ 566
GAMMELL, James 224
GARDNER, ___ 10
GARMAN, ___ 382
GARNER, Samuel 246
GARRETT, Rhichard
GARRISON, Stephen 251
GARVEY, Patrick 4
GASKINS, Adam 106
  Malachiah 512
GASTER, Jacob 447
GATEWELL, Ann 595
GATEWOOD, Philemon 116
GATHIER, Basil 294
GAUTIER, ___ 216
  J. N. 517
GAUZE, Needham 503
GAZLEY, Charles 251
GAZZAM, ___ 17
GEE, Polly 549
GELSTON, ___ 619
  David 630
  John 116
GENET, ___ 552
  Edmund Charles 539
GEORGE, Brittain 246
  Lewis 251
GERMAN, Rachel 30

GERRY, Samuel Russel 210
GETTMAN, George 52
  John 52
  William 52
GEYER, ___ 82
GIBBES, ___ 82
GIBBS, George 203,606
  J. 606
GIBSON, John 116
  Stephen 523,579
GILBERT, Jesse 321
  W. W. 619
  William W. 630
GILCHRIST, John 537
GILL, John 246
  Robert 251
GILLCHRIST, John 595
GILLESPIE, Robert 327
GILLESPY, ___ 450
GILLUM, James 566
  Thomas 566
GILMAN, ___ 349
  Peter 511
GILMOR, Robert 585
GILMOUR, Stephen 551
GINSINGS, George 251
GLASCOCK, George 138
GLASGOW, J. 279
  James 579,595
GLASS, Becky 445
  Levi 445,482
GLASSELL, ___ 153
GLISSON, D. 106
GOBBLE, Frederick 294
GOELET, John 92
GOLDING, Isaac 545
GOOD, John 251
GOODEN, Willie 251
GOODHUE, ___ 355
GOODIN, Robertson 251
GOODMAN, David 92
GOODRICH, ___ 192
GORE, N. 151
GOUDY, William 296
GRAHAM, Alexr. 485
  Duncan 559
  Eliza 485
  Francis 246
  John 246
  Stephen 436
GRANBERRY, Josiah 88
GRANBERY, Josiah 62
GRANDY, Charles 212
GRANT, John 251
GRAVES, Stephen 566

GRAY, 410
GRAYSON, William 155
GREEN, John 358
  Randolph 246
  S. 462
  Samuel 420
  William 191, 537
  Wm. 108
GREENE, Adam 532
  Charles 550
  Nathaniel 172
GREENFIELD, 51
GREER, David 405
GREGG, Andrew 443
GREGORY, James 92
  John 295
GRENVILLE, Thomas 43
GRICE, Charles 105
GRIFFIN, Richard 527
  Samuel 266
  William 246
GRIFFITH, Roger 286
GRINNAGE, John 251
GRIST, Richard 309
GROSEE?, James 595
GROSS, James 519
GROVE, 384,555
  W. B. 323
  William B. 121,317,579
  William Barry 126,293,
    347
  Wm. Barry 385
GUENN?, Samuel 251
GUERARD, Rebecca 133
GUIAN, Leuis 92
GUILD, Benjamin 20
GUION, 268
GUNBY, John 116
GURGANUS, Willie 30
GURLEY, Joseph 246
GUTHERY, William 395
HABERSHAM, John 116
HABLET, Wm. 334
HADDOCK, Andrew 251
  John 595
HADLEY, Simon 384
HADSOCK, Peter 246
HADSWORTH, William 251
HAGER, 475
HAINS, 71
HAINY, Frederick 52
HALL, Edmund 313
  George Abbot 116
  James 295
  John 251

HALL (Cont.)
  Thomas 633
  William 117,566
HALLETT, Richard 606
HALLIDAY, Samuel 537
HALLING, Solomon 143
HALSTED, John 116
HAMILTON, 619,630
  Alexander 125,222
  Archibald 644
  John 117,212,3.5
  Paul 380
HAMMOND, Geo. 617
  Joel 579
HAMSBURGER, Peter 52
HAND, Elizabeth 186
  Joseph 246
HANDY, 309
HANKINS, Thomas 86
HANLY, Samuel 499
HANSON, Samuel 116
HAR , Henry 50
HARDIN, 412,429
HARDWICK, Richard 246
HARE, John 406
HARGROVE, Hezekiah 251
HARLEY, R. 374
HARMAN, John 566
HARMER, 307
HARNETT, 247
HARPUR, J. 324
HARRAMOND, Henry 74
HARRINGTON, Henry 406
HARRIS, Benjamin 246
  David 583
  Edward 251
  Richard 116,212
  Samuel 362
HARRISON, Thomas 309,313
HARRY, James 512
HART, Adam 246
  John 154
  Samuel 251
HARTMAN, Jacob 436,621
HARVEY, John 50
  Joseph 117
  Joshua 246
  Neal 19
  Thomas 275
HASKILL, Jonathan 17
HASLIN, Thomas 268
HASWELL, 439
HATCH, Durant 60
  Edmund 30
  Joseph 30

HATHAWAY, 558
  James 80,100
  Woolsey 80
HATHORN, Cader 488
HAUGHTON, Tamer 50
HAWKINS, Benjamin 286,375
  Ephraim 251
  Philemon 275,296
  Wyatt 277,278
HAWKS, Francis 55
HAWLEY, Elizabeth 259
  Isaac 254,259,579,595
  Samuel 249,254,259
HAY, 268
  John 293,308,315,490,
    506,589
HAYDON, Joseph 262
HAYWOOD, 53
  John 200,261,274,286,
    308,315,368,573
HEART, 131
HEASTY, Matthew 92
HEATH, William 246
HEATON, Thomas 512
HEISTER, 364
HEISTHER, Daniel 443
HENDERSON, J. 568
  John 618
  Pleasant 261,315,466
  Robert 246
  Thomas 277
  William 235
HENDRICKSON, 563
HENNANT, John 595
HENRY, William 425
HENSLEY, William 246
HENSON, William 251
HERMAN, Z. 568
HERMETT, James 295
HERNDON, 117
HERO, Ann 332
HERON, 133
HERRINGTON, Giles 246
  Samuel 251
HERRITAGE, 30
HERVIEUX, 582
HETH, William 116
HEWETT, Solomon 564
HICKMAN, Nathaniel 493
HICKS, Benjamin 593
  Martha 343
  Micajah 251
HIGH, Samuel 313
HIGHFIELD, Hezekiah 251
HILL, 117,301

HILL (Cont.)
  Aaron 117,522
  George 76
  Henry 212, 280
  Jer. 116
  Michael 76
  Nathaniel 223
  T. 166
  W. H. 348,564
  William 410,522
  William H. 347
  Wm. 106
HILLER, Joseph 116
HILLHOUSE, James 287
HILTON, Peter 658
HILTZHEIMER, Jacob 244
HINCHMAN?, D. H. 22
HINCHY, Thomas 406
HINDS, James 527
HINTON, Wm. 92
HITFELL, Joseph 70
HITSELL, Joseph 70
HOBDAY, William 234
HODGE, ___ 286, 422
  Michael 116
  Robert 255
HODGES, Phil. 396
HOGAN, Margret 475
  Mary 475
HOGG, ___ 335,459
  James 192,253,312,336,
    409,434,565
  John 422
HOLLAND, Bazil 251
HOLLINGSHEAD, Benjamin 251
  Thomas 251
HOLLINGSWORTH, Samuel 585
HOLLIS, James 246
HOLLOWAY, John 542
HOLMAN, Christopher 294
HOLMES, John Bee 633
HOLT, George 373
HOME, ___ 515
HOOD, Charles 251
HOOKER, Hymeric 313
HOOPER, ___ 189
  Ann 290
  George 506,589
  William 290
HOPKINS, ___ mon 50
  James 170
  Samuel 242
HOPKINSON, Francis 345
HORN, ___ 117
HORREGTON, Thomas 246

HOSKINS, Baker 94
  Henry 545
  James 84
  Richard 72,94
  Samuel 94
HOSTLER, Alexander 191
  Mary 191
HOUSMAN, ___ 658
HOUSTON, Hugh 406
HOUTON, James 406
HOWARD, ___ p.16,127,555
  Caleb D. 319
  Edward 500
HOWAT, ___ 453,506,560
  James 506
HOWDESHAL, Henery 566
HOWE, Arthur 311
HUBBARD, ___ 179
  James 383
HUBER, George 52
HUDSON, Miles 246
HUFFEY, Stephen 116
HUGER, Peter 52
HUGHES, William 36
HUGHS, Samuel 251
  Willis 251
HUKMAN, Jacob 246
HULEHAN, Jame 92
HUNT, John 261,466
HUNTER, ___ 30
  Isaac 92
  Timothy 50
HUNTINGTON, Jedediah 116
  Roswell 648
HURLEY, John 246
  Joseph 246
HUSSEY, Stephen 116
HUTCHINSON, Isaac Storr 540
INDIANS
  Bowles 57
  Broken Arrow, of the 227
  Coosades 227
  Farmer's Brother, the 558
  Hanging Maw 478,479,532
  Keanna 478
  Lasley 532
  Little Turkey, the 478
  MC GILLIVRAY, Alexander
    227,235
  Mad Dog of the Tuckabatches
    557
  Noon Day 532
  Okaysoys 227
  Pocahunta 77
  Powhatan 77

INDIANS (Cont.)
  RINNARD, John 557
  Standing Turkey 479
  Warrior's Son, the 479
  WATTS, John 478,480
  Whit's Liutenant 557
INDIAN TOWNS
  Alabama 227
  Big Tallisee 227
  Chota 479
  Cowetas 227
  Coyatee 479
  Cusetah 227
  Estanaula 479
  Hitchets Town 557
  Little Tallisee 227
  Natches 227
  Toquo 532
  Tuckabatchy 227
INDIAN TRIBES
  Cherokee 327,383,455,
    479,480,499,526,532
  Creek 227,235,455,478,
    480,532,557
  Seneca 558
  Shanese 455
  Shawanoe 307
  Wyandots 412,429
INGLES, ___ 235
INGRAHAM, Jos. 92
INGRAM, ___ 189,507,515
  John 111,114,293,504
IREDELL, James 110,145,
  333
  Thomas 522
IRONS, ___ 414
ISAACS, Jacob 196
ISLAR, John 30
IVES, James 246
IVY, Curtis 261
IZARD, Henry 227
JACKSON, ___, Sr. 595
  Coleby 251
  Ebenezer 246,251
  James 410,523,579
  William 69,125,251,654
JACOCKS, John 50
JAMES, ___ 638
  George 620,635,636
  John 595
  Vachel 251
JANSON, C. W. 92
JARMAN, Hall 30
  Thomas 406
JARRET, ___ 52

JAUNCEY, James 183
JAY, John 430
JEFFERIES, ___ 479
JEFFERS, Paul 267
JEFFERSON, Thomas 187,227,
  548,617
JENAVIER, Jacob 295
JENNET, Christian 106
JENNINGS, Thomas 92
JERVIS, John 566
JETT, James 644
JOCELIN, ___ 288,374
JOHN, Nathaniel 564
JOHNSON, ___ 127
  Charles 117,333
  Crawford 246
  Frederick 246
  Thomas 493
JOHNSTON, ___ 117
  Benjamin 441
  Charles 212
  Francis 234
  Jacob 30
  John 117,231,495
  Joshua 210
  Samuel 110,117,286,595
  William 633,658
JOHNSTONE, ___ 536
JOINER, Benjamin 246
JONES, ___ 17,117
  Edward 315
  Elias 595
  Ezekiel 251
  John Coates 116
  John Paul 419
  Joseph 105,246,632
  Moses 251
  Nathaniel 595
  Paul 265,440
  Richard 30,427
  Thomas 633
  William 405
  Willie 591
JORDAN, ___ 306,595
  Caleb 246
  Celia 33
  Charles 444
  D. 486
  Fountain 246
  Nicholas 33
  Philip 251
  Wm. 50,92
JORDON, Melatiah 116
JOSHUA, ___ 30
JOYE, James 30

JUDGES
  CHASE, ___ 52
  DRAYTON, William 195
  HAYWOOD, ___ 53
    John 573
  IREDELL, James 145
  JAY, John 430
  JOHNSON, Thomas 493
  MORRIS, Richard 227
  PARSONS, Samuel H. 131
  PENDLETON, Nathaniel 493
  PERRY, William 210
  PETERS, ___ 43
  PUTNAM, Rufus 177
  SITGREAVES, John 347
  SPENCER, ___ 573
    Samuel 514
  STOKES, John 199,210,239,
    347
  WILSON, ___ 345
JUSTICES
  FELPS, Thomas 286
  M'KAY, Tho. 326
  MOORE, J. 393
  WILKINS, Mar. R. 506
  WINSLOW, J. 559
KEAN?, David 251
KEATON, Joseph 117,212
KEDDIE, James 393
KEELER, Benjamin 366
KEITH, ___ 1
KELLEN, Thomas 579
KELLER, John 579
KELLUM, George 246
  John 246
KELLY, ___ 496
  Hanson 595
  James 246
  John 50
KENNEDY, Henry 67
  John 580
KENNON, Richard 506
KENSEY, Andrew 92
KENT, ___ 30
KER, William 579
KERBEEN, John 255
KERR, ___ 431
  William 523,595
KERVIN, ___ 595
KEY, Philip 331
KEYS, Jonathan 30
KIDDS, John 251
KILLPATRICK, Efler 255
  John 255
KILPATRICK, Hugh 251

KINDALE, ___ 117
KING, ___ 496,619
  Edward 246,523,579,595
  Rufus 630
  Thomas 262
  Vincent 251
  William 31
KINGSBURY, J. 422
KIRK, Lewis 645
KIRKPATRICK, Elizabeth
  631
  William 631
KIRWIN, ___ 523,579
KITTERA, John W. 443
KITTERELL, Jonathan 280
KLINE, Daniel 52
  Jacob 52
  John, Jr. 52
KNIGHT, Miles 246
  William 92
  William Powers 339
KNOX, H. 292
  Henry 125,227
KUDER, Valentine 52
L NEIR, Isaac 537
LA FAYETTE 572
LABOYTEAUA?, Wm. 50
LADNER, George 16
LALLERSTEDT, ___ 126
LAMB, Gibbs 246
  John 116
LAMBERTZ, Enoch 246
LAMMON, Malcolm 523
LANCER, ___ 362
LANDRAM, ___ 395
LANE, J. 483
  Joel 481
  William 246
LANGDON, ___ 492
LANIER, Barl 362
  Lewis 212
LANSING, Jeremiah 116
LAPSLEY, Thomas 660
LAREY, Patrick 246
LARHO, Francis 246
LASHER, John 116
LASSITER, Aaron 522
  Ezekiel 522
LATHAM, Daniel 50
LAUGZE, Phill. 225
LAW, John 251
LAWRANCE, ___ 364,377
LAWRENCE, ___ 349
  ter P. 50
LAWSON, Thomas 414

LAYMEUR, ___ 665
LEACH, John 246
  Joseph 315
LEE, ___ 355,587
  Charles 116
  James 246
  John 116,246
  Richard Henry 379,452
  Richard Mand? 266
  William 523,579,595
LEECH, James 30
  Joseph 280
LEGGET, Absolem 579
LEGGETT, Absalom 246
  David 406
LEIGH, John 280,315
LENOIR, ___ 117
  W. 297,315
  William 260,466
LEONARD, James 393
LEPARD, William 251
LESLEY, John 246
LESLIE, W. 489
LESTIE, Ann 50
LEUIS, Archibald 92
  Elizabeth 92
LEVERING, Abraham 24
LEVY, Jacob Franks 435
LEWIS, ___ 484,535
  Isaac 246,529
  J. V. 637
  Joel 262
  John 207
  Josiah 193
  Thomas 17
  William 116
  William T. 219
LILLETON, William 246
LILLIBRIDGE, Joseph 595
LILTON, Cloid 251
LINCHE, ___ 398
LINCOLN, Benj. 116
LINDEN, Patrick 251
LINDSAY, ___ 223
  William 116
LINDSEY, James 246
LINGHAM, James M'Cubbin 116
LITTLE, John 99
  William 296,658
LITTLEJOHN, Thomas B. 47
  Wm. 98
LIVINGSTON, B. 619
  Brockholst 619,630
  F. R. 630
  I. R. 619

LIVINGSTON (Cont.)
  John 405
  Maturn 619
  Peter 619
  Peter R. 630
  W. 377
LOCK, ___ 192
  Matthew 315,481,498
LOCKWOOD, ___ 401
  Armwell 25
  Holland 25
  Isaac 92
LOLLER, John 251
LONDON, John 405
LONEY, John Lewis 170
LONG, ___ 280
  William 246
LONGCANNER, Anna Wilhelmina
  Elizabeth 364
LONGINO?, John T. 262
LORD, ___ 334,373,461
  W. E. 405
  William E. 310
LCRING, Peleg 295
LOUDON, ___ 1
LOVE, Kenan 106
  William 406
LOVELL, James 116
LOVICK, John 658
LOW, Thomas 251
LOWDER, Samuel 545
LOWRAN, Robert 326
LOWREY, John 122
LUCAS, George 568,646
LUCY, Burrell 246
LUDWICK, Lewis 251
LUNT, James 116
LUTEN, Absalom 65
LUTTERLOH, E. H. 468
  H. E. 250
  H. I. 134
  Henry E. 349,387
  Henry Emanuel 296
  Henry Lewis 276
LUU?, Warren 92
LYLE, Matthew 338
LYON, E. 50
LYTLE, Archibald 658
M'ALISTER, John 246
M'AUSLAN, ___ 220
  Duncan 322,399,570
M'AUTHUR, Patrick 595
M'BRIDE, Archibald 255,595
M'CABE, ___ 536
M'CALL, John 406

M'CANTS, William 380
M'CEIN, Moses 443
M'CLAIN, John 443
M'CLELLAN, William 313
M'CLOSKEY, ___ 480
M'CLOUD, John 251
M'CONNELL, John 594
M'CORKLE, Sam. 490
M'COY, Spruce 308
M'CRANEY, Neil 255
M'CULLOCH, Henry Eustace
  658
  Robert 658
  Thomas 658
M'CULLOH, John 532
M'DONALD, Archibald 595
M'DONERIGH, James 19
M'DUFFIE, Archibald 300
M'DUGALD, Angus 554
  Archibald 406
M'ELDERY, Thomas 585
M'ENTIRE, Robert 660
M'FARLAND, Duncan 325,595
M'FARLANE, ___ 404,501
  Duncan 509
M'FEDRAN, John 595
M'GILLIAVARY, ___ 526
M'GILLIVRAY, ___ 428
M'GUIRE, ___ 555
M'INTOSH, Adam 595
M'IVER, Alexander 322,602
M'KAY, Archibald 595
  Daniel 595
  Robert 595
  Tho. 326
M'KENZIE, John 226
M'KINLAY, James 570
M'KINSEE, Gilbert 595
M'KINSEY, Alexander 246
M'KINZEE, Andrew 595
M'KINZIE, J. 405
M'LARRIN, Daniel 246
M'LEOD, Donald 406
  John 595
M'LERAN, ___ 291,406
M'LOCHLAN, Daniel 559
M'MILLAN, James 595
M'NAUGHTON, ___ 216
  Aulay 570
M'NEIL, John 595
M'NIEL, David 453
M'PHERSON, John 192,253
  Malcolm 595
  Ronald 595
M'QUEEN, Hector 595

97

M'QUEEN (Cont.)
  Murdo 595
M'RAE, D. 567
  Duncan 562
M'REA, Duncan 149,524,537
MC ALLESTER, Charles 406,
  523
MC ARTHUR, Alexander 406
MC BRYDE, Alexander 523
MC CALL, Alexander 406
  John 579
MC CRAW, Roger 246
MC DEARMID, Angus 595
MC DONALD, Arthur 246
  James 579
MC DOUGAL, ___ 280
MC DUGALD, Archibald 579
MC ECHRAN, Duncan 579
MC FARTER, Daniel 246
MC FEDRIAN, J. 580
MC GILLIVRAY, Farquhar 235
MC INNES, Murdock 406,579
MC INTIRE, James 246
  William 246
MC INTOSH, Adam 523,579
MC INTYRE, Andrew 523
MC IVER, James 406
MC KENNY, Robert 246
MC KENSIE, Andrew 523
MC KENZIE, William 280
MC KERACHIN, William 406
MC KINSEY, William 246
MC KINZEE, Andrew 579
MC KOY, John 602
MC MALIAN, Dugald 523
MC MELLAN, James 406
MC MILIN, Renal 523
MC MILLAN, Dugald 579
MC NICOLL, ___ 501
  Donald 158,159
MC PHERSON, William 523
MC REA, Murdock 579
MC VAY, Eli 246
MAC ALLESTER, Alexander 353
MAC ASLAN, Duncan 469,470
MAC AUSLAN, ___ 453
MAC CALL, John 523
  Thomas 406
MAC CORKLE, Margaret 327
  Samuel 327
MAC DONALD, John 523
MAC FARLANE, Peter 406
  Robert 158
MAC KAY, Archibald 406
  Robert 579

MAC LEOD, Donald 523
  John 523
MAC LERRAN, Duncan 523
MAC LOCHLAN, John 406
MAC NAUGHTON, Aulay 469
MABERRY, ___ 527
MACALSTER, Alexander 595
MACAUSLAN, ___ 560
  Duncan 114,487,506,571
  John 618
MACHENHIMER, John 449
MACKAY, ___ 595
MACKEY, Archibal 579
MACLAE, Walter Ewing 570
MACLAINE, A. 293
  Archibald 247,316
MACNAUGHTON, ___ 506,580
  A. 224,487
  Aulay 470,506,521,571
  W. 528
MACNEILL, David 497,577
MACON, John 481
  Nathaniel 351,498
MACOY, Spruce 317
MACPHERSON, William 21
MACREA, Duncan 394
MACURD, ___ 28
MADDISON, James 346
MADISON, ___ 377
  James 266
MADREY, Darling 251
MAINER, John 50
MAINES, Frederick 251
MALLETS, ___ 653
MALLEY, Matthew 500
MANDERS, William 251
MANNING, John 251
MANSFIELD, Isaac 349
MANTON, Edward 108
MARBLE, Wm. 92
MARE, John 117
MARKS, Conrad 52
  Conrod 43
  Solomon 30
MARRETT?, Drury 251
MARTIN, ___ 257,307
  Alex. 298
  Alexander 245,246,263,
    274,277,279,286,297,
    p. 51
  F. X. 143,268,283
  Francis Xavier 213
  Gabriel 251
  James G. 35
  Thomas 116

MASK, John 406
MASON, George 155,178
MASSEY, Joseph 251
  Philip 251
  William 532
MATHERS, James 17
MATHEWS, John 633
  William 406
MATLOCK, Ty. 182
MATTHEW, ___ 556
  William 579
MATTHEWS, William 393
MAXWELL, Peter 133
  Robert 455
MAYORS
  FOSTER, Seth 102
  VARICK, Richard 227
MEAD, Robert 377
MEARS, James 319
MEBANE, A. 296,603
  Alexander 268
  Thomas 498
MEDLOCK, Charles 343
MELOTT, Jacob 251
MELTZTEAR, John 251
MELUGEN, John 512
MELVIL, Thomas 116
MENDINALL, Elisha 523,579
MENG, William 134,236,270
MERCER, ___ 457
MEREDITH, David 4
  Samuel 116,477
MERIWETHER, J. 543
MERKIN, ___ 541
MERRICK, John 92
MERRIDITH, William 246
MERRIFIELD, Abner 173
MERRITT, Hezekiah 30
  Stephen 595
  William 516
MICHAEL, Abner 251
MICKLEJOHN, ___ 280
MIDDLETON, Solomon 246
MILL, John 50
  Thomas 50
MILLEN, Alexander 91
MILLER, ___ 658
  Asher 116
  C. B. 627
  Christopher 251
  Edward 392
  George 251
  Henry 246
  John 447
  John B. 20

MILLET, ___ 216
MILLS?, ___ 311
MILLS, James 280
MILNE, Joseph 487,521
  William 216
MILNER, James 658
MITCHELL, William 251
MIX, Timothy 349
MONK, James 251
MONTGOMERY, Andrew 295
  R. 212
  Robert 117
  William 443
MOODY, ___ 27
  Robert 66
MOORE, ___ 355,393,414,461,
  507,564,595
  A. 481,490,603
  Alfred 296,347
  Elijah 246
  George 523
  J. 393
  James 149,246,322,600
  John Spotswood 116
  Maurice 10
  Richard 644
  Samson 251
  Simeon 246
  Thomas 346
MORE, A. 534
  James 398,448
  John 612
MORFITS, Hannah 406
MORGAIN, William 30
MORGAN, Bennet 246
  Morris 246
MORRIS, ___ 541
  Nathan 246
  Richard 227
  Robert 96,315,333
  Will 251
MORRISON, Alexander 246
  George 334
MORSE, Elisha 523
  Jedediah 1
MORTON, William 246
MOSELY, William 401
MOTT, Isaac 116
  Joseph 399
MOTTE, Benjamin 246
  Edgarton 246
MOW, John 251
MUCKLEYEA, William 251
MUDD, Zachariah 233
MUHLENBERG, F. A. 162,137

MUHLENBERG, Frederick A. 123
  Peter 443
MUIER, John 116
MULLIN, Lancelot A. p. 78
MUMBOWER, George 52
  Henry 52
MUMFORD, J. 458
  R. 147,319,343,473,474
  Robinson 653
MUNFORD, Gurden 619
  Gurdon 630
MUNROE, Alexander 406
  John 559
  Lewis 595
MURCHISON, ___ 424
  K. 489
MURDOCH, David 593
MURFREE, H. 426
  Hardy 117
MURLE, Samuel 113
MURLEY, Samuel 112,525,607
MURPHEY, Edward 579
MURPHY, ___ 6
  Edward 523
  Maurice 11
  Thomas C. 204
MURRAY, William Vans 331
MURRY, Alexander 380
MUSE, ___ 50
  Hudson 116
  William T. 37,95
  Wm. T. 96
NALL, Richard 579,595
NASH, Abner 60
NAYLOR, John 180,363
NEALE, Abner 570
  Thomas, Jr. 311
NEELY, William 566
NEFF, ___ 553
NEGROES
  Aaron 29
  Abraham 272
  Ben 285
  Bob Woods 126
  Brandy 85
  Bristo 75
  Charles 219,326,447,465,
  569
  Cooper Natt 410
  Cuff 625,628
  Douglas 397
  Emelia 488
  Emilia 445,482
  Frank 256,580
  Gabriel 520

NEGROES (Cont.)
  George 563
  Hannah 445,482,488
  Harper 370
  Hector 38
  Isaac 60,446,563
  Jack 488
  Jacob Spelman 60
  Jame 528
  Jem 161,465
  Jim 411
  London 284
  Lowdon 126
  Lusey 410
  Nancy Oxindine 613
  Natt 410
  Ned 445,482
  Peter 281
  Plymouth 551
  Rhodey 445,482
  Rose 445,482
  Quak 76
  Roger 171
  Sam 76,445,482
  Sambay 15
  Sampson 396
  Sarah 396
  Thomas Bowser 483
  Tim 396
  Toby 157
NEILSON, Alexander 595
NELSON, Thomas 355
NESBIT, David 117
  John Alexander 333
NESBITT, John Alexander
  315
NEVILLE, John 391
NEWBY, Mark 313
  Matthew 246
NEWELL?, Andrew 12
NEWMAN, Thomas 165
NEWTON, Edward 251
  Thomas 93
  Tho's. 35,102
NICHOLAS, ___ 82
NICHOLS, John 50
  William 24,251
NICHOLSON, ___ 619
  Peter 406
NICOLS, Wm. 43
NIEL, John 406
NIGHT, Samuel 406
NIXON, ___ 31
  Elias 630
  F. 619

NOBLES, John 246
NORCOM, ___ 50
  Edm. 79
NORFLEET, Elisha 26,32
NORRIS, William 453
NORRISS, Rob. 264,269
  Robert 531
  Wm. 264,269
NORTH, Joseph 513
NORWOOD, John 280
NOTH ___, John 50
NOURSE, Joseph 125
NOYES, ___ 423,463
  J. 463
NUTT, William 356
O'BRIAN, ___ 295
O'DONNALD, James 595
O'DONNELL, John 585
O'MALLEY, ___ 79
  Matthew 500
  Myles 500
OCHELTREE?, Duncan 594
OCHELTREE, Duncan 146
  Hugh 406
ODRISCOLL, Matthew 380
OGG, ___ 635
OLMSTEAD, Gideon 582
ORDER, Peter 246
OSBORN, Adlai 308
OSGOOD, ___ 619
  Isaac 355
  Samuel 630
OSTUN?, William 246
OTIS, David 92
  Joseph 116
OTT, Philip 424
OUTLAW, ___ 478
OVERALL, ___ 512
OVERTON, ___ 555
  John 334
  Thomas 268,523
  Thos. 595
PACA, William 185
PAGE, John 266
  Solomon 246
PAINE, Ebenezer 44
PALMER, Jonathan 116
PALMORE, Elisha 246
PARKE, Samuel 611
PARKER, ___ 566
  Abraham 251
  Jacob 92
  John 579
  Josiah 266
PARKINSON, James 659

PARKS, Elizabeth 418
  James 251
  William 251
PARSONS, Samuel H. 131,177
PATERSON, Joseph 316
  William 295
PATES, John 499
PATTEN, John 251
PATTERSON, ___ 217,408
  Alexander 413
  Isaac 464
  James 406,579,595,605
PAYFORD, William 246
PAYNE, Michael 39
  Wm. 50
PEACOCK, ___ 565
  Jesse 388
PEALE, ___ 198
PEARSON, Richmond 372
PEASE, John 116
PEMBERTON, James 135
PENDLETON, Nathaniel 493
PENNINGTON, Edward 330
  Isaac 330
PERKINS, Thomas H. 314
PERRY, ___ 212,289,359,422,
  453,574,595,610
  Benjamin 117
  Burrill 595
  P. 574
  Peter 120,248
  William 210
PERSON, ___ 50,268,644
  Thomas 296
PETERS, ___ 43
  John 92
PETRICE, Peter 246
PETTES, James 251
PETTIE, John 246
PETTIGREW, Charles 45,280
  Chas. 50,92
PEYRINNAUNT, Francis 90
PEYRINNAUT, Francis 89
PHARR, ___ 566
PHELPS, ___ 89
PHIFER, Caleb 296
PHILLIPS, Aaron 251
  Sherrod 53,54
PICKENS, ___ 455
PICKERING, Timothy 24,400,433
PICKETT, ___ 212
  Thomas 446
PICKMAN, W. 116
PIERCE, Abner 246
  John 663

PIERSON, Richmond 334
PILAND, Peter 251
PILE, Frederick 116
PINCKNEY, Charles Cotes-
  worth 633
  William 331
PINKHAM, Jhubald 92
PLATT, John 246
POINDEXTER, William 238
POLK, Charles 262
  William 389,394,537
POLLOCK, George 30
  Jesse 251
PONDER, Thomas 246
POPE, ___ 82
  Edward 116
POPPLESTON, John 104
PORTER, ___ 423,463
  D. 192,253
  J. 223
  R. 541
  Samuel 541
  Virginia 401
  William 481
PORTERFIELD, ___ 220,555
  J. 370,505
  James 209,322,437,453,
  504
  John 142,257
PORTIVIEET, Joseph 564
PORTIVIRNT, James 564
POSTELL, Benjamin 380
POSTMASTERS
  PICKERING, Timothy 400,
  433
  SIBLEY, J. 579,595
  John 403,406,523
  STANDIN, Hend. 64,92
POTTER, Daniel 251
  John 401
POTTS, ___ 141,142,318,
  334,373
  Jesse 504,588,595
  Zebulon 198
POWELL, ___ 532
  Nathan 329
  Richard 139,579,595,
  624
POWERS, John 516
PRAVEY, Nehemiah 246
PRESSTMAN, Geo. 585
PRICE, James 405
  John 97
  Jonathan 97
  William 246

PRINCE, Job 152
PRINDLE, Joseph 508
PRINGLE, John Julis 633
  Robert 380
PRIVET, William 251
PROGER, John 251
PROVOST, Samuel 442
PRUIT, St. Clair 512
PUGH, Francis 92,117,212, 526
PURVIANCE, Robert 116
PUTNAM, Barth 116
  Rufus 177
PYBURN, John 622
PYNE, Joseph 579,595
QUINCE, Parker 401
  Richard 405
  Richard, Jr. 401
  Susannah 401
RAINEY, John 268
RALLY, Hanson 523,579
RAMCKE, Frederick 73
RAMER, Francis 566
RAMSAY, ___ 455
  D. 1
  David 633
  Joseph 633
RAMSEY, Allen 87
RAND, Walter 579,595
RANDALL, Thomas 349
RANDOLPH, Beverley 340
RASHIER, Hardy 246
RAVENAL, ___ 82
RAWNS ___, John 50
RAY, Daniel 559,595
  Zachariah 262
REA, John 595
READ, ___ 478
  James 394
  John 175
READING, ___ 212
  Thomas 117
REAMS, William 251
REARDEN, John 142
REDMAN, John 367
  Vincent 116
REED, George 92
REESE, ___ 566
REEVES, George 188
RELFE, Enoch 117
RELL, Joshua 246
REX, John 579
REYLEY, William 246
REYNOLDS, Ann 92
RHODES, J. 592

RHODES (Cont.)
  Jacob 620,635
  John 608
  Zachariah 210
RICE, Joseph 130
RICH, John 384
RICHARDS, John 313
  Nathaniel 116
RICHARDSON, ___ 479
  Andrew 246
  Archibald 116
  J. 223
RIDGE, Thomas 313
RIDGEWAY, Nathaniel 493
RIESCH, Adam 52
RIGDON, Stephen 608
RIGGEN, ___ 212
RIGHTEN, William 117
RIPLEY, S. 22
RITCHIE, ___ 153,192,243,252, 470
  James 286,313,470,487,506, 521,570,571
RIVERS, Benjamin 246
ROAN, Christian 116
ROBB, Alexander 552
ROBERS, Chas. 50
ROBERTS, Ann 349
  Chas. 92
  Owen 349
  Richard 246
ROBERTSON, George 384
  John 246,295
  William 167
ROBESON, John 246
ROBINS, William 538
ROBINSON, Charles 329
ROBISON, Jonathan 537
ROGERS, Hezekiah 116
  John 510
  Joseph 79
  Parker 246
  Philip 585
  Thomas 106,245,246,263
ROMAN, Thomas 251
ROSIER, John 246
ROSS, Daniel 406
  John 116
  Joseph 422
  William 447
ROULSTONE, George 221
ROUNDTREE, Jesse 246
ROUTLEDGE, Thomas 328
ROWAN, John 311
  Mary 311

ROWAN (Cont.)
  R., Jr. 492
  Robert 121,504,652
ROXBURG, John 20
RUFFIN, Etheldred 313
RULEY, William 251
RUNNELS, Amos 281
RUSH, ___ 345
  Benjamin 596
RUSSEL, Eleazer 116
  Mark 278
RUSSELL, Wm. 92
RUTGERS, H. 619
  Henry 630
RUTH?, Phillip 52
RUTHERFORD, ___ 566
  Griffith 296
  Robert 536
  Thomas 251
RUTLEDGE, Edward 633
  John 633
  John, Jr. 227,633
RYALL, William 246
RYAN, Cornelius 246
SALMON, Vincent 246
SAMBLY, Philip 251
SAMPSON, Michael 650,659
SAMSELL, Abram 52
SANDERLIN, Robert 246
SANDERS, ___ 161
  Henry 246
SANDERSON, William 216
SANDS, C. 377
  Comfort 17
  J. 377
SANTEE, Caesar 246
SARGENT, Eps 116
  Winthrop 364
SAUL, John 30
SAUNDERS, Benj. 92
  Ebenezer 71
SAVAGE, George 116
  Thomas 246
SAWYER, ___ 50
  Enoch 212,313
SAYRE, Isaac 345
SCARBOROUGH, Nathan 246
SCHAW, Robert 150,302
SCOTT, ___ 307
  Abraham 246
  Dennis 251
  Drury 246
  John 116
  Richard 116
  Thomas 246

SCOTT (Cont.)
 W. 50
 William 315,333,443
SCULL, John G. 310
SEAGRAVES, John 251
SEAGROVE, 557
SEALE?, Robert S. 537
SEAMAN, Thomas 34
SEATON, William 477
SEAWELL, 106
SELBY, Samuel 92
SENEY, Joshua 331
SESSIONS, Isaac 454
SETGREAVES, John 308
SEVIER, 479
SEWEL, Thomas 537
SEWELL, Thomas 491,590
SEYERS, Benjamin 246
SEYES, 31
SHAFLER, Richard 566
SHAMS, Abram 52
SHARP, Wm. 102
SHARPE, Benjamin 246
SHAVER, Frederick 246
SHAW, 206,455
 Samuel 152
 William 579
SHEED, George 235
SHELBY, Evan 337,512
 Isaac 381
 Moses 512
SHEPARD, William 246
 Willoughby 246
SHEPERD, Bird 251
 John 246
SHEPPARD, J. 405
SHEREDINE, Upton 331
SHERIFFS
 CASWELL, Benjamin 313
 COLLIER, John 658
 DEBERRY, Henry 161
 DOTY, Lemuel 31
 HATCH, Edmund 30
 ? ROBERTS, Chas. 92
 WRIGHT, Thomas 138
SHERMAN, Betsey 228
 Roger 287
SHINE, Daniel 30
 John 30
SHIPMAN, Daniel 285
SHIPPEN, Edward 345
 Thomas Lee 227
SHIPPER, 31
SHOBER, Gotlieb 124
SHORT, Peyton 116

SHURBERN, Jacob 92
SIBELUS, 556
SIBLEY, p. 16;127,555,591
 Elizabeth 242
 J. 166,578,579,595
 John 114,127,215,221,242,
  p. 51;403,406,438,504,
  523,p. 78;606
SIDE, William 95
SIFFIN, William 516
SIMMONS, Charles Howell 406
SIMONS, James 633
SIMPKINS, John 246
 Joseph 251
SIMPSON, 619
 George 102
 Samuel 304
 Solomon 630
SIMSON, Edward 468
 John 246,411
 Samuel 246
SINGLETARY, Joseph 561
SINGLETON, Alexander 564
SISK, James 246
SISSIN, William 516
SITGREAVES, John 347
SKINNER, 292
 Dorothy 83
 John 117,218
 Joshua 50,212
 Samuel 493
 W. 5
SKIPWORTH, George 92
SLADE, Nancy 45
 Nathan 246
 William 45,67,89
SLAUGHTER, A. 35
SLEIGH, John 92
SLOAN, Philip 295
SLUCKEY, Arthur 564
SMALL, John 12
SMARTT, Littleberry 284
SMEDLEY, Samuel 116
SMILIE, John 443
SMITH, 50,53,54,77,360,
 390,406,453,510
 B. 481
 Benjamin 296,298,520,595
 Burrel 251
 Daniel 136,579
 David 209,251
 Ezekiel 246
 George 295
 Henry 52
 Ignatius 233

SMITH (Cont.)
 Jacob 251
 James 92,246
 John 251,523,579,595
 Jonathan B. 443
 Joseph Allen 227
 O'Brien 380
 Robert 275,579,595
 Samuel 1,251
 Stephen 116,246,595
 Thomas, Sr. 211
 W. 382
 William, Jr. 640
 William S. 630
 Wm. 619
SMYER, Michael 52
SNEAD, Robert W. 310
SOLOMONS, 446,569
 Levi 465
SOUTHERLAND, Ransom 644
SPAIGHT, Richard Dobbs
 481
SPEAR, O. 634
SPEARMAN, George 246
 William 141
SPEARS, 455
SPECK, Henry 449
SPENCER, 573
 Samuel 514
SPICER, John 310
SPILLER, F. 614
 James 621
SPOTSWOOD, 1
 W. 1
SPRINGFIELD, Aaron 251
SPRUILL, S. 212
 Simeon 117
SRINGER, Hezekiah 246
ST. CLAIR, 412
ST. JOHN, 550
ST. LAWRENCE, 425
 P. 407
 Patric 334
STACY, Robert 92
 Thomas 50
STAHLER, Anthony 52
STAIERT, S. 243,252,643
STALLINGS, Shadrach 310
STAN , Hend. 50
STANDIN, Hend. 64,92
 Lem. 66
STANEFORD, Jeremiah 116
STANLEY, James 246
STANTON, Christian 531
STARR, James 135

STEDMAN, Nathan, Sr. 202
  Winship 202
STEEL, Robert 406
STEELE, Elizabeth 327
  John 176,262,317,327,357
  William 327
STEPHENS, ___ 295
  Levy 71
  William 405
STEPHENSON, Thomas 92
STERRETT, Andrew 19
  Charles 19
  Samuel 331
STEVEN, James 595
STEVENS, James 579
STEWARD, Thomas 212
STEWART, Charles 251
  Charlotte Jeanett 369
STEWART?, Dempsey 251
STEWART, Duncan 310
  John 50,369
  Thomas 117
  William 523,579
  Wm. 595
STILES, Josiah 540
STILLARD, Peter 251
STIMPSON, James 295
STITH, B. 422
STOBY, ___ cy 50
  L. 50
STOCKS, ___ 52
STODARD, ___ 545
STODDARD, David 449
STOKES, ___ 240,352
  Barry 453
  John 199,210,239,347,372
  Montfort 422,466
STONE, David 117,212,490
  Elias 192,253
STORM, John 537
STOTT, Ebenezer 618
STREET?, John 210
STREET, Richard 268
STRINGER, John 246
STRONG, Caleb 107
  Peter 248,299,402
  Return 595
STROUD, John 615
STUBBINS, Joseph 651
STURGES, Jonathan 287
STURTEVANT, Eliajah 51
SULLIVAN, ___ 198,587
SULLIVANT, John 246
SUMMERS, S. 355
SUMNER, Francis 251

SUMNER (Cont.)
  James 2
  Joseph John 106
  Rufus 12
  Tobias 106
SUTTON, ___ 2
  Ashb ___ 212
  Ashberry 117
SWAIN, John 553
SWAINE, Shubael 364
SWAN, John 117
SWEAT, David 246
SWIFT, John 92
SYKES, James 246
  Samson 246
SYLVESTER, Nathan 251
TAGERT, John 50
TALBURT, John 246
TARBE, ___ 289,359,422,574,
  595
  P. A. 574
  Peter 126
TASH, ___ 7
TATOM, A. 324
TAYBOINE, Joel 246
TAYLOR, ___ 17,286
  George 255
  George R?. 632
  J. L. 481,555
  James 30,278,298,315,347,
    481
  John 452,655
  John L. 573
  John Lewis 308,466
  John Louis 577
  Kinchen 84
  Philip 501
  Robert 102
  Thomas 660
  William 246
TEDFORD, ___ 532
TENBROOCK, John 116
TERRELL, Harry 262
THACKSTON, ___ 306
  James 190
THAMES, Joseph 631
THAYER, Simon 364
THEAMS, Joseph 575
THOMAS, ___ 127
  Abisha 296
  Abishou 317
  Caleb 246
  Elisha 7
  William 137,246,604
THOMPSON, Abraham 228

THOMPSON (Cont.)
  Geo. 634
  John 499
  William 373
THOMSON, Charles 443,663
  J. 632
  James 310
  John 251
  William 251
THORNEY, ___ 82
THORNTON, Thos. 30
THRESHER, Richard 526
THURSTIN, William 246
TICHENOR, Isaac 81
TINDALE, James 117
TINER, Lewis 537
TININ, Hugh 512
TINNEN?, Carnes 660
TIPPET, Georg 251
TIPTON, Joshua 556
TITCOMB, Jonathan 116
TOMKINS, Jonathan 216
TOMMY, ___ 192,253
TOMPKINS, ___ 133
TONEY, Anthony 246
TOOMER, ___ 301,311
  Henry 247
TOTTEN, Joseph 523
TOURTEL, Nicholas 564
TOWE, ___ beth 49
TOWERY, ___ 526
TOWNE, Benjamin 581
TRAVER, ___ 658
TREDWELL, S. 59
TRENT, William 251
TREVETT, Richard 116
TROY, Matthew 186
  Michael 164
TRUAN, Francis 225
TRUEMAN, ___ 412
TRUMBULL, Jonathan 287,
  379
TRUSDEL, A. 530
TRUXTON, Thomas 18
TUCKER, James 132,246
  Joshua 246
  Thomas Tudor 633
TULLWOOD, John 405
TURNER, Amey 193
  David 212,313
  James 117
  John 193
  Jonathan 313
  Polly 313
  Simon 313

TURNER (Cont.)
  William 313
TUTLE, John 106
TYLER, Helen 296
TYLOR, Owen 246
TYNER, William 246
TYSON, Thomas 310
UBANKS, Thomas 318
ULIAS, ___ 658
UMSTEAD, John 282
UNDERDOO, Dempsey 246
UNGER, Lawrence 251
UNIVERSITY 484,603,611
  North-Carolina, of 298,
    490,534,564,605
UPDIKE, Daniel Eldridge 210
URQUAHART, ___ 404
  Alexander S. 432
  Henry 487,506
URQUHART, Alexander 158
  Henry 158,159,247
UTLY, ___ 192
VAIL, Benners 50
  John 58
  Thomas 6
  Thos. 92
VAN, ___ 325
VANCE, David 251
VANDERZEE, ___ 344
VANN, William 388,465,520
  Wm. 527,551,563,642
VARICK, Abraham 630
  M. 619
  Richard 156,227
VASSERE, Lemvel 251
VENABLE, ___ 266
VERNER?, ___ 371
VICK, Jacob 251
VICKORY, Luke 251
VINING, John 381
VOLLINTINE, J. 9,14
  Joseph 14
WADDELL, Hugh 133
  John B. 525
WAGUNSALES, Fer inand 251
WAID, Elisha 251
WAITE, John 96
WALKER, ___ 350,564
  Arthur 595
  Benjamin 116,595
  James 405
  John 178
  William 246
WALL, John 77
  Llewellyn L. 626

WALL (Cont.)
  Pocahunta 77
WALLACE, ___ 172
WALLICE, John 92
WALSH, Daniel 406
WALTER, Nathaniel 251
WALTERS, Solomon 246
WALTON, Timothy 92
WARD, ___ 492
  Elijah 246
  James 50
  Jas. T. 65
  John 246
  William 251
WASHINGTON, ___ 69,101,110
  George 110,123,162,182,187,
    227,379
  William 633
WATERS, W. 324
WATS, John 156
WATSON, E. 14
  James 559,619,630
  John 521,523
  Lotte 246
  Richard 133
  William 116
WATT, Samuel 17
WATTERS, William 311
WATTS, ___ 657,661
  John 450
  Robert 493
WAUGH, James 421
WAYMAN, Edward 116
WEBB, ___ 50
  John 406
  Lewis 251
  W. C. 377
  William 116
WEBSTER, ___ ard 50
WEEB, Jos. 540
WELCH, William 246
WELLS, John 246
  Richard 154
  Robert 512
WELSH, John, Jr. 240
WEST, James 251,511
  Richard 236
  Samuel 246
WEST ?, John S. 49
WESTBROOK, James 30
WESTERDALE, Francis 246
WESTLEY, Henry 595
WHALEY, Ezekiel 246
WHARTON, Robert 71
WHEATON, Daniel 31

WHEELOR, David 251
WHIDBEE, Elizabeth 50
WHIPPLE, John 291
  Joseph 116
WHITAKER, Robert 251
WHITE, ___ 136,341,583
  Alexander 266
  Anthony 551
  Benajah 537
  Benjamin 246
  Churchill 246
  David 246
  James 206,502
  Joel Sawyer 540
  John 47
  John D. 92
  Joseph 595,649
  Mathew Roan 255
  T. 488
  Thomas 3,482
WHITEHEAD, John 251
WHITEHILL, Robert 443
WHITEHOUSE, Anthony 246
WHITFIELD, Willis 246
WHITLOCK, William 632
WHITMORE, Samuel 116
WHYTE, Conyers 377
WICKS, James 30
WIGGANS, ___ 50
WIGGINS, Arthur 251
  Levy 246
  Mathew 251
WILCOX, John 471
WILKINS, Mar. R. 506
WILKINSON, Frances 660
  John 160
WILLET, Marinus? 227
WILLIAMS, ___ 29
  B. 106
  Benj. 395
  Benjamin 92,406
  Edward 246
  Francis 246
  James 608
  John 406,564,579,595
  Nicholas 475
  Otho H. 116
  S. 15
  Stephen 246
  Thomas 92
  Thomas Pool 313
  William 251,321,608
  Williby 313
  Wm. 92
WILLIAMSON, ___ 250

WILLIAMSON (Cont.)
  Hugh 1,117
  John 506,521,570
WILLIS, ___ 243,307,339,
  423,636
  J. 397
  John 201,320,388,418,
  620,635,638
  Sarah 595
WILLKINGS, Marshal R. 601
WILLS, ___ 286,422
  H. 91
  Henry 63,78,83
  James p. 3,8;68
WILLSON, William 595
WILSON, ___ 280,345,520
  James 92,345
  James L. 280
  John 214,251
  Stephen 585
  Thomas 19,251
  William 566
WINCHESTER, ___ 566
WINDSLOW, Tisdale 144
WINFIELD, Joel 593
WINGATE, Cornelious 523
  Cornelius 597
  Joseph 523
WINNE, Zachariah 251
WINSLOW, Edward 649
  J. 559
  John 286,313,342,504
WINSTON, Joseph 334,498
WIRE, ___shua 50
WISTLAY, Robert 595
WITHERS, Thomas 226
WITHERSPOON, D. 315
WOBSON, Joseph 251
WOFF, George 92
WOLCOTT, Oliver 125
WOOD, ___ 311
  Charles 246
  James 92,516
  Reuben 117
  William 251,466
  Willis 246
  Zeb. 117
WOODARD, Benjamin 92
WOODS, William 212
WOODWARD, Benjamin 263
  David 251
  Edward 246
WORK, John 256
WORREL, John 251
WORTMAN, T. 51

WOTY, Isaac 251
WOWDLE, John 251
WRAY, Jacob 116
WRIGHT, ___ 1,125
  Ewell 251
  Thomas 138,150,302,405
WYATT, George 50
WYNNS, Thomas 117,212
YATES, John 406
YELLOT, Jeremiah 585
YELLOTT, Jeremiah 18
YOUNG, ___ 658
  Alex. 289,305
  Daniel 75
  John 92
  Michael 251
  Robert 116
  W. P. 382
YOUNGBLOOD, Peter 380
YOUNGER, ___ 350
YOUNGHUSBAND, P. 28
  Thomas 28
YOWEL, David 451

ALAMANCE, Great 658
ALLIGATOR, Great 80
BANKS, Blue 595
BAY, South 82
BEAVERDAM 30
BLUFF, Donohoe's 649
  Indian 564
  Long 406,446
  Mares 622
BOROUGH, Biddeford 116
  Pepperell 116
BRANCHES
  Allegator 311
  Beaver-dam 564
  Great 30
  Joshua's 30
  Miry 30
  Pometer 30
  Rattlesnake 30
  Reedy 30
  Roaring 529
  Tocohoe 30
BRIDGES
  Ballard's 79
  Cochran's 319
  Lewis's 484
  Little-River 171
  Moore's 414
CANAL, Dismal Swamp 35,93
CAPES
  Fare 595
  Fear 401,446,589
  Hatteras 106
CARAWAY 658
CATFISH 401
CITIES
  Albany 116,230,344,365
  Baltimore 1,18,20,102,116,
    185,346,435,449,511,585
  Boston 7,12,22,107,116,
    129,144,152,173,228,232,
    332,390,415,493,511,619
  Charleston 1,82,116,161,

CITIES (Cont.)
  Charleston (Cont.) 195,225,
    235,339,382,398,428,455,
    480,517,530,544,550,563,
    576,582,633,640
  Hudson 116,344,390
  New-Haven 1,116,228
  New-York 1,16,51,70,71,116,
    123,129,162,170,176,184,
    187,194,227,230,280,317,
    349,366,390,442,477,540,
    583,587,619,630,638,639,
    663
  Philadelphia 1,17,20,24,30,
    43,52,62,71,81,102,108,
    109,115,116,125,130,135,
    168,174,175,182,198,210,
    227,244,295,330,345,367,
    375,376,379,381,382,386,
    400,433,449,455,475,477,
    530,539,541,552,581,583,
    596,617,619,641
  Raleigh 106,591,620,635
  Richmond 416,479
  Washington 511
COUNTIES
  Albermarle (Va.) 178
  Alleghany (Pa.) 391,443
  Anne-Arundel (Md.) 457
  Anson 212,321,362,394,406,
    514,527,537
  Beaufort 76,85
  Berkeley (Va.) 536
  Bertie 4,117,212
  Bladen 126,193,203,206,
    216,255,285,310,311,316,
    369,401,406,445,502,523,
    525,537,561,595,606,649
  Brunswick 298,310,311,401,
    503,517,537
  Buck's (Pa.) 24,43,52
  Burke 485
  Caecil (Md.) 457

COUNTIES (Cont.)
  Camden 36,105,212
  Caroline (Va.) 452
  Carteret 212
  Caswell 309,313,595,653
  Charles 233
  Chatham 141,188,236,
    237,258,276,286,318,
    334,352,371,395,406,
    407,425,471,501,506,
    568,595,605,618
  Chowan 3,6,26,38,42,66,
    79,94,117,212
  Craven 30,313,537
  Cumberland 171,181,300,
    353,394,406,471,487,
    523,524,537,554,559,
    579,594,595,628,631
  Currituck 106,313
  Davidson 315,595
  Dobbs 313
  Duplin 31,106,310,328,
    537,593,595
  Elegan 595
  Erelin 595
  Fayette (Pa.) 391,443
  Franklin 280,595
  Franklin (Ga.) 480,526
  Gates 50,62,88
  Glasgow 537
  Gloucester (N.J.) 378
  Granville 280,313,467,
    644
  Greene 479
  Hartford (Md.) 457
  Hawkins 136
  Hertford 117,212
  Hyde 106
  Iredel 406,595
  Iredell 256,278,296,326
  Jefferson 595
  Jefferson (Tenn.) 556
  Johnston 309

COUNTIES (Cont.)
Jones 30,31,60,313,537
Jonston 537
Kent (Md.) 457
Knox (Tenn.) 566
Lanchister (Va.) 447
Lenoar 537
Lenoir 106
Lincoln 406
Lincoln (Va.) 513
Martin 10,15,280,595
Mecklenburg 406
Mecklinburgh 284,337,
362
Montgomery (Pa.) 24
Montgomery 117,157,161,
406,625
Moore 138,240,310,394,
406,447,537,559,595
Morgan 317
New-Hanover 31,247,310,
487,537,545,564
Northampton (Pa.) 24,
43,52
Northampton 106,285
Onslow 30,31,310,537,
595
Orange 188,282,332,484,
595,603,611,645,658
Pasquotank 25,37,49,95,
96,97,117,212
Perquimans 5,117,212,218
Perquimens 2
Pitt 321
Prince Edward (Va.) 542
Princess Anne (Va.) 414
Randolph 117,523,595,
611,658
Richmond 325,394,406,
509,537,559,595,604,620
Robeson 482,488,537,595,
620
Robinson 212,320,352,406,
523
Rockingham 313
Rowan 113,286,294,313,
372,594,595
Rutherford 406
Sampson 310,394,537,590
Samson 281
Stokes 595
Sullivan 595
Surry 219,238,454
Tennessee 566
Tyrrell 80,84,89,90,117,
212

COUNTIES (Cont.)
Wake 313,579,595
Warren 280
Washington (Ga.) 526
Washington 447
Washington (Pa.) 443
Wayne 422,537
Westmoreland (Pa.) 391,
443
Wilkes 117
Yesdell 595
York (Mass.) 417
COUNTRY, Cumberland 136
Western 198
COURT HOUSES
Currituck 28
Ga es 13
Granville 644
Guilford 172
Hawkins 532
Randolph 658
Wake 483
CREEKS
Bachelor's 30
Back 188,658
Beaver 131,479
Big Sugar 284
Black 465,569
Blunt's 605
Brown 362
Bullock's 406
Cane 406
Chawgee 526
Crooked 499
Cross 192,253,278,406,519
Dry 236
Gardner's 10
Goodrich's 192
Gray's 410
Gun 658
Half Pone 512
Holly Shelter 31,401
Hunters 30
Island 30
Landram's 395
Linche's 398
Little Cypress 30
Lock's 192
Long 564
Mill 30
Moore's 564
New-Hope 484
Old Town 226
Rockfish 631
Shaking 31

CREEKS (Cont.)
Smith's 406
Suttons 2
Sycamore 566
Tocohoe 30
Town 401
Traver's 658
Tyrrel's 237
Ulias's 658
Verner's? 371
Wood's 311
DISMAL 29
DISTRICTS
Edenton 6,275,333,481,
522
Fayetteville 343,466,
473,474,481
Halifax 53,481
Hillsborough 481,652
Maryland 185
Mero 512,566
Morgan 481,652
Newbern 481
North-Carolina 55,62,218,
333,347,389,394,537,
570,577
Pennsylvania 24,43,391
Rhode-Island 232
Salisbury 262,275,481,
652
South-Carolina 195
Wilmington 427,481,564
DIVISIONS
Cape-Fear 310,323,347
Centre 351
Yadkin 357
ENOE 658
FERRIES
Adkin's 192
Mackay's 595
Rigdon's 608
Wright's 125
FLATTS 458
FOLLY, Lockwood's 401
FORDS
Island 326
Old Nation 284
Papo 479
Shallow 454
FORK, Grove 526
FORTS
Montgomery 349
Washington 429
HAYMOUNT 253
HAWFIELDS 188,401,653

HILLS
  Beech 550
  Laurel 509
HOOK, Sandy 51
INLET, Shallow 503
IRON WORKS, Allen's 219
ISLAND, Long 366,587
LAKES
  Catfish 30
  Heron 406
  Otsego 230
  Phelps 89
  Waccamaw 203
  Wacomaw 270
LANDINGS
  Campbellton 319
  Convent 80
  Coryman's 344
  Old Tar 4
  Rock 428
LICK, Salt 131
MARSHES
  Prown 523
  White 606
MATTAMUSKEET 422
MILLS
  Cochran's 120,359,453
  Robert RUTHERFORD's 536
  White's 136
  Winchester's 566
MINGO, Black 551
MOUNTAINS
  Cumberland 566
  Powell's 532
  Ragged 451
NECK, Virginia PORTER's 401
NINETY-SIX 411,465
OCCACOCK 44
PEDEE, Great 622
  Little 595,615
PIGEON, Little 556
PLAINS, Fair 509
PLANTATIONS
  Bluff Point 3
  Den, The 589,590
  Indian Wells 646
  Mount Vernon 449
  Old Town 226
  Rocky Point 247
  Spring Hill 293,589,590
  Summerton 203
  Sunsberry 88
  Three Forks 658
POCOSINS
  Back Swamp 31

POCOSINS (Cont.)
  Black Swamp 30
  Devil's 31
  Dover 30
  Herritages 30
  Juniper 30
  White Oak 31
POND, Flat 31
PORTS
  East Greenwich 210
  North Kington 210
  Patuxet 210
QUARTER, Stinking 658
REEF, Eaton's Neck 366
RIDGE, Long 31
RIVERS
  Annapolis 130
  Atkin 628
  Black 206,311,326,564,
    595,606
  Broad 526
  Cape-Fear 192,253,311,361,
    398,401,524,538,564,625,
    631,646,649
  Cashie 41,74
  Catawba 326
  Chowan 4
  Clinch 479,532
  Cumberland 512
  Dan 309,313
  Deep 188,268,314,406,501,
    594,608
  Elizabeth 401
  French-Broad 383,450
  Glaze 412
  Hawe 188
  Holston 532
  Hudson's 344
  Little 396,485,503,523,
    554,595,658
  Mayo 313
  Meherrin 9
  New 31
  North-East 247
  North-West 150,302,311,
    589
  Nuse 313
  Oconee 526
  Ohio 210,450
  Pee Dee 446,593
  Red 512
  Roanoak 296
  Savannah 161
  Saxapahaw 658
  Scuppernong 89

RIVERS (Cont.)
  South 502
  St. Joseph 307
  Susquehanna 125
  Tar 644
  Tenesee 479
  Tenessee 383,532
  Trent 30,313
  White Oak 30,31
  Yadkin, Forks of the
    294,372
ROADS
  Country Line 653
  Cross 52
  Deep-river 594
  Kingsbridge 70
  Nine Mile 31
ROAN-OAK 370
ROCKFISH 406
RUNS
  Big-Stony 595
  Bull 566
SAVANNAH, Cypress 564
SETTLEMENT, Cox's 406
SHOALS, Muscle 383
SHOCHEAL 406
SOUND, Albemarle 3,61
SPRINGS
  Cool 118,121,505,594,
    598
  Dripping 512,566
  Mineral 407
  Rockingham 277
STATES
  Connecticut 116,287,
    366,651
  Delaware 116,210,381,
    392
  Georgia 1,116,225,294,
    384,480,587
  Kentucke 478
  Kentuckey 376
  Kentucky 381,412,512,
    566
  Louisiana 127
  Maine 390
  Maryland 115,116,210,
    294,331,435,442,585
  Massachusetts 20,107,
    115,116,127,128,173,
    332,417,441,533,584
  New-Hampshire 7,115,116
  New-Jersey 116,345,373
  New-York 115,116,125,
    156,210,227,390,540,
    587

STATES (Cont.)
  Pennsylvania 17,24,115,
    116,198,379,412,443,530,
    541,552,581
  Rhode Island 108,173,196,
    210,242
  South-Carolina 115,116,
    125,145,157,161,195,211,
    239,326,349,380,398,411,
    446,465,517,526,550,551,
    569,593,613,615
  Vermont 81,365,413,439,
    510,529,535
  Virginia 101,115,116,155,
    178,225,263,266,326,340,
    346,390,414,429,447,479,
    536,538,542,593,618
STATIONS, Gamble's 479
  Greenfield 566
  M'Tear's 566
SWAMPS
  Black 30
  Buckhorn 595
  Dismal 93
  Gum 30
  Lebanon 29
  Pasquatank River 313
  Raft 406,595
TERRITORIES
  South of the river Ohio
    210,450
  Western 131,177,245,364
TOWNS
  Alexandria 1,116,153
  Annapolis 71,116
  Augusta 493,526,543
  Averieborough 595
  Averysburg 538
  Barnstable 116
  Bath 116
  Beaufort 85
  Bellsville 313
  Belvidere 298
  Bennington 529,535,558
  Bermuda Hundred 116
  Bethlehem 24
  Beverly 116
  Brunswick 401
  Burlington 116,378
  Butchertown 82
  Cambelton 595
  Campbellsburgh 4
  Campbleton 469,487
  Charlestown 116
  Charlotte 337

TOWNS (Cont.)
  Cherry-Stone 116
  Chester 116
  Clarksville 512
  Colesbridge 595
  Columbia 145
  Concord 533
  Cooper's town 230,330
  Culpepper 451
  Cumberland 478,480,566
  Danbury 245,246,263
  Danville 381,412
  Dover 7
  Dumfries 116
  Duxbury 20
  Edenton 1,4,6,11,12,23,32,
    34,39,42,44,48,57,58,59,
    61,63,66,72,73,75,77-80,
    83,86-92,98-100,104,117,
    212,280,333,422,500
  Edgartown 116
  Elizabeth-Town 206,216,255,
    525,606
  Fairfield 116
  Fayetteville 111-114,117,
    118,120-122,125,126,133,
    134,137,139,140,142,145,
    147-149,154,158,159,163,
    165-167,169,176,180,183,
    186,189,190,192,194,199,
    201-203,209,214,217,220,
    221,224,226,236,239,241,
    242,245,248,249,253,254,
    257-260,264,266,269-271,
    273,274,279,282,286,291,
    293,296,298-300,303,304,
    305,307,310,311,312,313,
    315,317,318,319,322,323,
    325,331,333,334,337,338,
    347,350,351,354,357-359,
    361,363,367,372,375,376,
    384,385,388,389,393,397,
    398,402,403,406,408-411,
    415,420-424,428,434,436-
    439,444,446,448,453,456,
    461,644-466,469-472,481,
    482,486,487,491,492,494,
    498,504,507,512,520,521,
    523,525,527,528,531,543,
    546,549,551,554,555,559,
    560,562,563,567,569-571,
    574,577-580,586,588,589,
    595,597,598,600,605-607,
    609,610,612-614,618,620-
    623,626,627,634,637,641-

TOWNS (Cont.)
  Fayetteville (Cont.)
    643,649,652-654,656
  Flushing 587
  Fredericksburg 153,451
  Fredericksburgh 116
  Frenchman's Bay 116
  George-Town 116,233,
    465,582,613
  Germantown 152
  Glahago 131
  Gloucester 116
  Greensville 422
  Gunbury 116
  Hager's town 475
  Halifax 53,54,280,285,
    422,582,591
  Hallowell 513
  Hampton 116
  Harrisburg 644
  Hertford 65
  Hill 593
  Hillsboro' 645,655,567,
    660,662
  Hillsborough 188,268,
    275,290,313,324,368,
    371,401,422,467,471,
    647,648,650,651,653,
    658,659-661,664,666
  Huntington 366
  Ipswich 116,584
  Kennebeck 640
  Kinsale 116
  Kiokee 526
  Knoxville 383,450,479,
    499,532,556,566
  Lazy-Hill 29
  Lexington 381
  Liberty-town 475
  Louisville 116
  Lumberton 320,352,397,
    508,592,595,620,624,
    635,638
  Lynn 441
  Marblehead 116,210
  Martinburg 536
  Mechias 116
  Medway 173
  Middleton 116
  Moravian 528
  Murfreesboro' 9
  Murfreesborough 426
  Muskogee 57
  Nanjemoy 116
  Nantucket 116

TOWNS (Cont.)
  Narraganset 129
  Nashville 512
  Natchetoches 127
  Neff's town 553
  New-Baltimore 344
  New-Bedford 116
  Newbern 55,56,58,60,143,
    169,213,234,239,268,
    280,387,395,422,466,
    573
  New-bury-Port 116
  New-Durham 7
  New-Garden 172
  New-London 116
  New-Orleans 225,428
  Newport 116,196,242
  Niagara 558
  Nixonton 29,95,96
  Nole-Chucky 595
  Norfolk 22,102,103,116,
    132,223,390,414,640
  Nottingham 116
  Oxford 116
  Passamaquody 116
  Penobscot 116
  Pensacola 57,526
  Perth-Amboy 116
  Petersburg 139,326,334,
    452,542,618,632
  Petersburgh 116
  Pitsore 605
  Pittsborough 395,407,618
  Pittsburg 131
  Pittsburgh 568
  Pittsford 413
  Plymouth 116
  Portland 116
  Port-Royal 116
  Portsmouth 116
  Port-Tobacco 233
  Pownalborough 513
  Princeton 1
  Prospect 344
  Providence 102,108,129,
    173,197,232
  Quaker Town 52
  Richmond 49,225
  Rochester 144
  Rutland 413,439
  Sagg-Harbour 116
  Salem 116,124,207,584
  Salisbury 164,186,240,
    262,272,327,422,489,
    528

TOWNS (Cont.)
  Sanford 390
  Savannah 116,235,493,557,
    640
  Sherburne 116
  Snow-Hill 116
  South-Key 116
  Stanford 366
  St. Mark's 116
  St. Mary's 557
  Stockbridge 128,229
  Stonington 116
  Stono 349
  Suffolk 116
  Sunderland 529,535
  Sutton 127
  Swansborough 422,595
  Tappahannock 116
  Tarborough 280,313,422
  Town-Creek 116
  Tugalo 526
  Urbanna 116
  Vandersee's-Landing 344
  Vienna 116
  Wadesborough 321
  Warren 418
  Warrenton 201,471
  Washington 76,422
  West-Point 116
  Wilmington 116,129,133,
    134,138,150,158,160,166,
    167,181,190,191,203,208,
    216,224,226,231,247,270,
    288,293,301,302,311,316,
    348,350,356,374,401,405,
    410,432,444,460,476,487,
    495,517,520,521,545,559,
    564,580,582,589,601,618,
    629,646,649
  Winchester 450,512,536,
    553
  Windsor 4,75
  Winton 4
  Wiscasset 116
  Yeocomico 116
  York 116
  York-Town 116
UHAREE 658
YARD, Moore 10

111

www.ingramcontent.com/pod-product-compliance
Lightning Source LLC
Chambersburg PA
CBHW031130020426
42333CB00012B/311